P9-DDW-129

Leading Self-Directed Work Teams

A Guide to Developing
New Team Leadership Skills

Kimball Fisher

Cofounder
Belgard • Fisher • Rayner, Inc.

McGraw-Hill, Inc.
New York   St. Louis   San Francisco   Auckland   Bogotá
Caracas   Lisbon   London   Madrid   Mexico   Milan
Montreal   New Delhi   Paris   San Juan   São Paulo
Singapore   Sydney   Tokyo   Toronto

Library of Congress Cataloging-in-Publication Data

Fisher, Kimball
    Leading self-directed work teams / Kimball Fisher.
        p.   cm.
    Includes index.
    ISBN 0-07-021071-3
    1. Work groups.   2. Leadership.   I. Title.
    HD66.F56   1993
    658.4'036—dc20   92-28418
                                                    CIP

1 2 3 4 5 6 7 8 9 0   DOC/DOC   9 8 7 6 5 4 3 2

ISBN   0-07-021071-3

*The sponsoring editor for this book was Karen Hansen, the editing supervisor
was Fred Dahl, and the production supervisor was Pamela Pelton. It was set in
Baskerville by Inkwell Publishing Services.*

Printed and bound by R. R. Donnelley & Sons Company.

This book is printed on recycled, acid-free paper containing a minimum of 50% recycled de-
inked fiber.

To Reenie
My wife, my colleague, and my best friend

"Don't mourn what you aren't,
celebrate what you are."
                                        —*Mareen Fisher*

Contents

Part 1. A New Kind of Leader for a New Kind of Business Environment

Part 2. Building the Foundation for Change

Part 5. The Team Leader Workout

Part 6. Common Problems and Uncommon Solutions

Foreword

Empowerment and teams have taken the world by storm. Managers have found that to remain competitive means tapping into the vast, underutilized resource of knowledge within their workforces. Furthermore, customer responsiveness through total quality management requires greater integration across functional groups. Cross-functional teams have, thus, become commonplace as organizations strive for reduced product to market times and continuous improvement throughout the value chain. But making teams function effectively has remained an elusive dream for many organizations.

The American culture, to a great extent built on individualism and a diversity of interests, runs counter to teams. Teamwork requires pulling a group of diverse individuals together to work toward a common goal. Some managers take the phrase "self-management" literally and expect it to happen, somehow by magic. But teamwork does not just emerge. It requires strong leadership throughout the entire organization.

Managers at several new plant start-ups believed they could run their operations without supervisors or first level managers only to find they needed to add the level of management as their operations failed to perform. A manager at one plant which eliminated their first level supervisors noted that things run fairly smoothly four out of five days a week but the plant could really use supervision on that fifth day. He was afraid, however, to reinstitute a leadership role because he did not know how to keep team leaders from reverting back to traditional supervisors. Even if it were possible to define the role, which he doubted, he, along with many of his contemporaries, argues that leaders are born and that it is nearly impossible to create leaders.

For years, organizational consultants have used the terms coach, trainer, facilitator, and resource to describe the leadership role. Coach and trainer are at least fairly familiar phrases, but facilitator and resource often sound like terms from another world. They are ambiguous terms. Worse yet, the role evolves as teams mature. Making sense out of this new environment is far from easy. Much confusion still exists as to what the role of team leadership is all about.

Kim Fisher helps to elevate us out of the jargon with real world examples and tips to make the transition. He has seen what works and what doesn't from first-hand observation—both as a team leader in a successful self-directed team operation and as a consultant in helping organizations transform from traditional to empowered work systems. He is thus able to provide a roadmap on how organizations can create an environment which promotes the development of team leaders.

But as Kim so rightly stresses, it is insufficient to merely develop leaders at the first level of management. Leadership must occur at every level of the organization, including the top executive suite. And as difficult as it may seem at the first level of management, the task of changing to team leadership at the middle management and executive levels is even harder. Fortunately, Kim provides a vision for how to make the journey.

Jan Klein[1]
GLOUCESTER, MA

---

[1] Jan Klein has taught operations management at the Harvard Business School and MIT's Sloan School of Management. Over the past decade, she has been studying the changing role of managers and supervisors in organizations.

Preface

In the spring of 1980 a senior manager of Procter & Gamble extended me an offer of employment as a team leader for the Downy Process work team located in the Lima, Ohio soap plant. He concluded our meeting with a discussion about future career opportunities. "Kim," he said, "there are two possible career paths open to you if you come to Lima: One, you can continue to work in line management assignments, or, two, you can work in staff positions as an internal consultant." He jokingly added that someone could also make a career someday out of writing a book about the amazing plant in Ohio.

His observation turned out to be a foreshadowing of my future work life, which with the completion of this book includes all three career paths. This book talks not about the specifics of the Lima, Ohio plant. (Many P&G executives still consider such specifics proprietary with the same competitive advantage of a product formulation or patented manufacturing process.) Instead, it describes the amazing energy and effectiveness of the self-directed work teams and team leaders in Lima and similar organizations. From these innovative workplaces we have many lessons to learn—lessons that are especially important as we approach the unique challenges of the modern work environment.

Why This Book?

We are witnessing a pivotal point in modern organizational history, a time when the structures and assumptions of traditional workplace management are once again being questioned. Some experts have dubbed it the "second industrial revolution" because the pervasive, classic U.S. workplace design—with its stovepipe functions, rigid bureaucracies, chain-of-command reporting relationships, and encumbering policies and regulations—may be becoming obsolete. In all fairness, this kind of workplace management has often worked and was once revered worldwide for its remarkable organization, control, and efficiency. But as the work environment has changed, many of these traditional organizations have proven too slow, too expensive, and too unresponsive to be competitive. Corporations have devolved into flatter and more flexible versions of the norm. Many current organizations have questioned not only the structure, but the basic paradigm of hierarchical work systems. They have been using an "empowered" workforce, which has assumed many of the traditional responsibilities of management in order to increase worker commitment and flexibility. In many cases corporations have been paid back with increased quality, productivity, and cost improvements, while workers have seen commensurate gains in the quality of their work life. It has become increasingly evident that these empowered teams may well be replacing the traditional workplace management practices that have characterized organizations since the turn of the century.

Effective team leadership is the key to creating and sustaining an empowered work force. But team leaders who are looking for clarification of their responsibilities in these nontraditional work groups have only a few sources that provide much useful information.

I wrote this book to help fill that void. The questions I want to discuss are some of the same ones that I struggled with as a new team leader at P&G:

- What are team leaders?
- How are they different from supervisors?
- What is required to be successful in this role?
- What does it take to change from a supervisor to a team leader?

Who Should Read This Book?

This book is written for team leaders and for those who support or study them. Although many of the examples and discussions are about team leaders at the first level in the organization (people who would have been called "supervisors" in a traditional organization), the book is also written for middle and senior level managers who are changing their roles from high level supervisors to teachers, coaches, and leaders of management and professional teams. It will be particularly useful for people who are moving toward the more advanced forms of worker empowerment called "self-directed work teams." Students and internal or external consultants who are helping supervisors change their role to team leaders will probably find the chapters on the change process particularly useful.

How Is the Book Organized?

The beginning chapters introduce the need for a change in the traditional supervisory role. The book continues with a discussion of team leader values, laying the foundation for the ensuing chapters, which clarify the new role. The latter chapters present specific skill requirements, problem-solving ideas, and suggested tasks. Readers who are already familiar with the basic theory and philosophy of team leadership may be more interested in the pragmatic topics found in the last sections of the book.

However, a note of caution: This role is characterized first and foremost by a set of values and assumptions rather than by a special set of behaviors. Those who are tempted to skip ahead and employ the behaviors or skills of the team leader discussed in the later chapters, while still believing in the traditional values and assumptions of the supervisor, will have a most unpleasant experience. Trust me on this one. It is a pretty good idea to review the chapters in Part 3 before experimenting with any of the skills or projects in Parts 4 and 5.

The specific structure of the book follows:

- *Part 1: A New Kind of Leader:* To show that these role changes have been driven by new business realities.

- *Part 2: Building the Foundation:* To illustrate the perils of excluding supervisors and the benefits of including them in the work change process.

- *Part 3: Values and Assumptions:* To demonstrate the power of values and assumptions as the base of the new role.

- *Part 4: The Role of the Team Leader:* To clarify the team leader role and to differentiate it from the traditional supervisory role.

- *Part 5: The Team Leader Workout:* To identify typical team leader tasks and suggest some things to do to develop competence and confidence.

- *Part 6: Common Problems and Uncommon Solutions:* To identify typical team leader problems during the transition stages and recommend solutions.

- *Part 7: Team Leader Evaluation Tools:* To help team leaders assess their fit and effectiveness in empowered work systems.

Understanding the leadership roles in a high-performance work environment has been a passion of mine since I was introduced to the ideas of sociotechnical work systems in graduate school. As I have made friends with some of the great thinkers and practitioners in this field, and most importantly, as I have worked side by side with the men and women who labor in self-directed work teams across the United States, Canada, and Western Europe, I have been touched by the dedication and relentless tenacity of people who are consumed by this work. I hope this book finds a way to share with you some of the things my friends have taught me about managing workplaces characterized by dignity, purpose, and competitive advantage.

Kimball Fisher
FEDERAL WAY, WASHINGTON

Acknowledgments

No author creates something utterly original. Even the most "innovative" management writers I know often simply repackage the thinking of others or add an unusual insight or snappy vocabulary to an established body of knowledge. This book, in particular, is clearly an example of a collaborative effort rather than being an exclusive product of my own creation. In even the most original parts of this book, for example, I write some reflections on my own experience which I came to understand better only with the help of other team leaders, workers, consultants, teachers, artists, and taxi cab drivers. In other parts of the book I am even more indebted to a rich intellectual and experiential heritage, which I catalog in those chapters.

This book has also clearly been influenced by conversations with some of the great thinkers in this field including Jan Klein, Pam Posey, Alan Wilkins, Jack Sherwood, Marv Weisbord, Dave Hanna, and Gene Dalton. The writings of these pragmatic philosophers—along with those of Eric Trist, Richard Walton, Fred Emery, Lou Davis, William Westley, Ed Lawler, Len Schlesinger and Albert Cherns—underpin much of my thinking, although any possible misinterpretation of their work is solely my responsibility. I have been discussing many of the ideas in this book with my colleagues Bill Belgard and Steve Rayner for so long that it is now nearly impossible to determine who originally conceived many of the ideas and observations included in the book. In retrospect it is as though many of the models and postulates contained here sprang whole from what we call the "three-headed monster" at BFR, Inc.·

I actually started writing this book in 1983 when I was working as an internal consultant at the Procter & Gamble soap plant in Chicago. At that time I distributed a short white paper to selected P&G managers partly to communicate some ideas that I thought might be helpful to the people making the transition from supervisors to team leaders. But I mainly wrote it to create an excuse to force myself to write down some of the things I learned while working in the innovative Lima plant. Bits and pieces of what would later grow into the book have been surfacing ever since.

Parts of Chaps. 1, 5, 17, 18, and 19, for example, appeared in the University of Michigan's *Human Resource Management* under the title "Management Roles in the Implementation of Participative Management Systems" (Fall 1986. © 1986 by John Wiley & Sons, Inc.; used by permission of author). Sections of what later became Chaps. 5, 8, 10, and 11 were modified from an article entitled "Managing in the High-Commitment Workplace" (reprinted by permission of the publisher from *Organizational Dynamics*, Winter 1989, © 1989 American Management Association, New York; all rights reserved).

The case study on Kodak appeared originally as a chapter titled "Creating a High-Performance Management Team: Eastman Kodak's 13 Room" in *The Manager as Trainer, Coach and Leader* by Jerome M. Roscow and Robert Zager in 1991 (used by permission of the publisher). This is one of a series of excellent books published by the Work in America Institute on the topic. Edited excerpts from the original appear as Chaps. 6 and 7, with some bits from the original in Chaps. 1 and 2 as well. Although I am listed as a coauthor of this case, my authorship was more of a courtesy than a reality. Steve Rayner and I worked on the research and interviews together, and we formulated the primary learnings and basic message of the case as a team. But credit for the writing of this excellent piece belongs solely to Steve. I have used large excerpts from the original with Steve's permission.

Parts of Chap. 24 come from "Vision, Opportunity and Tenacity: Three Informal Processes That Influence Formal Transformation," which was coauthored with Steve Rayner and Bill Belgard [in R. H. Kilmann and T. J. Covin (eds.), *Corporate Transformation* (Jossey-Bass, 1988); used by permission of the publisher and coauthors]. Chapters 12, 21, and 22 and part of Chap. 5 were also originally commissioned by the Work in America Institute, though they have never been published before.

I would like to thank the publishers of these articles mentioned for permitting me to include them in the book.

Thanks also to the folks at BFR for allowing me to reproduce copyrighted models (Team Leader Role Model, Team Member Role Model, Transition Difficulty Model, and Change Response Model) and portions of published BFR Implementation Tools™ (*Assessing Team Leader Effectiveness*). They add significantly to the book. I sincerely appreciate the BFR staff for covering phones and team assignments for me while I needed time to write. Sheri Piercy, Kathy Braun, Raejean Rosatto, Susanne Eaton, Larry Welte, Mike Hunter, Bonnie Sabel, Barbara Brenneman, Terri Cone, Phil Bromley, Jim Armstrong, and Bill and Steve made it possible for me to finish this project.

Writing this book has been an interesting learning experience. In some ways the book has forced me to think more critically and clearly about these topics than I ever had before. It provided an excuse to send early drafts to other managers and consultants for thought-provoking argument, suggestions, and examples. Although I wrote this book, in some ways you might say that the book "wrote" me as well. The process reminds me of a poem that I wrote when I was about 14 years old:

Writing writes and rights the writer,
Authors author, fights the fighter.
Hand to mind to mind the hand,
Writing writes, refines refiner.

I appreciate the way this process has helped to refine my thinking about team leaders. I would especially like to thank those who helped with specific feedback about the book and my thinking. Thanks to Karen Hansen of McGraw-Hill and Fred Dahl of Inkwell Publishing for their editorial improvements. Marv Weisbord gave me needed encouragement and suggestions on craftsmanship. Jan Klein and I discussed several iterations of the book, and she helped to improve the flow and strengthen the message considerably. Special thanks to Alan Wilkins and Pam Posey for their endurance, caring, and tenacity. Alan gave me numerous helpful critiques and showed me how to buttress some weaknesses in logic that appeared in earlier drafts. Pam read the book three times and sent me more than 40 pages of detailed notes ranging from recommendations on voice and grammar to constructive criticism on fundamental themes and postulates. Her collegial support on this piece has been a rare and precious commodity in these times of "hurry up," "sorry I'm busy," "don't have time to help you."

In particular I would like to express appreciation to Mareen Fisher, my dear wife, to whom I dedicate this book. During the years that I have been learning about the role of the team leader, she has been my personal confidant, coach, and consultant. And this book has her touch on every page. She displayed both the patience required to offer continuous suggestions for improvement and the compassion to not make fun of my two-finger typing method on the Macintosh, which allowed me to progress on this manuscript with the sleep-inducing speed of a northwest garden slug. She has made this a better book and me a better team leader.

Kimball Fisher

PART 1

A New Kind of Leader for a New Kind of Business Environment

1
Bosses Who
Don't Boss

*The teams at Goodyear are now telling the
boss how to run things. And I must say, I'm
not doing a half-bad job because of it.*[1]
STANLEY GAULT,
Chairman of Goodyear

Empowerment has clearly become the latest in a long litany of vogue practices that have ebbed and flowed over corporations like the changing of the tide. Today it is estimated that virtually every major corporation in North America and Western Europe is using various forms of empowerment somewhere in the organization. Many are experimenting with self-directed work team concepts, the most advanced organizational form of worker empowerment. But empowerment, if taken seriously, is not just another fad. It renders obsolete the traditional methods of management that have dominated corporations for the last one hundred years. Unlike a number of other current management experiments, empowerment is potentially as profound a change in contemporary organizations as the first industrial revolution was at the turn of the century.

Empowerment Is the Second
Industrial Revolution

Workplaces that empower employees to assume many of the traditional management responsibilities are spreading across North America and Western Europe. Self-directed work teams (SDWTs), in particular, are now beginning to appear in a wide section of private and public operations in both blue collar and white collar settings. It is evident that this movement has replaced quality circles—which dominated the discussions and practices of managers in the late seventies and early eighties—as the great managerial panacea for the demands of the coming decade. And this workplace transformation is so potentially profound that it has already been dubbed the "second industrial revolution."[2]

In an interesting reversal, this second industrial revolution makes companies act more like big family farms than hierarchical bureaucracies, just as the first revolution took workers off the family farm and into big corporations. People assume numerous management tasks and work in flexible teams instead of in rigid functional departments. These are big changes, often causing managers to rethink fundamental hierarchical and bureaucratic practices and beliefs that are the skeletal structure for the organizational culture. Empowerment, when implemented seriously, is not just an incremental change; it is a transformation of the workplace.

Support for the empowerment transformation is coming from a wide cross section of managers, employees, union executives, and professionals in a number of industries and public agencies. It is not, of course, universally supported. But even managers like John Welch, Chairman of General Electric, are now preaching empowerment. Welch was once known as "Neutron Jack" for his autocratic style manifested in dictates like the one that laid off 100,000 G.E. employees in the 1980s. Like a corporate neutron bomb, the action left all the buildings intact but it eliminated the people. He was also infamous for making casualties out of people who couldn't turn their businesses into number one or two in their market segment. This isn't the profile of someone you might expect to tout the benefits of worker participation. But he is now talking about a very different way to wage business warfare. "The idea of liberation and empowerment for our work force," he says, "is not enlightenment—it's a competitive necessity."[3]

SDWTs Pose a Challenge to Traditional Management

SDWTs pose some very special challenges for managers at every level in the organization. I know they did for me. I worked as a production manager in what was arguably the most advanced self-directed work team organization in Procter and Gamble. But when I first went to the plant I was uncomfortable and unclear about managing a self-directed work force. It seemed like a contradiction in terms. How do you manage a self-managed team? Did they really need me? Was there any job security for me as a team leader when it seemed like the whole purpose of these operations was to eliminate management?

It soon became clear to me that management did, in fact, have a crucial role to play in the SDWTs. But it was not the role I was used to playing. Before I went to P&G, a brief stint as a manager with another organization had convinced me that traditional practices were the best way to manage. I soon found out, however, that many of the classic management practices were entirely inconsistent with SDWT requirements. Supervisory responsibilities I had previously performed in the other organization, for example, were handled in this operation by the team members themselves. And it seemed to be working just fine.

P&G Declares SDWTs a Trade Secret

The soap plant where I worked is located in Lima, Ohio. It was started up in the sixties as one of the first and most successful U.S. SDWT experiments. It tested the then little practiced theories of a small group of British, U.S., and Australian social scientists. How did it work? The results of the experiment were so good that P&G declared them trade secrets with all the same restrictions and security precautions associated with product formulations and marketing plans.[4]

The P&G Downy Fabric Softener team averaged 99.9 percent within quality limits, held numerous safety records, and could make, pack, and ship cases of product to our California Downy factory less expensively than what it cost the other factory to get it out to their own loading dock. Perhaps even more remarkable than the types of results this plant was getting was the fact that, by the time I had arrived, this SDWT "experiment" had already been operating very successfully for over a dozen years. This clearly was not a momentary flash in the pan. It was turning out sustainable improvements. And my experience convinced me that SDWTs required a nontraditional approach to management. What happens when traditional managers don't change? Consider the following:

Jack's Problem

Jack (not his real name) was a veteran middle level manager in a major consumer products company. He was well respected and had a very senior position. His facility had recently been gutted and all new equipment had been installed successfully. The technology changeover was also being used as a platform for implementing empowerment. Although it was surrounded by a 50 year old facility using traditional management practices, this business unit had been selected as the organization's first attempt to redesign a department into fully functional self-directed work teams (SDWTs). These teams would form nearly self-sustainable business units, in which workers would act more like partners than subordinates. Not many months after the equipment was operational, however, the work team part of the project was failing badly. Tempers flared, grievances were filed, and trust was eroding rapidly. Jack had heard in conversations with the supervisors reporting to him that they thought he was to blame for the sluggishness of the empowerment effort. The consultant had given him frank feedback about how his autocratic style was impeding the team effort, along with very specific suggestions about how to change his behavior to be more participative.

Jack had honestly tried. His intentions had been good, his concern for results was unquestionable, and he had taken what he thought were the necessary actions to create the work culture change that his superiors wanted. Within a short period of time, however, he was moved out of his position. To add insult to injury, his new replacement succeeded in getting the self-directed work teams to function properly. The replacement rebuilt employee trust by listening to team members' concerns and making some modifications to the work design process to accommodate them.

The Changing Workplace

Jack's career was ruined; he was branded an "old style" manager incapable of managing successfully in a facility using empowered work teams. His later assignments were a series of lateral arabesques that eventually took him so far away from corporate center stage that he couldn't even *see* the spotlight he used to occupy as a key manager. Jack's story is true.[5] And until managers and supervisors can be better prepared for the changes occurring in organizations today, Jack won't be the last needless casualty of the changing workplace.

Thousands of managers and supervisors like Jack have seen their worlds suddenly turned upside down. Tens of thousands of others will face the same situation in the years to come. Once at the power pinnacle of the work floor or office, these newly named team leaders are now required to support rather than direct employees. They bear a variety of titles such as "resource," "facilitator," or "advisor." Their new job descriptions use words like "lead," "coach," and "train" to replace the traditional hierarchical standbys like "plan," "organize," "direct," and "control." But for the majority of management this new role brings a host of new and sometimes uncomfortable demands. This is especially true in the organizations using self-directed work teams. As their name implies, self-directed work teams require a fundamentally different and seemingly contradictory kind of leadership: bosses who don't boss.

Team Leaders Don't Supervise

In later chapters we will be using the terms "supervisor" and "team leader" in an unusual way. Let me explain what I mean by the title supervisor. In my previous management assignment I had learned that a significant, though often unwritten, part of the traditional manager's responsibility was to "supervise subordinates." This is a euphamism for bossing. No one really sat down and told me this, but that was what nearly all the successful managers did. You don't have to be mean or even very forceful to supervise. You just have to control subordinates. Supervisors can do this by telling people what to do and then by making sure they do it properly. More subtle control methods include maintaining the right to authorize subordinate decisions or limit the information or resources available to them. Whatever the means used, the end is the same. Supervisors create organizations where employees are driven by management, not by customers, and where conformity becomes more important than creativity.

All Traditional Managers Are Supervisors

Whether they supervise welders as a night shift crew boss or regional sales managers as a corporate vice president of sales and marketing, all traditional managers *supervise*. Supervisors, managers, and executives have typically been given separate titles depending on the numbers of employees over whom they have stewardship. But classic corporations, built on the turn-of-the century notion of chain of command, have long required that a significant portion of the responsibilities of management at the bottom, middle, *and* top are supervisory in nature. In that way they are all the same. For purposes of this book, the title *supervisor* therefore refers not just to the first level of management but to all traditional managers who are charged to supervise a group of subordinates.

Supervisors at all levels have to change to team leaders or else they will impede the efforts of the teams.

Operations, Management, and Culture Team Leaders

Just as all traditional managers are supervisors, the term *team leader* will refer to all managers who support self-directed work teams at every level of the organization. SDWTs are used not only on the work floor, but on the top floor of corporate headquarters buildings as well.

Although most general team leader responsibilities are the same for all team leaders, some responsibilities differ, of course, from one type of team leader to another. For purposes of our discussion, when it is important to differentiate between team leaders, we will use the following titles:

- Those who lead teams of individual contributors will be called *operations team leaders*, because they interface directly with those who perform the core work of the organization. In the traditional operations these are the people who would have been called supervisors, lead people, or foremen.

- Midlevel managers who lead teams of team leaders will be called *management team leaders*, because they lead other leaders.

- The most executive level of leaders will be called *culture team leaders*, because they have the ultimate responsibility for organization-wide empowerment and cultural change.

  These distinctions are particularly helpful for the discussion of roles and responsibilities during transition of an organization from traditional work systems to increased levels of empowerment.

Summary

Empowerment is in vogue for the nineties. However, managers at every level of the workplace are required to change from supervisors to team leaders if empowerment is really going to work. These unique workplaces require a fundamentally different role for managers who have traditionally been responsible for supervising subordinates regardless of their management level in the operation.

I know from my own experience that changing the management role isn't easy. Traditional organizational forms and management perspectives have been so pervasive that, like the air we breathe, they have become invisible to most of us. Unfortunately, it is hard to change something that seems so normal that you can't even see it anymore. And it isn't until we start choking that we really understand how much we depended on the stuff that has been withdrawn. Nowhere are the changes effected by empowerment—the so-called second industrial revolution—more evident than in self-directed work teams.

To better understand these unique SDWT organizations, as well as the values and business conditions that have created them, the next chapter explores the characteristics and historical roots of the self-directed work team.

Endnotes

1. John Greenwald, "Is Mr. Nice Guy Back?" *Time* (January 27, 1992), p. 43. All quotes will use the titles of the individual at the time the statement was made. I expect them, of course, to change over time.

2. R. L. Ackoff, "The Second Industrial Revolution," unpublished white paper, date unknown, and Eric Trist, "The Evolution of Socio-technical Systems: A Conceptual Framework and an Action Research Program," Issues in the Quality of Working Life, a series of occasional papers No. 2, *Ontario Ministry of Labour and Ontario Quality of Working Life Centre*, (June 1981), p. 24.

3. John Renesch (ed.), *New Traditions in Business* (Sterling and Stone Inc., 1991) p. 42

4. Only in the last few years has the understandably tight-lipped company had more open discussions about their SDWT experience.

5. Most of the references and quotes from clients and associates come from personal interaction and interviews. Some of them will not be identified by name for various reasons. As these statements have not been published elsewhere, I will typically not footnote a reference such as this throughout the rest of the book.

2

Self-Directed Work Teams

What Are They and Where Did They Come From?

The great revolution of modern times has been the revolution of equality. The idea that all people should be equal in their condition has undermined the old structures of authority, hierarchy and deference.... But when rights are given to every citizen and the sovereignty of all is established, the problem of leadership takes a new form, becomes more exacting than ever before. It is easy to issue commands and enforce them by the rope and the stake, the concentration camp and the gulag. It is much harder to use argument and achievement to overcome opposition and win consent.[1]

ARTHUR M. SCHLESINGER JR.,
historian and former advisor to Presidents Kennedy and Johnson

Organizational rules are changing. Classic hierarchical work cultures, which functioned efficiently through the 60s and 70s, often became uncompetitive in the 1980s and 1990s, in the wake of increasing global competition which was quicker, more flexible, and more innovative.

Many cherished techniques of management instituted to organize and coordinate the work force became ineffective, if not counterproductive, in the rapidly changing work environment. Says John Stepp, undersecretary of the U.S. Department of Labor, about these lumbering organizations:

> There are too many rigidities that have slowed us down and hampered our effectiveness. We see top-down decision making. We see overly prescribed tasks and narrow job definitions. We see long, drawn-out labor contracts and negotiations that more closely resemble cease-fire agreements among combatants than a rational agreement for organizing work and work relationships. Our industrial relations system is hampered by too many restrictions; too many inhibiting work practices, work rules, and personnel policies.[2]

Why Are Organizations Changing?

Organizationally speaking, the decades of the 1980s and 1990s have been the best of times and the worst of times. The worst of times because it has become painfully clear that a lot of traditional work practices have slowed down many organizations and made them too inflexible to compete in the modern work environment. This includes the public sector as well. In the early nineties government agencies have come under especially heated attack for waste and inefficiencies caused by what many frustrated citizens believe is bureaucracy at its worst. The rapid infusion of new technologies, new worker expectations, and new customer demands of the last few years have not fit well with the restrictive job boxes, status-laden levels of hierarchy, and narrowly focused functions of traditional organizational thinking. Many organizations, including some of the mammoths that dominated the lesser mammals for years in the private and public sectors, just weren't working anymore.

But in some ways it has been the best of times, because we have been forced (sometimes painfully) to seek solutions that make us better. Unfettered by rigid organizational bureaucracies, some companies have demonstrated that they can effectively challenge anyone through speed, quality, and agility.

So what? There is an ancient Latin proverb that goes, *Tempora mutantur, nos et mutamur in illis.* Roughly translated it means, "The times are changed and we are changed with them." To paraphrase Bob Dylan (a more current philosopher), "The times, they were a changing." For many organizations, the times *demanded* that they redesign themselves into new forms.

How Are Organizations Changing?

A number of companies began to change. Some took desperate measures, closing down operations and laying off thousands of white and blue collar workers in an attempt to staunch the blood colored ink on their income statements. Survivors in these operations found themselves in so-called "lean and mean" organizations with decreased resources and increased responsibilities.

Other organizations began to move in a more measured manner to alternative practices, which promised more flexibility and responsiveness to the turbulent business environment. Many large corporations, for example, started incorporating just-in-time inventory reduction processes to eliminate various forms of waste, and concurrent engineering practices to reduce the time required to get a new product idea to the marketplace. Some bet the farm on new whiz-bang technologies and product designs. Service organizations recommited themselves to scrutinizing cost effectiveness and refocusing their operations on providing service excellence. Fortunately, almost everybody began incorporating total quality management perspectives into their operations with an emphasis placed on customer focus and continuous improvement.

People Are the Competitive Advantage

But the bottom line of all of this activity didn't surprise anyone. We learned that people, not programs, are the answer to increased competitiveness in the changing work environment. Reports Norman E. Garrity, Executive Vice President of Corning, Inc., "We found that if you don't pay attention to the people aspects, such as empowering workers to make decisions, you could only get 50 percent of the potential benefits of restructuring."[3] And in companies like Corning who have the active support of leaders Garrity and Houghton, the CEO, the new work culture change appears to be working. Says Robert A. Hubble a production worker in the Corning plant in Blackburg Virginia, "Everybody that works here is competitive. We're willing to work long hours. We want to be multiskilled and learn how we can make the product better so we can be the best in quality and service to the customer. And if we do that, this plant will be around a long time."[4] These skills and attitudes pay off. Blacksburg turned a $2 million profit in its first eight months of production, instead of losing $2.3 million as projected for the startup.[5]

Empowerment is also paying off in service organizations who are reforming themselves into nontraditional, empowered operations. "It's no longer coming to work and slugging data into a terminal," says Mary Vandehay, a member of an insurance rep team at Aid Association for Lutherans. "We have to work with each other. We can't pass problems up the line to managers. We have to be honest and up-front with our coworkers."[6]

The kind of attitude expressed by team members like Hubble and Vandehay may be the difference between the winners and the losers in the competitive marketplace. Tools, technologies, and projects are necessary but insufficient; they don't matter if people don't want to use them to full advantage. And almost everybody has access to the same tooling, technology, and funding nowadays. Competitive advantage comes from fully utilizing the *discretionary effort* of the work force, not from buying the latest gadget or using the latest management fad. Voluntary effort comes from employee commitment, and commitment comes from empowerment. It is simple human nature. Why? In the words of Weyerhaeuser Human Resources manager Doug King, "It's hard to resist your own ideas."

It is becoming increasingly clear that organizational responses like new product and service development, cross-functional projects, technology deployment, and initiatives like total quality management (TQM) require a flexible and empowered work force. Put more succinctly, without significant levels of empowerment, projects and programs won't deliver the promised results. Speed, quality, productivity, and new products and services come from people not programs. And the stakes are high. In a competitive work environment, only the winners survive.

Defining Empowerment

What is empowerment? It is a function of four important variables: authority, resources, information, and accountability. You might remember these variables by using the memory word ARIA, which is composed of the first letter of each variable. The beauty of the opera solo of the same name depends on whether the music is written, performed, and accompanied well. Similarly, the empowerment melody works only when all the variables are in complete harmony. To feel empowered, people need formal authority and all the resources (like the budget, equipment, time, and training) necessary to do something with the new authority. They also need timely, accurate information to make good decisions. And they need a personal sense of accountabilty for the work. This definition of empowerment can be expressed as follows:

Empowerment = f(**A**uthority, **R**esources, **I**nformation, **A**ccountability)

Empowerment = **0 if A**uthority or **R**esources or
Information or **A**ccountability = **0**

In this formula we can see that empowerment is a function of the four variables and that if any of the variables in this equation go to zero then there is no empowerment. This explains why some empowerment initiatives are a sham. Authority without information and resources, for example, is only permission. Telling team members that they should go ahead and make decisions or solve problems without providing them access to accurate business information and without providing them the skills training, budget, and time to accomplish the task is a prescription for volatile failure. Not sharing accountability is paternalistic and condescending. It sends the message that the empowerment isn't real. Only when all four elements are present do people feel responsible and act responsibly.

Defining Self-Directed Work Teams

Empowerment gives people greater control over their own destiny. And there are varying degrees of empowerment. It is not something you either have or you don't have. Visualize empowerment as a continuum of employee involvement with lower empowerment techniques like selected employee input on projects on one end, ongoing employee task forces and quality circles in the middle, and higher empowerment processes like SDWTs on the other end (see Fig. 2.1).[7]

Self-directed teams are the most advanced form of empowerment. Whether it is called employee involvement, a sociotechnical system, a high performance system, partnership, semiautonomous work teams, or any of the multitude of names referring to organizations based on SDWT concepts, parts of companies like Corning, Procter and Gamble, Esso, Rockwell, TRW, Aid Association for Lutherans, Monsanto, Martin Marietta, Digital Equipment Corporation, Sherwin-Williams, Honeywell, Weyerhaeuser, Shell and a host of others have been using them aggressively.

What are self-directed teams? Let's use a slightly modified version of the definition used by The Association for Quality and Participation for their study on the subject (referenced in the next chapter):

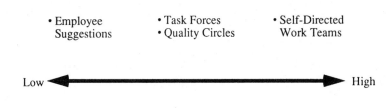

Figure 2.1. The Empowerment continuum. (*Adapted from "The Involvement Continuum,"* ©
1989 Belgard•Fisher•Rayner, Inc. Influenced by the work of John Sherwood.)

Self-directed team (noun): A group of employees who have day-to-day
responsibility for managing themselves and the work they do with a
minimum of direct supervision. Members of self-directed teams typically
handle job assignments, plan and schedule work, make production and/or
service related decisions, and take action on problems.

Where traditional work groups are typically organized into separate
specialized jobs with rather narrow responsibilities, these teams are made
up of members who are jointly responsible for whole work processes, with
each individual performing multiple tasks. Whereas a traditional organization might be divided into groups of functional specialists, for example, SDWTs are usually responsible for delivery of an entire service or
product, or they might be responsible for a geographic or customer base.
This is done to create (wherever possible) small self-sustaining businesses
that can be jointly managed by the organizational membership. At P&G
Lima, for example, we were divided into product organizations. The
team members made decisions about who would perform which task
rather than having each individual separated into jobs like operators,
mechanics, and trades people. Everyone had the same title, "technician,"
and everyone had a shared responsibility for the success of the team.
These are common elements of SDWTs. For other key differences between self-directed work teams and traditional organizations see Table
2.1.

SDWT Watchouts

A caveat is in order when defining SDWTs. It is critically important that
we recognize an enormous trap associated with overemphasizing the
structure (self-directed work teams) more than the process of empower-

Table 2.1. SDWTs vs. Traditional Organizations

Self-directed work teams	Traditional organizations
Customer-driven	Management-driven
Multiskilled work force	Work force of isolated specialists
Few job descriptions	Many job descriptions
Information shared widely	Information limited
Few levels of management	Many levels of management
Whole business focus	Function/department focus
Shared goals	Segregated goals
Seemingly chaotic	Seemingly organized
Purpose achievement emphasis	Problem solving emphasis
High worker commitment	High management commitment
Continuous improvements	Incremental improvements
Self-controlled	Management controlled
Values/principle based	Policy/procedure based

ment. For the sake of clarity and simplicity, this book, for example, spends a lot of time and attention on SDWTs as the unit of discussion. Inappropriate focus on the teams in the workplace, however, can cause serious problems.

Two problems in particular result from focusing too much on the teams themselves. First, we can begin to believe that the teams are the end instead of the means to an end. SDWTs are a method of improving results, not a substitution for them. This all too common means/ends inversion has caused some organizations to lose sight of their organizational purpose and to focus instead on the care and feeding of the structures. ("Sorry, our poor customer service is caused by the fact that everyone is in a team meeting right now.") This is obviously a bad mistake.

Second, overemphasizing the "self-directedness" of the teams can lead people down the wrong path. In fact, the name "self-directed work team" itself can be misleading. Some believe that it connotes an absence of management personnel (which is inaccurate). SDWTs means a change in the role of management, not an elimination of supervisors and managers. Others assume that the name implies that the team has complete latitude to do whatever it wants (which is equally inaccurate). All teams operate within appropriate boundary conditions. Probably a more accurate term is the one favored by my colleague Bill Belgard: *work centered teams*. Simply stated, these operations are ones in which skilled, well-informed people take direction from the work itself rather than from management. More on this later in the book.

SDWTs Outperform
Traditional Operations

Whatever you call them, if all else is equal these work cultures are often credited with outperforming their traditional counterparts. At a conference about these unique workplaces, Charles Eberle, a former vice president of Procter and Gamble, said:

> At P&G there are well over two decades of comparisons of results—*side by side*—between enlightened work systems and those I call traditional. It is absolutely clear that the new work systems work better—*a lot better*—for example, with 30 to 50 percent lower manufacturing costs. Not only are the tangible, measurable, bottom line indicators such as cost, quality, customer service and reliability better, but also the harder-to-measure attributes such as quickness, decisiveness, toughness, and just plain resourcefulness of these organizations. Importantly, the people in these organizations are far more self-reliant and less dependent upon hierarchy and control systems than in the traditional organization.[8]

The excitement caused by these kinds of reports has accelerated the development of self-directed work teams. To better understand this emerging role of the team leader and to determine whether self-directed teams are here to stay, let's briefly consider the history of these unique work cultures.

The Origin of Self-Directed
Work Teams

Most attribute the origins of self-directed work team concepts to the early work of an Englishman named Eric Trist. In the 1950s Trist coauthored a paper in which the term "socio-technical system" first appeared.[9] In this and other papers that were to follow, Trist challenged many of the fundamental assumptions of "scientific management," an idea developed by Frederick Taylor at the turn of the century and perfected by Henry Ford in the U.S. automobile factories of the 1930s. At that time, scientific management appeared to be the answer to the problems in rapidly growing industries caused by their dependence on a largely unskilled and illeducated work force. By breaking down job responsibilities into small specialized increments, the workers could become proficient more rapidly and a sense of order and predictability could be imposed on the emerging chaos of industrialization. This, coupled with having decision making and problem solving become the sole provenance of foremen and supervisors, facilitated the movement away from the little shops of independent craftsmen that characterized industry of the period and toward mass production and standardized factory work.

Scientific Management: Strengths and Weaknesses

Scientific management brought with it a number of advantages that current critics often fail to remember, including improvements in the quality and efficiency of work processes. It helped workers with little experience and education become fairly productive quickly. In fact, it often actually improved the work life of the employee who had previously been subjected to deathtrap mining operations, exploitative sweatshops, and capricious shop owner management. Although it facilitated industrialization, scientific management also had some very serious negative side effects. It separated the workers from the results of their work. It stripped them of an opportunity to understand the whole work process, participate in a variety of tasks, and do the planning, evaluating, and improving of work processes. Perhaps most detrimentally, it prevented them from understanding the customers who used their workers' products and services. These were all normal aspects of working in a small workshop or family farm. Consequently, workers became focused over time on their own jobs and job rights which were often, ironically, counterproductive to both the good of the enterprise and the individual.

Sociotechnical Systems

After discovering a remarkably productive coal mining team in postwar England, Trist suggested an alternative to scientific management. He said that by forming work teams that had complete responsibility for an entire operation, the interface between people (the social system) and their tools (the technical system) could be more fully optimized. This, he further postulated, would lead to job performance that was more rewarding and productive for the increasingly experienced work force.

About a decade later, these ideas took root in the United States. In the 1960s and early 1970s, experiments with what were called "semiautonomous work teams" or "technician" operations started in Procter and Gamble plants in Ohio and Georgia, a Cummins Engine facility in Jamestown, New York, and a General Foods plant in Topeka, Kansas. In these organizations academicians joined ranks with practitioners to create self-directed work teams, which demonstrated remarkable competitive and social advantages over scientific management. Since that time numerous other organizations have followed suit by creating or redesigning workplaces in which teams of employees get involved in operational decisions and in many of the traditional supervisory responsibilities of managing the day-to-day business. In these organizations the traditional barriers to maximum employee contribution, such as narrow job descriptions, restrictive functional distinctions, lack of ongoing business information, and hierarchically geared compensation and status systems, are minimized.

From Manufacturing to Service SDWTs

What started in a few manufacturing plants has also spread into the service sector in organizations like Shenandoah Life Insurance company and American Transtech, a company broken off from the AT&T monolith during the divestiture. These teams have even spilled over into public organizations and utilities like the financial arm of Seattle Metro, schools like those in the Dade-County, Florida "school-based management" program, into hospital and research organizations like the Mayo Clinic, and into tourist and recreation facilities like the San Diego Zoo.

Is worker empowerment another of the countless flavor-of-the-month business fads we see from time to time? No. For reasons to be discussed in the next chapter, empowered work systems like the SDWT are the next inevitable step on the ladder of workplace evolution.

Summary

Once cherished rules for the organizing and managing of people are becoming obsolete in today's rapidly changing world. Numerous organizations in a wide array of industry and service sectors have started using SDWTs in an attempt to respond to the demand for increased flexibility and responsiveness. Some operations have made mistakes by not understanding that empowerment requires authority, resources, information, and accountability [$E = f(A,R,I,A)$]. Others have misapplied SDWTs by focusing too much attention on the structure and not enough on the purpose of the operation. But overall, those who have used SDWTs— have been rewarded with significant organizational improvements. The first published writing about these remarkable workplaces is generally attributed to Eric Trist and other members of the Tavistock Group in postwar England. These unique workplaces have changed fundamentally the role of the supervisor at every level of the organization. And it looks like SDWTs—a commonsense idea that probably has been practiced by some people since the beginning of organizational history—are here to stay. A question asked by many team members and team leaders alike is, "What took so long?"

Endnotes

1. Arthur Schlesinger, "On Leadership," in Roger Burns, *Abraham Lincoln* (Broomall, Penn. Chelsea House Publishers, 1986), p. 9. Used by permission.

2. John Stepp, from a speech presented at the *Ecology of Work Conference* sponsored by the Organization Development (O.D) Network and NTL, June 24–26, 1987, Washington D.C.

3. John Hoerr, "Sharpening Minds for a Competitive Edge," *Business Week* (December 17, 1990), p. 78. Used by permission.

4. Hoerr, p. 72. Used by permission.

5. Hoerr, p. 72. Used by permission.

6. Hoerr, p. 78. Used by permission.

7. Jack Sherwood, a prominent STS consultant, introduced this idea to us at Tektronix in 1983. We found it a simple and effective way to describe empowerment choices to people.

8. Charles Eberle, "Competitiveness, Commitment and Leadership," a speech delivered at the *Ecology of Work Conference*, 1987.

9. Eric Trist, "The relations of Social and Technical Systems in Coal Mining," paper presented to the *British Psychological Society*, Industrial Section, 1950.

3

Team Empowerment

Passing Fad or the Future of Work Design?

No matter what your business, these teams are the wave of the future.[1]

JERRY JUNKINS,
CEO of Texas Instruments

Self-directed work teams have clearly not displaced traditional operations as the predominant organization type. But in the next few years we will see these teams replacing many of their more traditional counterparts. SDWTs will not be a short-lived fad for two reasons: (1) they have been around a long time, and (2) they get results.

SDWTs Have Been Here for Decades

Unlike fads, which tend to be popular for a few years and then fade away into obscurity, these self-directed work teams have been around for decades. Multiple corporations have actively used these teams since at least the early 1960s and arguably earlier. Several companies have also reported that they originally used SDWTs at the startup of their organizations or new ventures. As they grew, they usually moved away from the self-directed work teams to the management philosophies and structures in vogue for organizations of their size and type. A lot of them are now trying to get back to their roots.

SDWTs Work

The second and more powerful reason that self-directed work teams are here to stay is that (all else being equal) they get better results than their traditional counterparts. In a review of organizations that had transitioned from traditional work systems to SDWTs in seven countries, John Cotter, a prominent sociotechnical system consultant, found that:

Ninety-three percent reported improved productivity.

Eighty-six percent reported decreased operating costs.

Eighty-six percent reported improved quality.

Seventy percent reported better employee attitudes.[2]

Reports from organizations within American Transtech, DEC, Tektronix, Mead, TRW, James River, P&G, Martin Marietta, General Electric, Esso, Ford, and other corporations confirm these findings and indicate that SDWTs frequently outperform comparable traditional operations. Unlike a number of other corporate initiatives that have promised fire but delivered mostly smoke, SDWTs often improve many of the key organizational measures by 30 to 50 percent.

When SDWTs Don't Work

SDWTs don't always, of course, get sterling results. Although I am not aware of any studies to confirm this, SDWT consultants normally suggest that empowerment has about a 50 percent success rate. That is, for every 100 companies that begin this work, about half of them fail to get the desired improvements. Why? The single biggest reason is a lack of management commitment to the whole change process. Impatience or an unwillingness to make the personal management changes necessary to make it work has foiled many attempts to create sustainable SDWTs. Another typical shortfall is the organizational unwillingness to provide the necessary budget and time for training to help team leaders and team members acquire new skills.

But sometimes, even when SDWT implementation and support are flawless, failures can occur. No organizational design or management style can guarantee success. The airline People's Express, for example, was well publicized for using self-directed work teams effectively just prior to its failure. But caught in a whipsaw between rapid growth and a questionable market, the airline went bust. Similarly, both DEC and P&G have shut down SDWT organizations. Although these operations in the eastern United States and Europe were more cost and quality effective than traditional facilities, they were not good enough to compensate for major declines in the market or for distribution advantages of other locations, respectively. SDWTs are not a substitute for sound business basics. If you have a product or service no one wants to buy, teams won't necessarily help. Nor will they help if you are in the wrong business or if you don't have the right technology. They can only give you a better chance to be successful by more efficiently leveraging the human potential across the whole of the organization.

SDWT Results

While leveraging human potential can't guarantee anything, it does provide enormous benefits. Many organizations in the consumer products, aerospace, and paper industries are actively using these teams because they believe SDWTs provide significant competitive advantage. David Swanson, a P&G senior vice-president, confirmed this in a closed meeting at Harvard in 1984. He stated that the P&G SDWT plants were, "30–40 percent more productive than their traditional counterparts and significantly more able to adapt quickly to the changing needs of the business."[3] Adds Ted L. Marsten, Cummins Engine vice-president, "this is the most cost-effective way to run plants . . . the people felt a lot better . . . and we got a much higher quality product."[4] GM has actually used references to their teams in their Saturn automobile ads, apparently assuming that the advantages in quality, service, and/or cost effectiveness will be obvious even to consumers who may be completely unfamiliar with organizational alternatives.

These teams aren't just for the megacorporations either. Johnsonville Foods, a sausage manufacturer in Sheboygan Wisconsin claims that their productivity has improved 50 percent since the company started using teams. Nor is the SDWT revolution limited to manufacturing companies. Federal Express claims that a team of clerks found and solved a billing problem that was costing the company $2.1 million per year.[5] Insurance companies like Aetna and Shenandoah Life Insurance have reduced cost and improved service through empowered teams. And American Transtech office teams can process twice as many forms as they could under the traditional work system. Consider the following illustrative SDWT results in Table 3.1.

Table 3.1. Examples of SDWT Results

Organization	Results	Source
P&G manufacturing	30–50% lower manufacturing cost.	Eberle
Federal Express	Cut service glitches (incorrect bills and lost packages) by 13% in one year.	Dumaine, p. 54
Shenandoah Life Insurance	Case handling time went from 27 to two days. Service complaints "practically eliminated."	Hoerr and Pollock, p. 70
Sherwin-Williams Richmond	Costs 45% lower. Returned goods down 75%.	Fisher
Tektronix Portables	Moved from least profitable to most profitable division within two years.	Fisher
Rohm and Haas Knoxville	Productivity up 60%.	Hoerr and Pollock, p. 75
Tavistock coal mine	Output 25% higher with lower costs than on a comparison face. Accidents, sickness, and absenteeism cut 50%.	Trist, p. 16
Westinghouse Airdrie	Reduced cycle time from 17 weeks to one week.	Sherwood, p. 16
AT&T Credit Corp.	Teams process 800 lease applications/day vs. 400/day under old system. Growing at 40–50% compound annual rate.	Hoerr and Zellner, p. 59
General Electric Satisbury	Productivity improved 250%.	Hoerr and Zellner, p. 58
Aid Association for Lutherans (AAL)	Raised productivity by 20% and cut case processing time by 75%.	Clipp. p. 21
Cummins Engine Jamestown	Met Japanese $8,000 price for an engine expected to sell for $12,000.	Fisher
Xerox	Teams at least 30% more productive than conventional operations.	Hoerr and Pollock, p. 75

Table 3.1. Examples of SDWT Results (*Continued*)

Organization	Results	Source
Best Foods Little Rock	Highest quality products at lowest costs of any Best Foods plant.	*Productivity*, p. 1
Volvo Kalmar	Production costs 25% less than Volvo's conventional plants.	Hoerr and Pollock, p. 74
Ford Hermosillo	In first year of operation, lower defect rate than in most Japanese automakers.	Sherwood, p. 5
Weyerhaeuser Manitowoc	Output increased 33%. Profits doubled.	Sherwood, p. 20
Northern Telecom Harrisburg	Profits doubled.	Zenger
General Mills	Productivity 40% higher than traditional factories.	Dumaine, p. 55
Honeywell Chandler	Output increased 280%. Quality stepped up from 82% to 99.5%.	Sherwood, p. 16
American Transtech	Reduced costs and processing time by 50%.	Sherwood, p. 16

SOURCES:

F. Paul Clipp, "Focusing Self-Managing Work Teams, *Quality Digest* (April 1990), pp. 20–22, 24–29.

Brian Dumaine, "Who Needs a Boss?" *Fortune* (May 7, 1990).

Charles Eberle, "Competitiveness, Commitment and Leadership," a speech about P&G, *Ecology of Work Conference* (June 24, 1987).

Kimball Fisher, Personal interviews.

John Hoerr and Michael Pollock, "Management Discovers the Human Side of automation," *Business Week* (September 29, 1986).

John Hoerr and Wendy Zellner, "The Payoff from Teamwork," *Business Week* (July 10, 1989).

Productivity, "An American Miracle that Works" (November 1982), pp. 1–5.

Sherwood, John, "Creating Work Cultures with Competitive Advantage," *Organizational Dynamics* (Fall 1988).

Eric Trist, "The Evolution of Socio-technical Systems: A Conceptual Framework and an Action Research Program," *Ontario Ministry of Labour and Ontario Quality of Working Life Centre* (June 1981).

John Zenger, Presentation at American Society of Training and Development (ASTD) Annual conference, 1991.

SDWTs Are the Probable Future

Will the SDWT become the predominant organizational structure of tomorrow? A *Business Week* cover story suggested that it "appears to be the wave of the future,"[6] while a report in *Fortune* magazine boldly proclaims it *is* the wave of the future.[7] But whether they completely displace traditional work systems or not, self-directed work teams are clearly growing. In a study done in 1988 by the Center for Effective Organizations at UCLA, for example, researchers found that 67 percent of the organizations they surveyed who said they were using empowerment techniques were also using SDWTs somewhere in their organization.[8] In a related 1990 study by *Industry Week*, The Association of Quality and Participation (AQP), and Development Dimensions International, a remarkable 83 percent of the companies experimenting with SDWTs at that time said they planned a considerable increase in their use by 1995.[9]

The bottom line is this:

1. It seems that almost everybody is using some form of empowerment.

2. Most of the organizations using empowerment will eventually experiment with SDWTs in parts of their organizations.

3. Once they use SDWTs somewhere, most corporations say they want to expand them into other parts of their operations.

This trend is clear in the recent survey of 476 Fortune 1000 companies published by The American Quality and Productivity Center. The study showed that, while only about 7 percent of the current workplace was organized into SDWTs, a full half of the companies questioned said they would rely much more on SDWTs in the years ahead. And as these numbers increase there tends to be a ripple effect as companies see their competitors and collaborators using the approach. Everybody wants to "keep up with the Joneses"—especially when the Joneses can deliver the same products and services quicker, with higher quality, and with lower cost. After P&G used the teams on the soap side of the company effectively, Colgate became interested and involved. Improvements on the pulp and paper side of the company were not unnoticed by competitors (now SDWT devotees) James River, Crown Z, Champion and others. Why isn't everybody doing it yet?

For most firms, the lack of movement comes either from a lack of information or from resistance to the concept. It is too early to tell whether the vast majority of managers will be able to make the personal changes necessary for such universal transformation from traditional to SDWT operations. These SDWT organizational practices are often in direct contradiction to the management philosophies and styles that catapulted powerful supervisors into their current positions of control and responsibility at every level of the corporation. Nor is it clear that other people will be able to change from the comfortable and pervasive work practices of the past. John Myers, Human Resources Vice President for Shenandoah Life, suggests that "bureaucratic organizations become habit-forming, just like cigarettes."[10] Supervisors and "supervisees" alike often just can't bring themselves to change. The majority of contemporary organizations are still on the fence watching the SDWT parade go by. Some of them may wait too long.

SDWTs are clearly on the rise, not because they are more humane and not because altruistic managers find SDWTs morally compelling. To paraphrase Winston Churchill, SDWTs are the worst form of organization except for all the others. They are frustrating and messy and chaotic. But they work. They get results. Some organizations are excitedly leading the charge; others are moving cautiously, while still others are being dragged into a SDWT future by customers, competitors, or technologies. But they will go. Because as long as somebody can figure out how to improve results using SDWTs, others will have to figure out how to keep up with them.

Summary

Many supervisors at every level of the operation can see that the handwriting on the wall for their organization says self-directed work teams. SDWTs are not just another passing fad. There have been successful examples of these operations around for decades. In the last few years in particular, numerous organizations have used the teams to improve results by 30 to 50 percent. SDWTs have clearly now matured from a small handful of applications into numbers well into the thousands. Other current social and technical trends (discussed in the next chapter) clearly suggest that these operations are more consistent with contemporary organizational and social realities. If these trends continue, it is unlikely that a supervisor who fills multiple assignments during her career will not have a chance to act as a team leader. For many whose companies are making stronger commitments to these teams, the days of traditional supervision are already gone.

Endnotes

1. Brian Dumaine, "Who Needs a Boss?" *Fortune* (May 7, 1990), p. 52. © 1990 by The Time Inc. Magazine Company. All rights reserved. Used by permission.

2. John Cotter, "Designing Organizations That Work: An Open Sociotechnical Systems Perspective," *John J. Cotter and Associates, Inc.*, 1983.

3. John Hoerr and Michael Pollock, "Management Discovers the Human Side of Automation," *Business Week* (September 29, 1986), p. 74. Used by permission.

4. Ibid., p. 74. Used by permission.

5. Brian Dumaine, "Who Needs a Boss?" *Fortune* (May 7, 1990), p. 52. © 1990 by The Time Inc. Magazine Company. All rights reserved. Used by permission.

6. Hoerr and Zellner, p. 57. Used by permission.

7. Brian Dumaine, "Who Needs a Boss?" *Fortune* (May 7, 1990), p. 52. © by The Time Inc. Magazine Company. All rights reserved. Used by permission.

8. Wright, R. and Ledford, G., "High Involvement Organization Study," conducted and published by the Center for Effective Organizations, Graduate School of Business Administration, University of Southern California, Los Angeles, November 1988.

9. Richard Wellins et al., "Self-Directed Teams: A Study of Current Practice," *Industry Week*, The Association of Quality and Participation (AQP), and Development Dimensions International study, 1990.

10. Hoerr and Pollock, p. 72. Used by permission.

4

The Classic Supervisor Is an Endangered Species

It can be argued that the traditional supervisor is an anachronism and an impediment to productivity.[1]

PETER F. DRUCKER,
Consultant and Author

In a recent survey at Monsanto's Krummrich plant in Sauget, Illinois, supervisors were asked if they believed that the traditional supervisory function would continue into the foreseeable future. Eighty percent replied that self-directed work teams were inevitable and that significant changes in their responsibilities would rapidly render the traditional role for supervisors obsolete. Other managers have echoed this prediction for their own companies as well. I remember the apprehension we felt as management in P&G's Chicago soap plant, for example, when in 1983 we received a memo from a senior officer of the company suggesting the eventual closure of facilities that did not make the transition to self-directed work teams with the necessitated change in the supervisory role. Says Bob Condella, Director of the Administrative Center at Corning, "Corning and American Industry are moving to empowerment. It is a competitive edge." What is the implication of this for traditional supervision? "We are absolutely looking for different qualities in leaders today," he says.

Are these examples isolated instances, or are they harbingers of the future of management? Are traditional supervisors the dinosaurs of the coming decade of workplace evolution destined to be placed in museums of natural history rather than in living organizations?

The Supervisory Role Is Evolving

We will likely see a broad-based organizational evolution toward highly empowered work teams and away from the traditional hierarchical and bureaucratic organizations of the past. We may be witnessing, in fact, the single most significant change in the role of management since the first industrial revolution created the job of professional supervision.

These changes will greatly reduce the need for traditional supervisory jobs because the teams will perform most of those supervisory responsibilities themselves. Peter Drucker, a consultant who has had an uncanny ability to anticipate future management trends, has predicted the demise of the traditional supervisor for some time. Edwards Deming, the father of the quality movement, has also suggested that traditional management practices are not only obsolete but actually detrimental to the contemporary work force. Known more for his clarity of thinking than his tact, he says, "Our prevailing system of management has destroyed our people."[2]

Is the traditional supervisor an endangered species? Yes. Does this mean the people who are supervisors are no longer needed? No. But the role must evolve into something else. If the role of supervision stays static in the changing workplace, it will cease to add appreciable value to the organization. This is true, of course, for all levels of traditional supervision in the organizations attempting self-directed work. And understanding and becoming competent in these evolving team leadership responsibilities is becoming more important in corporations, schools, and public organizations for a number of reasons.

Why Empowerment Practices Will Continue

We have already reviewed why SDWTs are not just another management fad because of their remarkable (and sustainable) competitiveness. But there are at least three other reasons why the practices of empowerment will accelerate dramatically in the mid-1990s and consequently displace traditional supervisory practices at all levels of the organization:

1. Empowerment is an idea whose time has come.

2. Technology now makes empowerment practical.

3. Basic human needs make worker participation inevitable.

An Idea Whose Time Has Come

Empowerment tends to be most effective in precisely the kind of environments that many organizations find themselves in today. Although these work systems are not a new idea, they are an idea whose time has come.

Many people argue that SDWTs are not as useful in settings where the work is highly mundane and repetitive and where consistency is more important than innovation. Nor, they say, do they provide much benefit where performing the work requires little interdependence, where technologies are forgiving, and where single experts are best qualified to make independent decisions. SDWTs aren't for organizations in which stability is more important than flexibility, they say. But even if we accept these arguments, there are fewer and fewer of these kinds of organizations around anymore. And although there is some merit to these arguments, I do know of successful examples of SDWTs in each of the disputed categories. Lots of organizations, for example, use the teams to get rid of unnecessary mundane and repetitive work. By rotating from job to job each team member gets a chance to learn a number of skills and avoid the boredom that comes from performing the same task ad nauseum. In fact in many companies, managers who believe that SDWTs aren't appropriate for them (because of the reasons just cited) are simply dragging their feet while competitors in their own industries are already using the empowered teams.

Different Business Environments Require Different Organizations

This is a new day in which complex work assignments usually require the input and buy-in of multiple people. The watchwords of responsiveness, quality, customer orientation, speed, productivity, and quality of work life have become more important than the previous unspoken workplace mottos of control and regulation. Many people are finding that, even though they may have come from an organizational setting where empowered work teams may not have been as useful in the past, changes are being caused by customer demands, employee expectations, competition, government intervention, public pressure, environmentalism, technology, or any other of a host of possible reasons. They find themselves in a

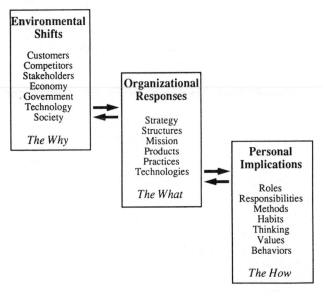

Figure 4.1. Responding to change. (*Belgard•Fisher•Rayner Inc.* © *1989. All rights reserved. Used by permission.*)

new world where empowered teams make a lot more sense now than they did before. These new realities require organizations to evolve and roles to change, as illustrated in Fig. 4.1.[3] Look at some examples.

Tektronix Responds to Time-to-Market Pressures.   One division of Tektronix faced significant challenges from Japanese portable oscilloscope competitors who were quicker to the market and less expensive. For certain Tek divisions, market demands for development speed and manufacturing flexibility required a change to self-directed work teams. Traditional work systems simply would not have allowed the innovation and, more importantly, the speed required.

Historically, Tek design engineers had taken about five years to develop a new product technology. As long as we could keep a product family in the marketplace for about ten years, this was not a problem. But during the 1980s, increased competition from numerous well financed and technologically advanced organizations changed the rules forever. Major product technologies were becoming obsolete in two years instead of ten. The technologies that new electrical and software engineers learned in school were, in fact, often obsolete twelve months after graduation. Product development simply had to be done much more quickly.

Designers no longer had time to waste in lengthy management reviews. Budget approval and tooling purchase couldn't wait for hierarchical red tape. There certainly wasn't time or money for major product and process rework once designs were finalized. Being first or second to the market (with a quality product) was important for capturing early market share with a longer revenue stream.

Once a new technology was introduced by Tek or by one of its able global competitors, there was less than 800 days to recoup the investment and make a profit. Looked at in this light, every day of lost opportunity caused by bureaucratic slowdowns was costing the company thousands of dollars.

Design teams of engineers and assemblers were empowered to make design decisions within certain boundary conditions. Approval-type activities were minimized and manufacturing team members were included early in the design process to lessen the downstream redesign work. Empowered manufacturing workers put a customer "hot-line" on the floor to respond to customer questions directly, and they put their workstations on wheels to allow for frequent reconfiguration of the workplace to correspond to ever changing process improvements. Most of the changes were instituted in real time by the empowered product SDWTs of manufacturing, marketing, finance, and engineering employees, who often couldn't afford to wait for management approval. The results? Several design teams brought new test and measurement products to market in one half the time it used to take. The need to redesign existing product lines to make them more manufacturable has decreased significantly.

Boeing Cuts Design Time.   Boeing 777 design teams are another example of empowered teams being used to improve the speed and quality of product delivery. The teams are cross-functional groups of engineers, assemblers, finance, and marketing people. Decisions are made in real time without the traditional wasted periods while one department waits for the reactions or approval of another. Rotating leadership of the teams depends on the phase of the project. At the time of this writing, the leadership of the teams comes from design engineers because the primary product of the early phases is a good design for the new airplane. But as the project nears the production phases, the leadership will formally shift to the manufacturing team members. Boeing believes that these empowered teams will significantly improve the time to market of what has been called the largest industrial project of this type in the world.

Cost Drivers at Corning.   Stan Zelleck, the plant manager of the Corning plant in Oneonta, New York, described some of their reasons for moving to work cells (their version of the SDWT). In an employee meeting he walked up to the newsprint pad and began writing down the names of three competitors in the biotech and medical research plastic labware industry. He then wrote a comparison of financial data obtained from annual reports for the Corning plant and the competitors. The demonstration showed the difference in gross production costs for a large company like Corning and for small companies like some of their competitors.

While competitiveness has always been important, the new business challenges created by the global marketplace, small but well capitalized competitors, and significantly higher customer expectations can't be met in this plant with traditional bureaucratic solutions. They are too slow, too rigid, and too costly. With pressures from insurance companies to lower medical costs and from colleges to lower research costs, only dramatic increased productivity and rapid, ongoing process improvement can help them be competitive. The plant couldn't compete if everybody did one separate job in the traditional way. It couldn't afford equipment downtime while operators waited for engineers to fix them. It couldn't afford the expensive material waste caused by not empowering workers to make real time improvements to their processes. They were having to offset the lower wage cost and lower overhead costs of their competitors by acting differently. Although it is still to early to determine if the strategy is working, the plant expects the kinds of cost improvements other Corning facilities have obtained (in the neighborhood of 30 to 50 percent as mentioned in earlier chapters).

Cost pressures are affecting a number of similar operations. Says Jimmy Bilodeau, the plant manager of the new Apple Computers plant in Fountain, Colorado, "We have to show that we can still make quality, cost competitive products at U.S. labor rates. That's what we intend to prove here with our teams. We can compete globally by using empowerment."

Reduced Defense Spending

At companies like Martin Marietta and Texas Instruments one of the driving factors for empowered project teams is the dramatic change in defense spending. The end of the cold war has affected millions of defense jobs across the globe. Only the most effective organizations, those who capitalize on the full potential of their human and technical resources, will survive. Executives like Pete Teets and John Adamoli in the Astronautics Division of Martin and Steve Leven of TI's Defense System Group realize that this kind of effectiveness cannot be mandated by management but must be generated willingly by the work force who are empowered to take action on process improvements to lower cost and improve speed, quality, and responsiveness.

New Social Complexity

Many other elements in the current business environment drive organizations towards teams and make bureaucracies and hierarchies obsolete. Though many of these pressures have been around for years, they have a new and immediate impact on organizations. You hear it everywhere. Customers are changing; they want more quality. There are more competitors. We are in the midst of a technology and information explosion. There are heightened environmental concerns. Both public utilities like Iowa Public Service and corporations like Monsanto for example, are looking for ways to cover the cost of conformance to stricter pollution laws through work redesign improvements by teams.

Current complexities are affecting noncommercial enterprises as well. What is teaching school like today? Consider the speed with which important education information changes now. How would you like to teach social studies when even cartographers, the people who make maps, can't keep up with all the country name and border changes of modern society? For the last several years there have been periods of only a brief few months when even the latest world globes were accurate. Can traditional centralized curriculum committees plan classes and purchase texts anymore, or do SDWTs of teachers have to make these calls real time? Consider this. Steve Posner, a former USC professor now has a monthly periodical for high school students called *Fast Times*. The periodical has a distribution of more than 19,000 schools with a readership of more than a million students. Its purpose? To supplement social science texts, which can't keep up with the changes in today's world. Texts can't be printed fast enough to be relevant, let alone accurate, in today's quick paced world.

Changing Work Force Expectations

Some organizations are finding that they need SDWTs to recruit top-notch talent. Highly trained technical talent nowadays wants more than money. They want influence and high quality of work life too. This is affecting a number of operations. In parts of the United States, for example, the baby boom workers are gone. For R. R. Donnelley and Sons in the Los Angeles area, the reason for empowerment is attracting and retaining skilled talent, workers who are no longer willing to accept the quality of work life of a traditional printing operation.

There are other human reasons, of course, for moving away from traditional operations. The General Manager of the financial division of the Seattle Metro public transportation organization, Tracey Petersen, is supporting the SDWT concept because she believes it is now a moral imperative. Today's work force has higher expectations for involvement and is better educated and more capable than ever before. This human potential is often vastly underutilized in traditional organizations which treat workers as hands and backs instead of whole human beings with minds and hearts.[4] "They deserve better," says Petersen, "I have come to believe that I have a moral responsibility to manage the work force in a way that allows them more influence over their work life. It's the right thing to do for our staff and it has given us better results for our customers."

Adapting to Change

For these and other reasons in the modern work environment, SDWTs are a timely idea. In fact some operations are using the teams primarily for their proven flexibility and adaptability to almost any change. While we don't know what specific changes will be in store for us, the last decade has taught us that we can depend on constant change. The nature of the future—the "constant whitewater" described by Professor Peter Vaill, consultant Tom Peters and others—is such that more and more organizations find self-directed work teams newly appropriate for their evolving needs.

Technology to Support Empowerment

The second major reason why these nontraditional work organizations and work roles will become more prominent in the future is team-facilitating technology. Now, with user-friendly personal computers, faxes, and telephone networking alternatives, there are cost-effective technological options that allow the increased utilization of meaningful work team involvement. A whole new information systems software genre, dubbed "groupware," has emerged to facilitate team involvement as well. These packages include:

- Electronic messaging systems (electronic mail, teleconferencing, etc.).
- Decision support systems (automated Delphi and nominal group techniques, etc.).
- Systems to support collaboration (shared authoring processes, bulletin boards, etc.).

- Most importantly, business information systems that make timely cost, quality, and project status information available to all team members.

These technologies facilitate group decision making, problem solving, information gathering, and information assessing. Technology can also provide some substitutions for the information passing and coordination role of the traditional hierarchy. This allows teams to be directed by the work and information rather than by managers. Each of these facilitating factors deserves some elaboration.

Team Decision-Making and Problem-Solving Technologies

In a front page story of the *Seattle Times* a reporter noted that Boeing had begun replacing "imperious, turf-minded supervisors with self-regulating, cross-discipline teams" in various parts of the corporation.[5] The move will continue on a grand scale in the new 777 design operation, which will be organized into multiple teams of eight to ten designers, production experts, customer support personnel, and finance specialists. "The idea," the paper reports, "is to have each team consider the aircraft as a whole and to empower each team to act quickly on ideas, free from the chain-of-command second-guessing." To do this has required a technology that until recently was not cost-effective. "Computer modeling," the story continued, "... is a linchpin tool. The teams have the capability, via a computer screen, to design and match up parts for the entire aircraft, minimizing the need for expensive mockups" and time-consuming management authorization "to see if parts fit and alterations work."[6] These technologies have enabled the teams to make decisions and solve problems that would have required a traditional supervisor before.

Other technologies can help teams with additional decision-making tasks as well. Apple Computers, for example, now has developed a software package that facilitates team staffing decisions. Included in the spider network are complete work and education histories of employees everywhere in the search area. Motorola uses computer polling to allow groups to do assessments and to display results real time as charts and graphs. The technology will also help in training. Teams can use photographic white boards to display and copy their meeting notes. Soft technologies like the search conference[7] and large group information and decision-making processes are used widely by companies like Corning to enable groups of 200 people or more to participate in real time decision making.

Team Information Systems

All these technologies, if used properly, provide processes that can focus teams and define legitimate opportunities for action. Effective utilization of these and other decision-making and problem-solving technologies depends, of course, on the quality of the data used. Thankfully there are also technologies to aid teams with information gathering, sharing, and evaluation. This eliminates much of the ineptness that often characterizes the ineffective groups that are "unburdened" by timely and relevant facts and data. Those are the kinds of groups we have ridiculed in the past. (Question: What is a camel? Answer: A horse designed by a committee.)

In the past, organizations that wanted to include team members in decisions had a difficult time getting so many people good information in a timely way. But group information sharing is no longer the logistical problem it once was. My colleagues Steve Rayner and Mareen Fisher and I were duly impressed, for example, when we visited an NEC factory in Toyama, Japan in 1987 to see the work area filled with terminals, which could be accessed by anyone on the floor at any time. These terminals were linked to a file server containing information on goal achievement, cost, quality, waste sources, machine efficiencies, and specific project indicators, which was updated every 40 minutes. Armed with this kind of timely data, people can become significantly involved in the management of the business in ways that were not practical before the introduction of these technologies. In the U.S., several companies are developing similar systems. At the Elkton, Maryland, Air Products and Chemicals polymers chemical plant any employee on site can access real-time information on new orders, production status, quality, schedules, and a variety of other production information.

Information Gathering

TV and VCR technologies also make information gathering for teams much more practical. Communication from customers, vendors, and other people in the company can be done in a way that is more accurate, more understandable to the team and more human than memos or supervisory monologues. One organization design team from Northern Telecom, for example, took a film crew with them as they searched the world for cutting edge organizational alternatives in Canada, the United States, Japan, and Korea. The video was a much more powerful way for the representatives to communicate their findings than a lecture from a supervisor or human resource professional would have been.

Information Is Power

These technologies have facilitated empowerment because ultimately information *is* power. Information is the power to foresee trends, to solve or avoid problems, and to make good decisions. Participation without information is a sham. But with good information (as well as legitimate authority and resources to act on that information), people can effectively get involved as partners in their organizations. In fact, information not only supports involvement, it causes it. I have seen numerous examples of team members who have been drawn into improving a longstanding work process, for example, simply because they learned that there was a better way or because they found out for the first time how much money the process cost. I have seen people at every level of the organization—*even though it sometimes meant personal inconvenience*—decide to do things differently when confronted with the facts.

Technology Substitutions for Hierarchy

These same technologies can often complete some of the traditional tasks of supervision. Control equipment in factories, for example, can provide operators with up-to-the-minute information that previously had to be communicated by the boss. Computers in service operations can help professionals synthesize and prioritize information in a way that was possible before only by depending on the supervisor. Federal Express drivers carry palm sized computers that give them pickup and delivery addresses for overnight packages. These digital readouts substitute for supervisory-determined job assignments, which, by the way, would be too slow.

Other technologies are allowing substitutions for the oversight and coordinating functions of a traditional hierarchy as well. CEO T. J. Rodgers of Cypress Semiconductor, for example, has a computer system that allows him to review the goals of all 1,500 employees in four hours. He does it weekly. He then telephones and chats with people. He doesn't call to supervise but to offer the help his position/clout allows. This substitutes for layers of expensive bureaucracy to align teams towards common goals and to minimize overlapping efforts in different parts of the operation.

Technology Helps But Is Not the Whole Answer

As always, technology by itself is not the answer. In their upcoming book *Teams and New Technology*, authors Don Mankin, Tora Bikson, and

Susan Cohen argue that advances in information technology cannot unleash the full potential of collaborative work unless complementary changes are made in work flow, team structure, supervisory styles, and work cultures.[8] But if teams apply and customize the technologies appropriately, the technology can become a tremendous tool for real empowerment, which until recently was unavailable.

AT&T, for example, is putting many of their salespeople into "virtual offices." The virtual office concept means that sales professionals will work almost exclusively out of their cars and homes: no common offices, no clustered desks, no weekly staff meeting on site. Only a few years ago this organizational design would have required a hierarchical approach to management. Someone (presumably the boss) would have to approve decisions, solve problems, and maintain consistency and control across the sales force. With modern technology, however, they have other alternatives to a single boss coordinating everything. Cellular phones, portable faxes and computer networks allow the rapid transmittal of information from one salesperson to others. Teleconferencing makes meetings and real time group decisions possible for people who are located all over the globe. While it will certainly still have its challenges, AT&T virtual office members can be self-directed work teams. That would have been nearly impossible in even the recent past.

Worker Participation Is Inevitable

The third and perhaps the strongest reason of all to question the long-term viability of the traditional supervisory role is that some form of worker participation is inevitable. Look at the remarkable world events of the late 1980s and early 1990s. Forever etched in the minds of the observers of communism and authoritarian governments is a nearly incomprehensible television picture: the mobs tearing down the Berlin wall with crowbars and fists as the guards look on passively. Many of us thought that event would not occur in our lifetime. And that was only one of the remarkable events of these last few important years. We saw Boris Yeltsin calling successfully for the Soviet people to stand up against the military leaders who kidnapped Mikhail Gorbachev in a coup attempt designed to stave off impending republican reform. We saw the limp body of an executed oppressive East European dictator, and the bravery of a single demonstrator attempting to block an approaching tank column in Tiananmen square. In countries in Eastern Europe and South America, democratic reformers have replaced totalitarian predecessors (with varying degrees of success). These demands have been heard in Africa as well. Polish unionist Lech Walensa catapulted from a workplace reform-er, without a prayer of a chance to affect change (we thought), to a high ranking government official in an extraordinarily short period of time.

The World of Democratic Reform

Think about the amazing political collage of these last few dozen months. In just a handful of years, popular revolutions have either toppled long-standing and seemingly unmovable autocratic governments or focused world attention on the population's demands for significant democratic reform. Why? Because the human spirit longs to be free. Repression is less tolerated in the modern world of human rights advocates supported by a world press. For all its weaknesses, people still want democracy. Some have been willing to die for it.

In a world that celebrates a rich diversity of cultural heritage, I find it interesting that virtually all cultures have stories or religious texts that are remarkably similar to what the Judeo-Christian cultures know as the "Golden Rule": to treat others as you want to be treated. Most people eschew even the subtle forms of human subjugation of one class of people by another. People will continue to seek equality, influence, and freedom.

Democratic Reform in the Workplace

This freedom will demanded increasingly not only from political systems but from organizational systems as well. The autocratic practices of tradi-tional organizations will simply be rendered obsolete as people demand the right to be included in the governance of their work life, just as the students and citizens of the world are demanding the right to influence politics. Modern-day revolutionary heroes like Thomas Jefferson are alive and well in today's workplace. And they are still saying the same thing. Consider the following only slightly modified version of a famous revolutionary document:

> We hold these truths to be self-evident, that all people are created equal, that they are endowed by their Creator with certain unalienable Rights, that among these are Life, Liberty and the pursuit of Happiness. That to secure these rights Management is instituted among People at work, deriving their just powers from the consent of the governed. That whenever any Form of Management becomes destructive of these ends, it is the Right of the People to alter or to abolish it, and to institute new Management, laying its foundation on such principles and organizing its powers in such form, as to them shall seem most likely to effect their Safety and Happiness.[9]

Worker participation is a manifestation of peoples' desire for democracy in the workplace. Legislated already in some Scandinavian countries, and discussed as a possible element of the European Economic Community initiatives, this trend will naturally follow the democratization of other political systems. SDWTs are typically the natural extension of this movement. Although they are not democracies in the strict sense of the term, they do allow the kind of influence on the workplace that has normally been unavailable in traditionally managed operations.

Summary

Because companies are replacing traditional organizations with self-directed work teams, a number of supervisors at all levels of the organization are in the middle of a major evolution of their work roles and responsibilities. This trend is not an aberration but instead a harbinger of the future. Why?

1. Empowerment is an idea whose time has come. Recent time-to-market pressures, cost drivers, social complexities, reduced defense spending, demographic changes, and regular unpredictable change are a few of the reasons that SDWTs are newly appropriate for today's workplace. Traditional workplaces just can't handle these situations as well.

2. Technology now makes empowerment practical.

3. Basic human needs make worker participation inevitable.

For many team leaders newly submerged in SDWTs, however, the transition is considerably more difficult than they expected. Managers newly introduced to team management often face predictable kinds of dilemmas, which are highlighted in the next chapter.

Endnotes

1. Peter Drucker, "Twilight of the First Line Supervisor?" *Wall Street Journal* (June 7, 1983).

2. Quoted in a presentation at the Association of Quality and Participation's annual conference by Peter Senge, April 7, 1992, Seattle, Washington.

3. This model is used with the permission of BFR, Inc. © 1989 BFR, Inc. All rights reserved.

4. Jack Sherwood has often used this terminology when working with clients.

5. Byron. Acohido, "Boeing's Bold Switch Toward Japanese-Style Work Teams: 777 Is Focal Point of Move to Put System into Effect Company-Wide," *Seattle Times*, Sunday (April 7, 1991).

6. Ibid., p. A8.

7. Marvin Weisbord, *Productive Workplaces: Organizing and Managing for Dignity, Meaning, and Community* (San Francisco: Jossey-Bass, 1987).

8. Mankin, Don et al., *Teams and New Technology: Developing Information Systems for Collaborative Work* (Cambridge, Mass: Harvard Business School Press, forthcoming).

9. Adapted from Thomas Jefferson, *American Declaration of Independence* (1776).

5

The Transition from Supervisor to Team Leader

A Rocky Road

Working through the corporation for 40 years under the autocratic system was a lot easier, particularly when you want something done quickly and you are convinced you know the right way to do it. It is a lot easier to say, "Okay, boys, we're going to Chicago tomorrow," rather than sit down and say, "All right, first of all, do we want to go out of town? And where do we want to go—east or west? And if we're going west, which of seven cities do we go to?" And we finally narrow it down and go to Cedar Rapids, Iowa, and I really didn't want to go there. I spend a lot of time working at participative management. But I have to be honest and say that I think we get better decisions out of it.[1]

ROGER SMITH,
former CEO of General Motors

Changing to a team leader is difficult. Not everybody makes it. Fred Eintracht, a manager who pioneered SDWTs at Texas Instruments puts it this way, "self-managed work teams are not for the faint of heart."[2] Consider a few of the predictable problems people encounter when they

44

are changing from a traditional manager (supervisor) to a leader of an empowered work team:

> The programmers Bob supervised at the insurance company had gone through a major organizational change to become a self-directing team. When he asked for clarification about his role, however, people would usually tell him what not to do: "don't control" or "don't direct people anymore." Or sometimes he would be told to "lead instead of manage" or to "be a coach instead of a boss." Was he supposed to just turn over all of his responsibilities to the team? Was there a job for him here any-more? What value did he add?

> Carlos, a rookie operations team leader in a progressive manufacturing plant in the southwest United States, was confused and frustrated by a recent workshop he attended. Titled "The Role of Team Leaders," the workshop made him feel that there was a right and a wrong style of management for self-directed work teams. The right style described by the instructors felt unnatural and awkward to Carlos. Was he supposed to act as though he was somebody else? He wondered if his decision to come to this plant had been a mistake.

> Mary was a management team leader for a division of an electronics company,which was changing to work systems based on a high level of employee commitment and participation. She saw the teams struggling with important issues about which she had extremely strong opinions. But should she say something to them at the possible risk of "taking over" and shutting down their emerging sense of involvement?

Typical Transition Problems

Bob, Carlos, and Mary are experiencing the painful but predictable transition problems associated with changing from a supervisor to a team leader. Some people make the switch almost effortlessly. Says Terri Volpe, a controller who became a team leader of an SDWT of finance and accounting professionals at Tektronix:

> For me it was major relief. It was finally the opportunity to do business the way I thought business ought to be done. Instead of hanging around the office every day checking to make sure that everybody was doing what I told them," people go off and do their jobs... and come up with some better results than what I originally thought they were going to go after.[3]

But this sense of relief is not a common sentiment for people who struggle with the personal change required. One team leader from Shell Canada, for example, described his feeling during the transition from traditional to team leader practices as being like having one foot on the dock and one foot on a boat. You're not sure whether to stay on the dock [which represents the stable, predictable management methods of the past] or whether to jump on the speed boat revving up to head off in a new direction [the uncertain and fast moving future]. In some ways it comes down to taking a leap of faith.

Paul Whitesides, the staff psychologist for the Highline School District near Seattle, Washington, says this is a very personal change for team leaders to make. He compares it to moving a cemetery. "You have to move one body at a time," he says. Changing traditional approaches to management requires far more than changing technique. For many of us it requires a fundamental reassessment of the hierarchical paradigm on which organizations have been based since the turn of the century. How do you know when you had made the switch successfully? One Tektronix operations team leader says it is harder than most people think. Many who claim they have always acted this way are fooling themselves. "If you think you are already there," she says, "you haven't even started." She adds that there is hope, however. "If you think you have a long way to go, then you're already on the way."

To further complicate matters, we have often developed our traditional approaches to management because it was required of us by the same organization that now wants us to change. Says Rick Nicholson, a human resources executive with Weyerhaeuser:

> ...one of the most difficult changes to make when implementing high performance systems is for the "manager" to become the "leader." [But]... they have been promoted, recognized, and rewarded for their controlling skills, not their delegation, coaching and facilitation skills.

Supervisors feel a little "schizophrenic" as they watch the leaders who built the system that created the need for traditional management practices in the first place (and who were often seen as the personification of them) turn around and call for change.

There is considerable evidence that changing from a traditional supervisor to a team leader can be very unpleasant. Prominent researchers like Rosabeth Moss Kanter, for example, have highlighted some of the typical concerns associated with this change[4] and while they were at Harvard, Professors Richard Walton, Leonard Schlesinger, and Janice Klein also cataloged the difficulty in numerous articles with titles like "Why Supervisors Resist Employee Involvement,"[5] "Work Restructuring and the Supervisor: Some Role Difficulties,"[6] and "Do Supervisors Thrive in Participative Work Systems?"[7]

It Is Difficult for Supervisors at Every Management Level to Change to Team Leaders

First level supervisors are not alone. Senior level and midlevel supervisors have also experienced some considerable difficulty in these transitional settings. At Honeywell, R. J. Boyle, a vice president, reported that upper management supervisors expressed discouragement when early attempts at empowerment created numerous task forces that were clearly "out of control."[8] Roger Smith, former CEO of General Motors, says it was easier just to tell people what to do than to manage his own team of direct reports this way. Midlevel management supervisors confess frustration with their ever increasing loss of control over work processes; senior staff supervisors dislike the premature challenge to their expertise made by others who take on responsibilities previously held only by them as functional experts. It just flat *ain't easy* for many supervisors to change to team leaders regardless of their position in the organization. In fact it is harder for management to change to SDWTs than for anybody else.

Changing to SDWTs Is Harder for Team Leaders Than Team Members

Based on research by the experts just mentioned, as well as my own experience with these transitions, the graph (in Fig. 5.1)[9] depicts the contrast in the ease of transition to self-directed work teams between nonmanagers and managers.[10] While the difficulty may not be manifested until later in the implementation process, it is almost always significantly more difficult for supervisors to make these changes than it is for the rest of the work force.

Unfortunately, to avoid these transition problems, some companies have given up and walked away from self-directed work team philosophies part way through the implementation process. Thinking that the medicine is worse than the illness, they have prematurely aborted the empowerment process before it has a chance to show a return on the financial and human investment they had already made. Some have abandoned the effort because they were more interested in maintaining management control than in taking the uncomfortable personal risks required to get improved results from empowerment. Others, like Jack's company mentioned in Chap. 1, have eliminated or steamrolled over

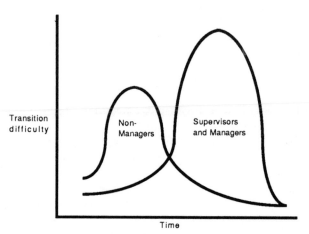

Figure 5.1. The relative difficulty of changing to self-directed work systems. (*Belgard•Fisher•Rayner Inc. © 1989. All rights reserved. Used by permission.*)

some supervisors to try to make the implementation work without them. Obviously, none of these options is the best way to resolve these difficult but predictable transition issues. When organizations are committed to this process they will take the time to work through the difficulties with supervisors in a way that makes the most sense for their set of circumstances. It doesn't make it easy, but it does make it possible.

Four Reasons the Transition Is So Difficult

Some supervisors are frustrated with the change to the team leader role because they have a fundamental, gut-level disagreement with this direction. They feel that it is an abrogation of management rights and responsibilities, which will lead their company on the sure path to chaos and destruction. Generally speaking, however, very few supervisors continue to have this disagreement once they really understand SDWT leadership. The four most common reasons for supervisor transition difficulty are:

1. It is frequently seen as a net loss of power or status for management.

2. The team leader role hasn't been well defined for most supervisors.

3. Some are concerned about losing their jobs due to SDWT.

4. In what might be called a "double standard" syndrome, many supervisors are expected to manage in a way that is very different from the way they are managed themselves.

Each of these issues deserves elaboration.

Dealing with the Perceived
Loss of Power or Status

The first reason that supervisors at every level of the organization resist these changes to team leadership roles is that they see it as giving up something. Two senior level supervisors I worked with at Monsanto, for example, had this difficulty. Both of them were asked to relinquish certain executive prerequisites to create an egalitarian climate more conducive to SDWTs. One of them hesitated to give up his preferred parking space and the other refused to give up a spacious office. When I asked them about their concerns, they both said that they had worked long and hard to get where they were. They felt they deserved the little extras commensurate to their positions. In either of these cases I don't think that the parking space or office was the real concern. It was the power, the prestige, or the status that these things symbolized.

"I miss the prestige, I can't say I don't," says Miles Majure who was a second level manager with Duke Power in Huntersville, North Carolina.[11] He helps to coach new teams now and likes it that the workers are happier than before. But he still has that sense that he has come down in the world. That is not an uncommon perception. Our societies often judge us by the work titles and responsibilities we have. People understand and respect "supervisor," "manager," or "vice president." "Team leader" they don't. It isn't common enough yet to have earned its own appropriate level of recognition.

Position Status

Once in a training class, as we were talking about the role of the team leader, a burly middle level supervisor from Shell Canada interrupted the discussion. "What am I going to tell my mother?" he asked. At first I thought he was joking. Then he continued. "How am I going to explain to my family and friends that I am not a 'Director' anymore? How can I tell them that I don't run this business?" He was genuinely concerned that his change in responsibilities and job title would be seen as a demotion by the people he cared about.

In our own consulting and training company, the absence of a traditional high status title was at one time actually affecting our ability to get the work done. Larry Welte, a former controller at Tektronix and Hewlett Packard, does SDWT financial system consulting and manages company finances for BFR. Like the other BFR consultants, his title is "principal." He found, however, that the general financial community was confused by his title. So he had two sets of business cards made up. One set, which says "Principal," he uses with clients and company team members. When he introduces himself to bankers for loan negotiations, however, he uses the other set of cards, which say "Chief Financial Officer." They understand that better, and they know he has sufficient clout to represent the company.

Dysfunctional Status Symbols

Some people might think these are trivial concerns. They are not. Some companies are now holding sessions for the families of former supervisors to help them understand the importance of the new roles and reduce the anguish of the transitioning leader. Even if these responses sound petty, I would suggest that many of us feel the same way even if we don't admit it openly. We all want to be recognized, rewarded, and important. But we can't let these normal desires interfere with workplace effectiveness.

Substituting the dysfunctional status symbols common to hierarchical organizations with more functional ways to meet these personal needs is very important. Some companies, for example, have team leaders mentor other people. These assignments help the organization by facilitating the transfer of skills and knowledge to a broader base of the population. But they also recognize teachers for their expertise. Other organizations have made them consultants or have given team managers key roles on important technical or business projects with high visibility.

Unclear Roles Cause Unnecessary Transition Difficulties

Most of supervisors' concerns about a loss of power or status are resolved when organizations create appropriate team leader roles and then make these roles clear. The feeling of disempowerment is often based on a misunderstanding (or on organizational misapplication) of the SDWT concept. They believe that empowerment is a win-lose game. Workers win and supervisors lose.

Much of the concern expressed by traditional supervisors at all levels of the organization, as illustrated in the stories of Bob, Carlos, and Mary, can be alleviated through ongoing discussions to clarify the new role of team leader (assuming, of course, that the role has been appropriately designed). The proof then is in the pudding. The organization must back up these discussions by reinforcing them through the reward and information systems. Successful organizations aid the team leaders in defining and becoming skilled in the new roles. Unfortunately, this is often not done very well. For the typical supervisor, a lack of organizational support and role clarity condemns them to what is becoming known as the "wing-walker problem."

The Wingwalker Problem

The predicament of many supervisors can be compared to that of the wingwalkers in the barnstorming days of early aviation. Like the wingwalkers, supervisors at all levels are asked to change positions on a moving biplane when they start using any significant form of empowerment. There is an important rule known by all wingwalkers, however, that is very useful for people in a similarly turbulent situation to know. The wingwalker rule is, *"Never let go with one hand before you grab hold with the other one."* All old wingwalkers know this to be a useful rule.

But this rule is often broken during the transition process. Supervisors like Bob are told what to let go of (e.g., "Do not control or direct anymore") rather than what to grab hold of. That is not good enough. The result is as devastating to the organization as it is to the wingwalker. The most common response is to hold on more tightly as the "wind velocity" of business demands increases (thereby struggling even harder to hold on to the comfortable but no longer appropriate role). Other supervisors simply let go and abdicate responsibility to ill prepared team members.

To use another analogy, being told what not to do is like trying to teach someone to ride a bike by telling them how not to do it. The results are almost always disastrous as the new bike rider keeps thinking, "Don't lose your balance and fall down." What usually happens? We do exactly the thing we are trying so hard to avoid. Supervisors at all levels need to have a clear understanding of the team leader role and how it differs from that of classical management. Moreover, we need to understand that this new role will change over time as the teams mature. Without this understanding, supervisors are left in the dark with unrealistic expectations for their teams and each other. This is a very serious problem, and the bulk of the next two chapters will deal with a better approach to this role clarification process.

Job Security Concerns Frustrate Supervisory Change

The third reason for frustration among supervisors in transition is that they often perceive self-directed work teams as organizations without a real role for them. For some it is a basic job security issue. Look at what we call these organizational structures. "Self-directed" or "self-managed" work teams sounds suspiciously like we do not need supervisors anymore. This notion is reinforced when companies like Dana Corporation publicly announce the reduction of management levels from 14 to 6 due to moving responsibilities "down" into the organization. General Mills claims that much of the productivity improvements they have realized from the SDWTs comes from the elimination of middle management.

Other companies, like Tektronix and Monsanto, have offered early retirement incentives to encourage management downsizing, and then engaged in efforts to create self-directed work teams because there were not enough supervisors to manage in the traditional way. All of this is, obviously, a matter of concern for supervisors.

Every Team Needs a Coach

While it is true that fewer policing and directing tasks are required in these organizations, there is a corresponding need in SDWT operations for an increase in group facilitation, skill development activities, and information gathering and dissemination. These work systems require a formal leadership role. Although numbers of organizations (both SDWT and traditional operations) are eliminating supervision positions, this doesn't necessarily mean an elimination of people. In fact, some organizations have discovered that they have taken out managers to the peril of the operation.

Tom Clark, a senior manager at Tennessee Eastman, notes that while self-directed work teams can be successful in sustaining their operations without management (they have had some examples of teams operating without managers), these "...Teams haven't improved their operation without the help of a team leader." His conclusion? We need team leaders. These are not supervisors who direct and control people, of course, but team leaders who teach and support them. In the Procter and Gamble plant where I worked as a team leader, a level of management that had been eliminated earlier was added back several months later. Was this a failure of the self-directed work team design? Certainly not. Our assumption about the elimination of management from the teams was naive. Every team needs a coach. Successful organizations normally change supervisory jobs into team leadership positions. They don't just strip the resources from the operation.

What Happens When There Are Too Many Supervisors?

Some organizations find during the transition that they have too many supervisors. Originally staffed for traditional operations, which required multiple levels of supervision, these organizations find they have more supervisors than new team leader positions. What do they do? Some operations have laid these supervisors off.

This is extremely unwise for several reasons. First, the unnecessary loss of the supervisors' expertise to the operation can be deadly to less mature teams. Second, management support is critical to the success of these implementations. We simply cannot expect support from managers who suspect that they will lose their jobs as a result of SDWTs.

What are some alternatives?

- When the Rohm and Haas Louisville Kentucky plant changed over to self-directing work teams several years ago, they had fewer team leader positions available than people who had been managers. To deal with this problem, they made a number of their supervisors into training coordinators who were responsible for managing the endless education requirements of the team.

- While most companies don't replace retiring supervisors in this situation, one company *hired back* some of the supervisors who took early retirement as part-time trainers.

- At another company supervisors agreed to provide 18 months of technical advice to the teams. At the end of that time the company agreed to place them into other positions.

- In still another company 25 supervisors participated in designing a SDWT system with only 10 team leader positions. Those who weren't selected for the jobs were guaranteed their existing salary package if they became a team member, or they had the option to transfer.

Other companies have used other solutions. Although there are no perfect solutions to these difficult business realities, these approaches minimized what could have been not only a serious disenfranchisement of the displaced supervisors, but also a great trauma to the survivors as well. Instead, these approaches institutionalized a process for skill, interpersonal and business development in the facilities and provided these supervisors a personal vehicle for providing their teaching and mentoring resources to the team members.

The Double Standard

The fourth common transition problem comes from the all too frequent perception that there is a double standard for treating team leaders and team members. The way some organizations implement self-directed work teams reinforces the notion that self-direction is only for the work team and not for the leaders. It is seen as something that "the top tells the middle to do with the bottom." Empowerment should work everywhere in the organization and not just for nonmanagement teams. If these participative systems are to endure they will have appropriate inclusion and roles for everyone.

Unfortunately, many organizations have introduced self-directed work team practices in a way that has greatly threatened supervisors—the most critical players in assuring the overall success of the SDWT effort. These shortfalls have created frustration and resistance, which are unnecessary when compared to what some organizations have encountered during the transition process.

Successful Team Leader Transition at Kodak

There are, fortunately, some good examples of successful transitions from the supervisor to the team leader role. Several team leaders at Kodak, for example, made what workers called "big changes." Most of the supervisors had three things going "against them," if one were inclined to believe these frequently repeated (but often inaccurate) stereotypes. First, they had military management backgrounds. ("When I say jump, you say how high?") Second, they worked in a company with a reputation for management techniques that were contrary to many of the SDWT concepts. ("It might work in some new companies in California, but it will never work here.") Third, they had held traditional supervisory roles for a number of years. ("You can't teach old dogs new tricks.") Despite these "three strikes," and although they had had reputations as successful autocratic supervisors, they had changed over several months to be very good examples of SDWT team leaders. This same story has been repeated in other companies by supervisors at other levels of the organization as well.

What was different for this group of supervisors? They managed their change process to assure the maximum possibility of success. They started a weekly study group, for example, to review the dozen books they had been reading as a group. These sessions ended up providing a lot of learning. They helped the supervisors to understand the changing nature of the Kodak business environment and to clarify the leadership role required to be successful in the future. Through their reading, they discovered that a number of different companies were facing challenges that could no longer be met successfully with a traditional approach to supervision. Consequently, through their discussions about the challenges facing their own business with strong competitive pressure from Fuji Film, they decided together that they needed to change the way they managed.

The supervisor team then made a number of changes. Traditional supervisory functions were assumed by the work teams as the teams were trained to accept them. Their job assignments then expanded to incorporate work tasks that before had only been done by higher level managers.

Performance appraisals were changed to support the new responsibilities of team leaders. Perhaps most importantly, they were led, empowered, and supported through the transition by a manager who modeled appropriate team leader behaviors. Much of the clarity they received about the new role came from watching their "boss" act that way himself. Rather than tell them, for example, that they needed to be sensitive to team input, he opened an early study group by requesting feedback on his own performance. Though initially cautious about giving the boss honest feedback, it gradually became a norm inside and outside of the study group. And once they saw it done, it was much easier to go out and do the same thing with their teams.

Summary

Changing from a supervisor to a team leader is a difficult process. In fact, it is much more difficult for supervisors at all levels of the operation to change to SDWTs than it is for anyones. In fact it is much more difficult for supervisors at all levels of the operation to change to SDWTs than it is for anyone else. Many supervisors have problems during the transition because (1) it is seen as a loss of power or status, (2) the new role is unclear, (3) they fear losing their jobs, or (4) this role isn't modeled by the leaders of their own management team. Despite what the name might imply, however, self-directed work teams do need team leaders. While these role changes are usually difficult, examples like the team leaders at Kodak show that they can be made very successfully.

A more detailed look at the "13 Room" department at Kodak in the next two chapters will begin to clarify some of the key transition learnings to consider when changing from supervisors to team leaders.

Endnotes

1. "The Painful Reeducation of a Company Man," *Business Month* (October 1989), p. 78. Reprinted with permission of *Business Month* magazine. Copyright © 1989 by Goldhirsh Group Inc., 38 Commercial Wharf, Boston, MA 02110.
2. Alan Cheney, "Self-Managed Work Teams," *Executive Excellence*, February 1991, p. 12.
3. Belgard•Fisher•Rayner, Inc. "The Leadership Role" Videotape © 1991. All rights reserved.
4. Rosabeth Moss Kanter, "Dilemmas of Managing Participation," *Organizational Dynamics* (Summer 1982), pp. 5–26.

5. Janice Klein, "Why Supervisors Resist Employee Involvement," *Harvard Business Review* (September–October 1984).

6. Richard Walton and Leonard Schlesinger, "Work Restructuring and the Supervisor: Some Role Difficulties," *Report to the Harvard Business School* (March 1978).

7. Richard Walton and Leonard Schlesinger, "Do Supervisors Thrive in Participative Work Systems?" *Organizational Dynamics* (Winter 1979).

8. R. J. Boyle, "Wrestling with Jellyfish," *Harvard Business Review* (January–February 1984), pp. 74–83.

9. This graph is used with the permission of BFR, Inc., © 1989 BFR, Inc. All rights reserved.

10. The sobering graph on management transition difficulty is based on the writing of Janice Klein, especially "Good Supervisors are Good Supervisors—Anywhere," *Harvard Business Review* (November–December 1986) and "Why Supervisors Resist Employee Involvement," *Harvard Business Review* (September–October 1984), along with the observations and research of William Westley, "Quality of Working Life: The Role of the Supervisor," *Employment Relations and Conditions of Work* (Labour Canada, 1981), Richard Walton and Leonard Schlesinger, "Work Restructuring the Supervisor: Some Role Difficulties," *Report to the Harvard Business School* (March 1978) and "Do Supervisors Thrive in Participative Work Systems?" *Organizational Dynamics* (Winter 1979), and K. Kim Fisher, "Management Roles in the Implementation of Participative Management Systems," *Human Resource Management* (Fall 1986).

11. Beverly Geber, "From Manager into Coach," *Training* (February 1992), p. 28.

PART 2

Building the Foundation for Change

6

The Kodak 13 Room Story

Empowering Team Leaders

The signal benefit the great leaders confer is to embolden the rest of us to live according to our own best selves, to be active, insistent, and resolute in affirming our own sense of things.... And they attest to the wisdom and power that may lie within the most unlikely of us.... Great Leaders, in short, justify themselves by emancipating and empowering their followers.[1]

ARTHUR M. SCHLESINGER JR.,
*historian and former advisor to
Presidents Kennedy and Johnson*

My colleague Steve Rayner and I were commissioned by the Work in America Institute to write a case about a successful SDWT of team leaders at Kodak. We discovered what we think you will agree is a remarkable story. Following are excerpts from that case, which was written primarily by Steve.

Housed on the grounds of Eastman Kodak's enormous industrial complex in Rochester, New York, is a manufacturing department known as 13 Room. Here color film for the consumer and professional markets is manufactured. Eastman Kodak's 13 Room offers a dramatic example of how to introduce self-directed work team management in a manner that draws strength from the management team rather than alienating it.

59

Background

The process of producing color film is very complex. Some 3,000 potential variances have been identified through the process flow—anyone of which can result in an unacceptable final product. To add to the difficulty of manufacturing, many of the steps done by the 13 Room employees are still performed manually. The critical step of formulating the chemicals, for example, is still done entirely by hand in a manner similar to the method devised by Mr. Eastman decades ago.

In 1987, after completion of a successful project with Eastman Kodak's International Operations, Ralph Olney became Manager of 13 Room. The organization he inherited consisted of nearly 200 operators, supervisors, and managers. Within the corporation the operation was seen as a solid and consistent performer.

During his project with International, Olney had the opportunity to broaden his perspectives of not only the film business, but of industry in general. He had witnessed dramatic competitive changes in a variety of markets and could see the traumatic impact they were having on many corporations. As Olney was reflecting on his new position and what he hoped to achieve, he began to recognize that a new management approach would be required. One that unleashed the energy and creativity of the work force by developing their capability. He needed a management team that was selflessly committed to transferring their knowledge and expertise to those who worked with them.

Management Practices Reflected the Military Background of the Supervisors

Historically, nearly 80 percent of the supervisors in the various film production departments at Kodak had backgrounds that included military service. As a result, many of the management practices seemed to reflect a military model. Typically the supervisor was the technical expert and gave directives that specified exactly what was to be done and how to do it. Orders were generally followed by subordinates without comment or question. The hierarchy was clearly defined.

Olney recognized that this perspective had some predictable consequences. First, supervisors tended to be so directly involved in the running of the work area that it was not uncommon for them to be on 24-hour call. If a process problem arose, regardless of the hour (day or night), it was likely that they would be called to fix it. Second, operators had come to believe the correct way to address a problem was to call the supervisor or some other technical expert for the solution. Generally, operators had been given little opportunity to take on expanded responsibilities and were sometimes punished when they did. Although 13 Room was unique in many respects, it was not immune to the impact of a work culture that had tended to reward tight, autocratic supervision, along with minimum operator development and involvement. As one operator described it:

> You were literally told what to do and how to do it. You never got any information about the business or even how the unit was performing. You were completely in the dark. And if you didn't follow up on a demand you'd been given and the foremen found out about it, the comment back would be "you don't need a badge to leave here."

An Environment of Trust Is Created

Olney's first words to his reports were, "Let's figure out a way to work ourselves out of our jobs." The comment was taken seriously by the majority of his staff. Olney quickly created an unusual environment of trust because he had worked with several of the supervisors before. As one staff member recalled:

> When Olney said that, I thought, "Sure, why not?" It never occurred to me to be concerned with job security or anything like that—I trusted Ralph [Olney]. I figured if I really could work myself out of my job there would be something better ahead.

The Change Process Begins with Education

The process of introducing self-directed work team management in 13 Room began with the formation of a study group. The group consisted of Olney and his five reports. Starting in June 1987, they met one or two days every month to discuss one of the 12 books that they had jointly decided were the "essentials" in understanding high performance work systems. During their discussions they would note specific concepts, learnings or models that were directly applicable to their operation. These observations from the readings later become the foundation for the vision, the operating principles, and many of the strategies that were specified in the 13 Room business plan. The study group continued through November.

Operators Become Interested in the Study Group

One of the interesting and unexpected benefits of the study group was the response of the operators. As one team leader recalls:

> People would ask, "Where've you been?" and I'd tell them about the study group sessions and what I was learning from the books we were reading. The next thing I know people were asking to read my copy after I was done. Then copies started appearing in the work area that people had gone out and bought on their own. Everybody was thirsting for knowledge.

Supervisor Group Empowered to Make Unit-Wide Decisions

Based on their learnings from the various readings, the staff decided to identify and eliminate the bottlenecks that were currently having a detrimental impact on the operation. The foremost bottleneck they identified was the flow of information and decision making from Olney's office. Decisions had historically funneled up to the 13 Room Unit Manager level for approval before any direct action was taken. This included decisions relating to budget, schedule, technology, quality, cost and safety—virtually everything relating to the operation of the organization was brought to the Unit Manager. As a group it was decided to formally eliminate this step and begin empowering the first level supervisors with the decision making authority and responsibility to address these issues. This was further augmented by having their direct involvement in setting the 1988 goals for 13 Room. These included goals for quality, delivery, cost, and safety.

Upon completion of the study sessions the staff set out to describe a vision and the operating principles for 13 Room. The vision that was developed looked three to five years out and was focused on five areas of responsibility: site, management systems, operations, personnel, and planning. To further the role expansion of the first level supervisors, each of Olney's five reports became responsible for managing one of these areas in addition to their regular responsibilities. The supervisor responsible for personnel, for example, developed the group's affirmative action goals, determined training needs, assured conformance to state and federal laws with regard to labor practices, and oversaw the compensation program. The supervisors regarded the chance to absorb these responsibilities as being "exciting opportunities" rather than "just more work." As one supervisor succinctly put it, "I was having fun for the first time in years."

The concentration on expanding the role of supervisors continued into 1988. During this period more and more emphasis was put on the importance of supervisors working toward developing the capability of their work groups. Initially this was primarily done in the form of increased information sharing. Olney began modeling this important aspect of their role by sharing pertinent business information at monthly assemblies. During these meetings, open to everyone in the organization, Olney would share the latest financial, quality, cost, and schedule data for the unit, as well as review strategies and customer feedback and address any other issues that might be of interest to the audience.

Organization Structured into SDWTs

The supervisors were starting to act like an SDWT of team leaders. They determined that a reorganization of the reporting structure would help facilitate information sharing and problem solving. Under the reorganization, teams were formed based on the flow of the product (formerly teams had been formed and managed based on their shift). This new structure created some immediate advantages including far greater visibility of bottlenecks and problem areas. It also had the advantage of creating a stronger sense of team identity among the operators. The newly formed groups were called "core teams."

Team Meetings and Training Critical

The operations team leaders began to hold regular meetings with their core teams. These meetings became focused on problem identification and resolution. They also served as opportunities for team leaders to share with their teams what they had learned from the study group sessions. In this way the meetings began to develop the capability of the work teams themselves. This was the critical piece of the overall role expansion equation: the team leader role could expand only to the extent the work group role absorbed many of the traditional supervisory responsibilities.

To further develop the skills and abilities of core teams, the team leader group became directly involved in developing a training package that included statistical process control, just-in-time (inventory and waste reduction) concepts, group interaction, goal setting, and consensus decision making. The training sessions, which were divided into 12 different modules, were taught by the team leaders themselves.

64

13 Room Declared a Business

To more fully describe how much the management of the operation had changed, the 13 Room staff declared itself a business in April 1988. From a legal standpoint nothing was really different—13 Room was still a manufacturing unit within Eastman Kodak—but from a psychological standpoint, everything had changed. Olney took on the title of "CEO" and each of his staff members became a "Director." They began to develop measurements, including financial data, that looked at 13 Room as if it were an independent business. They extended the focus of their role on more strategic, longer-term issues and put even more emphasis on developing their work groups. As one "Director" described it:

> The question we had begun asking ourselves was, "If this were my business what would I do?" After we declared ourselves a business it really began to feel like it was our own.

Results

The results of this effort are impressive. From 1987 to 1988:

- Overall product conformance to specifications improved 27 percent.
- Statistical process control improved 228 percent.
- Output increased 12 percent.
- Cost dropped 11 percent.
- Uptime increased 2 percent.
- Safety increased 67 percent.
- The department achieved the highest rating of any production in the Kodak's annual quality of work life survey.

No less impressive is the profound nature of the changes to the management role. Operations team leaders are now directly involved in strategic planning, goal setting, customer and vendor relations, and the continual development of their team. "Our role today is so different," stated one team leader, "that if a foreman from 10–15 years ago were to come here and see what we're doing he'd have a stroke."

Summary

We have much to learn from the 13 Room transition to self-directed work teams. Unlike many other organizational changes of this type, which have traumatized supervisors, these Kodak team leaders have been personally empowered through the process. The common thinking that suggests that empowering workers means disempowering team leaders proved wrong in this case. As a result of unusually high trust between the management team leader and the operations team leaders, coupled with specific acts that empowered them to perform important new responsibilities, these team leaders saw the transition as a personal win rather than a career loss. As these changes were supported organizationally through formal title changes (and by recognition systems reinforced through performance appraisals and project reviews with Olney and other team leaders), they became real.

In analyzing this example in detail, four critical factors that led to the successful transition of the supervisory role to the team leader role clearly stand out. These characteristics can be briefly described as:

1. Create an expanded role (not a diminished role) for team leaders.

2. Develop a true self-directed work team for team leaders, not just for workers.

3. Manage by vision and principles rather than by policies and procedures.

4. Make developing capability a priority.

Each factor will be covered in more detail in the next chapter.

Endnote

1. Arthur Schlesinger, "On Leadership," in Roger Burns, *Abraham Lincoln* Broomall, Penn.: Chelsea House Publishers, 1986) p. 9–10. Used by permission.

7

Overcoming Common Transition Difficulties

Four Learnings from the 13 Room

The worst thing you can do to a team is to leave it alone in the dark. I guarantee that if you come across someone who says teams didn't work in his company, it's because management didn't take an interest in them.[1]
JAMES WATSON,
Vice President of Texas Instruments

The 13 Room change process demonstrates how an organization can avoid many of the problems suffered by team leaders in transition. Consider the following:

Create an Expanded Role for Team Leaders

All too often the role of team leaders in self-directed work team organizations is described in terms of what they should not do (the "wingwalker problem"). Supervisors should not dictate; they should not make decisions for their group; they should not railroad decisions through; they should not take credit for the accomplishments of the group; they should not manage the attendance policy and vacation schedule and so forth. On the other hand, even the list of "shoulds" is typically filled with terms that have become cliches like "coach," "leader" and "facilitator." These terms, though perhaps accurate, are often not helpful to managers and supervisors who find themselves struggling with exactly how they should be spending their time and focusing their energies on a day-to-day basis. As a result many supervisors, faced with the transition to self-directed work team practices have a fairly concrete notion of what they should be giving up, but only an abstract idea of what they should be moving towards.

Avoiding the Wingwalker Problem

The wingwalker problem was clearly avoided in the 13 Room transition. The supervisory team saw themselves as the creators and architects of the new work environment rather than victims of it. They were first involved in expanding their own knowledge of technical processes and high performance work systems through the study group. This helped them to develop the vision and operating principles for the organization. Once the vision and principles were defined, they became directly involved in translating them into a business plan with clear goals, objectives, and strategies. Each step in the process built on the previous one, expanding both the personal capability of the team members and the horizons of their role as team leaders. It became natural for the operations team leaders to begin relinquishing many of their former administrative responsibilities and technical expertise to their team since the expansion in the capability of the team allowed them to further expand their own roles. The management team leader (Olney) did exactly the same thing for the team of leaders.

Using Symbols to Reinforce the Changing Team Leader Responsibilities

While to some the act of declaring 13 Room a business and forming a Board of Directors might seem silly, its significance on both a symbolic and literal level cannot be ignored. Symbolically it represented a clear break with the supervisory practices of the past and suggested a greatly expanded role for the team leaders. On a literal level it was representative of the kind of work that the former supervisors had begun to do: It was strategically oriented, directed more toward customer and vendor interfaces, and more fully focused on the development of people.

Develop a Self-Directed Management Team

The transition to self-directed work systems is generally described as being a traumatic, gut-wrenching experience for supervisors at all levels in the organization. It is viewed as requiring individuals who are introspective enough to recognize their own personal biases and the impact that their management style has on their team. In short, supervisors need to acknowledge how they must personally change before they are likely to become effective in the new team environment.

Applying SDWT Principles to Team Leaders

The 13 Room case helps to illustrate a dramatically different approach— one in which the management team served as the primary support mechanism during the transition. Instead of being a group of independent first level supervisors focused on the success of their functional organization and competing for the limited attention and resources provided by higher level supervision, these team leaders were treated as a self-directed work team themselves. They had common goals and multifunctional tasks, and they were responsible for making decisions and solving problems as a team.

Certainly one-on-one meetings between Olney and members of his staff were important, but far more critical was the interaction and feedback that the operations team leaders received from each other on an ongoing basis. Initially Olney, the management team leader, modeled this behavior by asking staff members to provide him with candid feedback about his performance during one of their team meetings. As Olney recalls,

> It was several months into our effort and several things were going wrong. So I went into the staff meeting and said, "I need some help. Give me some feedback." The initial response was silence. Not a word. Then I prodded the group a little and suddenly it all came flooding in. I left the meeting with a list of 30-some items.

At the next meeting Olney went through the items and described those that he felt were his responsibility and those he felt were the team's responsibility. He described what he was going to do with those items he felt were most important for him to personally address; he also facilitated the group through decisions on how to address those that were more the responsibility of the team.

The Importance of Example and Feedback

The 13 Room case demonstrates the power of feedback in a constructive, nondefensive manner. This power was further augmented by a two-week course, attended by the entire management group that was focused on how to effectively give feedback. The common experience greatly enhanced their ability and desire to give constructive criticism and support for one another's efforts. One manager described his relationship with the team succinctly by saying, "When I committed to the future state of this business I was accountable to the unit, not to Ralph [Olney]. My reinforcement comes from them."

The team that was formed among the group of managers was further enhanced by their responsibility structure. Since each had the dual responsibility of managing both a manufacturing operation and what traditionally would have been a site-wide staff responsibility (site, personnel, planning, operations, managing), a tremendous amount of interdependency existed among each member. If, for example, a training issue emerged in one core team the manager responsible for personnel would work directly with that group and their direct supervisor to address it.

Manage by Shared Vision and Principles

By having the team leaders develop the vision and guiding principles as a team, Olney ensured a common acceptance and common understanding of the direction of the organization. This was augmented by Olney's ability to model the importance of "managing by principle," one of the key attributes of team leaders, which we discuss at length later in the book. Rather than direct or regulate with policies or procedures (the preferred means of operating a traditional organization), Olney used the principles the team leaders had developed instead. During staff meetings, for example, Olney would ask questions that ensured that the principles were being considered before decisions were reached. This continued modeling led to the formalization of a proposal and business plan format which required that the relationship between the guiding principles and recommended actions were thought through and consistent. The management team saw an essential part of their role as being guardians of the vision and operating principles of 13 Room. This gave them another shared responsibility and kept them focused less on their individual teams and more on the shared purpose of the newly organized business.

Develop Capability

One of the things that immediately strikes the outsider who observes members of 13 Room is the emphasis put on developing the capability of the team. The phrase "building capability" means developing the business, interpersonal, and technical abilities of the work force far beyond the level considered adequate in a traditional organization. The phrase is uttered constantly. To the management team and core group members, the words are not lip service. They are truly obsessed with the idea. "*Everything* we do here," noted one team leader, "is directed toward developing more capability in each other."

Building Team Leader Capability

Developing capability takes on many forms in 13 Room. Initially, much of the capability development was directed at the management team. This was initiated by the study group sessions where, over the course of six months, 12 management books were read and thoroughly discussed. "It was like going back to school again," reflected one team leader of the intensity of the sessions. The books—which included *The Goal, A Passion for Excellence* and *Japanese Manufacturing Techniques*—served as "eye openers" to what is possible in a high performance work team environment.

The expansion of knowledge was tightly coupled with an expansion of responsibility. The management team was encouraged to begin applying what they had learned and given the necessary authority and responsibility to see the changes through. The team itself became engaged in developing the vision and principles for the operation and ultimately setting the business plan. Olney was particularly effective at encouraging this expansion and challenging the capability of each team member. According to one team leader, "He shares responsibility, which is very different from delegating. I have as much input as anybody."

Building Team Member Capability

Capability building was no less emphasized among the core group members. This was begun first by increasing the flow of information to the operators through monthly information sharing meetings. At these meetings Olney would share the current financial, quality, and output performance, as well as strategies that were being pursued or feedback from customers, with everyone in 13 Room. This flow of information was soon augmented by improvements in the computer information systems that gave operators up-to-the-minute status reports on the performance of the entire unit.

Training

In addition, a 12-module training program was begun that covered topics ranging from the basic concepts of self-directed work teams to the intricacies of process flow mapping and statistical process control. It is noteworthy that these training sessions were not conducted by a separate training department, but by the management team themselves. The sessions were cleverly designed, often using a game show format to make the learning experience more fun. The module on statistical process control, for example, followed a format identical to *Jeopardy* where teams were given the answer and then scrambled to be the first ones to push the buzzer and give the correct question.

The Importance of Ongoing Learning

The expansion in capability continued (and continues) in virtually all areas of the operation. Operators took complete responsibility for developing the training manuals that depict the correct methods for performing each sequence in the unit. They also determined the means for conducting cross training and set a realistic implementation schedule. More recently they have begun redesigning the work area to more effectively utilize existing space, and they were directly involved in creating a new performance evaluation document and describing the process for its use. Some team members have volunteered to become the "subject matter experts" for their core group in the area of quality management. These individuals are currently on an intensive one-year program, in which they are working and learning directly from the process engineering department about the complexities of color film manufacturing. After the completion of their program they will return to their core team where they will share their knowledge with their teammates. In this way the entire capability of the team will be enhanced through their experience.

As the increase in capability has occurred, so have the expectations that both management and peers put on one another. As one operator noted, "There was a time when you got rewarded for just knowing your name." Clearly that is no longer the case. The obsession with developing capability has greatly enhanced the current performance of 13 Room and promises to do so well into the future. As one engineer noted, "The problem now is keeping up with the demands for more knowledge. We aren't able to develop the capability in them as fast as people are able to assimilate it."

Summary

The four simple lessons are important themes to remember when introducing self-directed work team practices: create an expanded role, develop a self-directed management team, manage by vision and principles, and develop capability. Kodak was able to engage their supervisors where others have only frustrated them. More importantly, the expansion of their roles, as well as their participation in the transition process itself, improved the implementation of the SDWTs throughout the organization. The 13 Room experience demonstrates the importance of applying the concepts of self-directed work teams to management groups. In this way many of the typical transition difficulties reviewed in earlier chapters are rather neatly resolved before they become problems. We have also learned from Kodak that the role of the team leader is critical to SDWTs. The SDWT of team leaders would not have happened without a Ralph Olney. And the self-directed core teams would not have happened with the operations team leaders, Richard Burke, Miles Kavanaugh, Herb Melcher, Norm Roegiers, and Gerry Shepard.

In the next several chapters we will explore in more detail team leader characteristics and the role of leaders during the implementation. Many of these things have been highlighted briefly in this study. But the ability to effectively manage by principle, develop team capability, and model appropriate behaviors takes more than acting a certain way.

In the next chapter we will consider both the visible and the invisible parts of being an effective team leader.

Endnote

1. Brian Dumaine, "Who Needs a Boss?" *Fortune* (May 7, 1990), p. 58. © 1990 by The Time Inc. Magazine Company. All rights reserved. Used by permission.

PART 3

The Power of Values and Assumptions

8

The Visible and Invisible Elements of Team Leadership

The most difficult thing for me was giving up control. I was far more traditional than I thought I was.[1]

BOB CONDELLA,
*Director of the
Administrative Center of Corning, Inc.*

One of the reasons that the role of the SDWT leader is difficult to explain is that it is something more than just actions and activities. It includes the way leaders think and the things they value. We talk too often about the team leader's role as something that we *do* instead of something that we *are*. We focus on management behaviors or on styles without also discussing the things leaders care about, like their personal values and vision, or a set of core beliefs that influences their actions. The resulting picture is incomplete. It is not wrong, but it is not entirely right either. It is like trying to explain why a glove moves without discussing the hand inside it.

Problems with Focusing Only on Actions

Focusing exclusively on the behavioral part of this role implies that we want team leaders to learn a standard set of participative behaviors, or to mimic the style of other successful leaders. This is a deceptive if not a dangerous practice because an action that is entirely appropriate in one situation may be completely counterproductive in a slightly different one. And the problem with trying to exactly copy someone else's style, of course, is that pretending to be something you are not is an unhealthy, unsatisfying, and ultimately unsustainable effort. It is a sham.

Situational Leadership Does Not Help Much Either

Even the idea of situational leadership—the notion of selecting and applying a particular leadership style warranted by the situation—is not very helpful in clarifying the team leader role. Of course, different situations require different approaches. But telling someone to change their style suggests a sort of mechanical selection from a set of preprogrammed responses. That never felt very authentic to me. It comes off like play acting instead of really manifesting convictions. It is sort of like walking around in an uncomfortable, ill fitting mask just because it has the required expression for the moment. Peter Vaill, an authority on high performing organizations, expresses this idea succinctly. He writes:

> I would say a lot more clearly how bankrupt I think situational manage-ment is for understanding leadership in high performing systems. It is true that in high performing systems, leaders' styles "fit" the needs of the situation. It is not true that in high performing systems leaders have made any very concerted effort to change their style to fit the needs of the situation which is what situational theory says you're supposed to do. Leaders of high performing systems seem to understand instinctively that if you tinker with your style, you'll undercut your effectiveness.[2]

So where does that leave us?

The Role Is More Than a Style of Managing

We need more discussions about the inside stuff of managers; about what some team leaders call "managing with your gut." Understanding this role requires more than an understanding of the things we can see team leaders do. It requires looking at what happens inside of them as well. We have generally avoided these kinds of discussions about what goes on inside someone's mind, however, for some pretty good reasons:

1. Things like management beliefs cannot be observed. Since they cannot

be observed they cannot be touched, photographed, verified, or quantified. That makes them hard to talk about and impossible to measure.

2. What team leaders care about can be pretty personal. Delving into these issues may seem intrusive.

3. Things like values and vision sound pretty soft. They do not grab the attention of many busy, results-oriented leaders like well reasoned prescriptions about what to do and how to act.

Despite our discomfort with probing the internal stuff of team leaders, however, we need to do this to understand the role of the SDWT team leader and to show how it differs from the classic role of the supervisor. Supervisors have become frustrated with the contradictions and confusion caused by emphasizing only the visible parts of this role. That means we must look inside at the intellectual and emotional parts of management.

A Model for Discussing the Things You Cannot See

For purposes of this discussion it may be helpful to divide the various aspects of the management role into two parts: observable things (like an individual's behaviors, styles, and statements) and unobservable things (like someone's values, assumptions, paradigms, and vision). (See Figure 8.1). The unobservable things are examples of the core beliefs of the team leader. They include the invisible elements that create a personal code of rightness and wrongness in conduct.

In the model, the different elements of the team leader's role are divided into two boxes: the invisible box and the visible box. Elements in the boxes interact with each other. If a leader really *assumes* at gut level

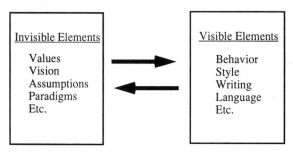

Figure 8.1. The invisible and visible elements of the team leader role. (*Adapted from K. Kim Fisher, "Managing in the High-Commitment Workplace" Organizational Dynamics, Winter 1989.*)

that team members have good ideas (things in the invisible box), for example, then the leader's *behavior* (things in the visible box) will likely reflect these biases. Thus the team leader who assumes that the clerks will do a good job hiring their peers is much more likely to invest in the training necessary to prepare them to manage the hiring process than the supervisor who doesn't believe they can do it.

In later chapters we will review the importance of these invisible elements of the role required to be successful as a team leader. At this point, suffice it to say that most unsuccessful team leaders have problems not with behavior or skill deficiencies, but rather with the invisible stuff of leadership. Jim Wessel, a vice president at Becton Dickinson, noted that some of their more problematic transitions were in changing their thinking, not just their actions. "We had to get over the mind-set that said, 'I'm not in control, so it must be out of control,' " he says.[3]

Just as the invisible elements of the role affect the visible elements, the reverse is also true. If a team leader actively practices the *behavior* of soliciting ideas from team members, for example, then that leader's *assumptions* and *values* about this topic will likely be influenced by these experiences. To go back to the hiring example, assume that a new team leader from another area is transferred to work with the team in the middle of the hiring process. Even if she wouldn't have assumed that this team could have done the hiring (and probably wouldn't have empowered them to do so if it had been her decision), her assumptions change when she sees them succeed. ("Hey, they did a great job, I'll do this again!")

Summary

Describing the role of the team leader requires more than a discussion of typical activities and behaviors. It requires looking at things that go on inside the team leader. Thus both things that are visible (like behaviors or management style) and things that are invisible (like assumptions and values) are important aspects of this role. Obviously, we cannot see what is in anyone else's "invisible box" except as it is demonstrated through visible behaviors. But we need to understand clearly how important the invisible elements are in driving effective team leaders. We also need to explore how a few commonly held values in traditional organizations inhibit the effectiveness of the team leader.

The next chapter focuses on some of those values that can either inhibit or accelerate team leader effectiveness.

Endnotes

1. From a presentation to the Corning Information System Group by Bob Condella, Corning, New York, January 14, 1992.

2. Peter Vaill, personal correspondence, 1986.

3. Brian Dumaine, "The Bureaucracy Busters," *Fortune* (June 17, 1991), p. 34. © 1991 by The Time Inc. Magazine Company. All rights reserved. Used by permission.

9

Theory X Assumptions and Control Paradigm Thinking

You Can't Get There from Here

In warfare, commanders like Captain Queeg, who rule by intimidation and monitor every maneuver from the top, have sometimes won battles and even wars. But from the German blitzkrieg to Asian guerrilla struggles, the most adaptable forces, and the most effective... have been those in which soldiers and subcommanders understood the objective and could be trusted to work toward it on their own.[1]

JAMES FALLOW,
Author

On the morning of July 1, 1916, British troops launched what was to become a horrifying suicidal assault on the Germans at the Somme. During the attack, troops emerged from their trenches and began marching in orderly rows directly into German machine gun fire. Several problems could be faulted for the unthinkable slaughter of that day. But Author Paul Fussell argues in *The Great War and Modern Memory* that

60,000 of the 110,000 British soldiers were killed or wounded during that battle largely because of the British class system and the assumptions it fostered:

> The regulars of the British staff entertained an implicit contempt for the rapidly trained new... "Kitchener's Army," largely recruited among workingmen from the Midlands. The planners assumed that these troops—burdened for the assault with 66 pounds of equipment—were too simple and animal to cross the space between the opposing trenches in any way except in full daylight and aligned in rows or "waves." It was felt that the troops would become confused by more subtle tactics like rushing from cover to cover, or assault-firing, or following close upon a continuous creeping barrage.[2]

Our Thinking Affects Our Behavior

Fortunately, business leadership assumptions rarely result in carnage of this magnitude, but our beliefs about people *will* affect our ability to work successfully in a SDWT environment. Our values, assumptions, and management paradigms will ultimately become our behavior. To test this idea ask yourself the question, "Do I know what is important to my boss?" Unless we are new or dysfunctional employees we almost always know what our boss *really* cares about through the subtle clues they give us—not the stuff they say they value, but what they really care about. They can use new behaviors, techniques, styles, or vocabularies for a short time, but ultimately they reward or punish us according to what they truly value. And sometimes we know what they value better than they do. The same is true of each of us. Until our beliefs about people change, for example, our actions towards them aren't likely to change. A Monsanto manager once told me that the difference between successful and unsuccessful SDWT leaders was more in what they thought than in what they did. It's perfectly natural. Like a Pop Warner football coach told me once: "Watch their navels, not their heads, their body will follow their navels." Similarly our actions will follow our gut-level beliefs and values.

If we honestly believe that everyone wants to do a good job, or in the words of Johnsonville Foods' CEO Ralph Stayer that, "they want to achieve greatness," we will treat people differently than if we are skeptical of their motives or abilities. There is a lot of truth to the Biblical adage, "For as he thinketh in his heart, so is he."[3] That is why the invisible elements of the team leader role are so important. This change requires a whole different way of management thinking, because blocking the pathway to effective team leader behaviors is the gate of personal values, assumptions and paradigms. Without first unlocking the assumptions of the traditional supervisory gate, the traveler cannot progress far on the journey towards becoming a team leader.

In this chapter we will review some of the invisible elements of leadership that are so important to the team leader. Specifically, we will examine the problems caused by Theory X assumptions and control paradigm thinking. To introduce these topics, consider the following example.

The Invisible Team Leadership Elements in Action

When Ricardo Semler became president of Semco, Brazil's largest marine and food processing machinery manufacturer, he had a problem. The company was close to financial disaster. After a few years of "hard work" and "good luck," however, the company became one of Brazil's fastest growing companies, with a profit margin of 10 percent on sales of $37 million in 1988. What happened to turn around the company?" Says Semler: "...most important were the drastic changes we made in our *concept* of management."[4] Specifically, Semler credits the three fundamental values on which some 30 management programs are based. The three values are democracy, profit sharing, and information.

Grand values like these that aren't acted on, of course, don't have any currency in the workplace at all. In fact, to the predictable detriment of the organization, they only create cynicism and mistrust. Some supervisors individually, and some organizations (apparently speaking for supervisors collectively), have articulated such values or principles or enlightened assumptions about the work force for years. Semler calls this "participatory hot air." I call it the *stated* values. What is important, of course are the *demonstrated* values and assumptions, the values we enact.

Demonstrated Values Are More Important Than Stated Values

When Semler, for example, *stated* that he assumed all workers were adults, he *demonstrated* the value by abolishing the norms, manuals, rules, and regulations that were inconsistent with that assumption. Flex time was established, dress codes eliminated, and collective decision making introduced. When it was time to make a decision about relocating the marine division into larger facilities, they closed up shop for a day, loaded up buses of employees, and took them to evaluate the three factories for sale nearby. Interestingly, the employees favored a different building than did the culture and management team leaders (they call them "counselors"). They moved into the building the team members wanted, however, and the division's productivity per employee improved significantly. It jumped from $14,200 per person per year in U.S. dollars in 1984 (the year of the move) to $37,500 by 1988.

Says Semler, "Employee involvement must be real, even when it makes management uneasy."[5] He speaks from personal experience. Employees convinced him to abort an acquisition process that he was sure was the right thing to do for the business. Reflecting on this trial of his "democracy value" and "adult worker assumption," he believes that the future of the acquisition would have been clouded because the people who had to make it work didn't think it was the right thing to do. So it was probably the best decision to stop the process. But that didn't make it any easier to swallow at the time. He wanted it and they didn't. He was the owner of the company and could easily have forced his will on the organization. But reinforcing the values was more important to him than having his way.

Would the Semco turnaround have been successful without these actions? It's unlikely. Would Semler have been able to take the actions with a traditional set of values and assumptions about the role of managers? It's doubly unlikely. "Corporate civil disobedience" (Semler's words) requires a courage and conviction that is born from a different set of invisible gut-level beliefs. It's a completely different mind set. Let's explore the differences by reviewing a particular piece of management wisdom that has withstood the test of time.

Theory X and Theory Y Revisited

Most supervisors are familiar with McGregor's famous Theory X (autocratic) management and Theory Y (democratic) management. But many still think these are management styles or techniques rather than management assumptions. They miss the point. Theory X managers are not necessarily mean or harsh; they simply assume that people are naturally lazy and need to be supervised. Some of the nicest, most gentle supervisors I have known were Theory X supervisors. Conversely, some of the toughest and angriest supervisors I have known are Theory Y managers who assume that people want to achieve and consequently hold them accountable for it. The distinction between Theory X and Theory Y refers not to management styles or behaviors, but to assumptions that we have about people (see Table 9.1).

Table 9.1. Differences in Management Assumptions

Theory X	Theory Y
Most people are lazy.	People like to work.
Most people need to be controlled.	People have self-control.
Most people need to be motivated.	People motivate themselves.
Most people are not very smart.	People are smart.
Most people need encouragement to do good work.	People want to do a good job.

SOURCE: Adapted from the work of Douglas McGregor, especially *The Human Side of Enterprise* (New York: McGraw-Hill, 1960).

Team leaders are Theory Y managers. But what does that really mean? Without Theory Y assumptions we are simply incapable of being effective team leaders because we cannot allow ourselves to do what needs to be done in a team environment. Whenever I have had Theory X assumptions about team members I have worked with, for example, I have resorted to blaming, accusing, and nonparticipative behaviors, which only limit the capacity of the work force by creating fear, confusion, or even worse, apathy in the workplace. When we believe that workers are lazy ("All he does is waste time if I'm not watching him") or stupid ("She'll never learn the computer, she's a high school dropout"), we don't take the time to develop or challenge them. Consequently our assumptions actually limit their potential performance.

Theory X in Action

Most of us know that our assumptions affect our behavior towards others. We can validate this, of course, in our own personal experience. It is blatantly clear when others have Theory X assumptions towards us. For example, U.S. federal and state income tax forms and procedures are clearly based on the assumption that people will cheat on their taxes. Some company paperwork or processes apparently assume that employees are not trustworthy (time clocks, certain kinds of expense reports, expenditure authorization processes, etc.). Have you had these experiences? How do they make you feel? Do you feel empowered?

A particularly frustrating experience with Theory X assumptions occurred outside the business setting. I was on an airplane that had been badly delayed when a harried flight attendant started chiding us on the P.A. system for standing in the aisles. "You know people," she said caustically, "we can't push back until everyone is seated." What were her assumptions about the passengers? Did she think we were hoping to delay the flight further by lallygagging aimlessly in the aisles? It was clear to me that we were laboring as quickly as possible to get our luggage into the overhead bins so that we wouldn't miss our connecting flights. What we needed was some help with our luggage, not a tongue lashing. Too often what we give team members is polite recriminations when what they need is help with the luggage.

We Get What We Expect

When we believe that workers need to be supervised, we will find ways to control them. For example, I once talked with several livid union members who were told that they had to bring in a doctor's excuse for each time they take a sick day. Although there may have been abuses in the system, this particular company chose to tighten up the policy instead of dealing firmly with the abusers on a one-on-one basis. What do you think was the message delivered to the work force by that decision? The workers assumed that the message was, "We don't trust you and we will treat you like children." Unfortunately, if we treat grown-ups like children, they tend to act like them. One employee quipped that although he couldn't afford to go to the doctor for every flu or cold that he got, he would satisfy the new requirement by getting a note from his mother.

Theory X Assumptions Can Be Anywhere in the Organization

Dave Hanna, while an organizational development executive at Procter and Gamble, noted an interesting related phenomenon at executive levels in organizations. When managers were newly promoted, they would soon start complaining about how their bosses failed to realize the competence of the managers at their level. When they were promoted again, however, they soon forgot their earlier frustrations and began to question the competence of their former peers. He began to realize that most managers had the assumption that the level of incompetence was always one level below them.

These assumptions prompt supervisors at all levels to create audit systems to check their subordinates. These systems then hinder the subordinate's ability to do the work and negatively affect their accomplishments. Instead of working, for example, the subordinates have to spend their time filling out reports or defending their decisions. This then reinforces in the superior's mind that the subordinates are incompetent. It's a vicious circle caused by Theory X assumptions.

How Theory X Assumptions Become Self-Fulfilling Prophecies

In his book *Managing in the New Team Environment,* Larry Hirschhorn makes a similar argument.[6] He describes the psychology of control as a self-fulfilling prophecy. Supervisor Anne, for example, assuming that her subordinates need supervision, closely monitors worker Bruce's performance. Over time Bruce begins to assume that he must need to be supervised closely or else Anne wouldn't do it. So he acts accordingly. The supervisor sees how he acts and lays on more supervision to compensate for the lower level of self-initiated work. Bruce sees the increased supervision and his self-esteem suffers further; he loses more interest in the work, and so forth. It creates a negative performance spiral which injures self esteem and causes unhealthy dependency. Anne's good intention to improve the performance of the operation either causes performance to suffer or requires her to continuously increase her supervision to a point of diminishing returns.

Try Some Different Assumptions on for Size

If you are like me and don't come naturally to a lot of these Theory Y assumptions, what do you do? When something goes terribly wrong (that is usually when our true assumptions about people surface), slow down and force yourself to assume that the event happened in spite of the team members doing the best they could with the skills, tools, and information they had at the time. You will approach the situation much differently than if you start from Theory X assumptions. I know this from personal experience. Try it sometime. It's worked for me.

Early in the startup of our company we had problems with our training materials arriving in time for the sessions. After several phone calls, in which I reprimanded (in a nice way) the "responsible" principal for not performing up to the standard of service we expected, I found out that the problems had been caused by a lack of timely notification about the sessions. In almost every case, the problem had been caused because I, not understanding the time required for mockups, printing, and shipping, had not given people enough notice to accomplish the work. I had been reminded again of something that I frequently forget: we normally need to fix the system, not the people. My assumption that someone else was at fault for the mistake was wrong.

Another invisible element of team leadership related to the assumptions we have about people is our paradigm of work. This deserves some elaboration.

Work Paradigms

Our life experience is translated into models or patterns of thinking, the dictionary definition of "paradigm." Paradigms provide our own personal interpretation of reality and act like glasses through which we see and make sense of the world around us. During the time of Columbus, for example, the flat world paradigm was dominant. Consequently, maps were drawn accordingly and sailors would rebel when they had been at sea too long for fear that their captains were running perilously close to the edge of the earth. The earth-centered universe paradigm was so prevalent during the time of Galileo that the scientist's life was threatened when he suggested a sun-centered theory of the universe.

Our paradigms are so powerful that Thomas Kuhn, while writing a history of science,[7] found that scientists (a normally rational and logical group of people) frequently ignored data that was inconsistent with the prevailing theories of the day. They actually screened out information that couldn't be explained by their scientific paradigms, ignoring the inconsistencies, which when finally understood, often later led to scientific breakthroughs. The adage, "I'll believe it when I see it," is wrong. When we understand the impact of our paradigms, we understand that, "I will see it when I believe it."

Paradigm Paralysis

Joel Barker, a noted futurist, calls this phenomenon "paradigm paralysis," a rigidity of thinking that doesn't let people see things outside their frames of reference.[8] An example of this is the Swiss watchmakers who, because of their domination of the watch market for decades, were literally blindsided when digital watch technology took over the marketplace and caused the Swiss to lay off thousands and thousands of watch workers. Ironically, they not only didn't see it coming, but they actually were the ones who had invented the digital technology that drove them to their knees in the 1980s. At a watch show, the Swiss R&D people displayed the digital watch they had invented, which because it had no mainspring or face hands, was not considered by the Swiss to be important enough to protect. Their analog watch paradigm blinded them to seeing the threat or possibility inherent in the digital watch. Seiko and Texas Instruments were at the show and the rest, as they say, is history.

People Who Don't Have the SDWT
Paradigm Don't Understand SDWTs

I saw this happen at P&G. After 20 years of successful experience with SDWTs, there were still some managers (some at very senior levels of the company) who couldn't see what made these organizations work so well. During tours when visitors came through the Lima, Ohio plant, for example, I saw several managers rationalize away the impressive business results of the facility. "Well, you guys are successful because of the new equipment you have," they would say, even though less successful plants had the same equipment. "This is primarily because people work harder in the midwest than in other parts of the country," some argued, but there were successful SDWTs all over the country. Still others said it was because the plant was a "greenfield," or start-from-scratch, plant even though P&G had retrofit or "brownfield" success stories even back then.

Some visitors argued that anyone could do this if they could hire the kind of people we found at Lima. Somehow they did not realize that the technicians at Lima had become so skilled through of the years of special education, coaching, and experience they had received at work, all of which would be unavailable to employees in a more traditional workplace. These employees did not have all these characteristics when they were hired. They had to learn them in the same way that team leaders learn how to make good decisions and solve problems: by doing it. Genetic coding didn't create these extraordinary team members; their raw talents were refined in the crucible of personal experience and through the assistance of their team leader mentors who made sure that the development opportunities were provided.

Why didn't people understand? It wasn't because they were stupid. These were bright, successful managers. They simply were incapable of understanding things that were so inconsistent with their paradigm of management. They were literally blind—like the scientists in Kuhn's book—to the data.

Control and Commitment Management Paradigms

Our work paradigms are firmly entrenched in our minds and then consequently manifested in our organization structures and practices. Noted employee involvement expert Richard Walton, for example, identifies the primary difference between managers in traditional organizations and managers in empowered work systems not as their actions but as their paradigms about management.[9] He suggests that most supervisors at all levels of the organization today operate with the "control" rather than the "commitment" paradigm, seeing their job as controling the work force through policies and punishment. It is a logical extension of Theory X assumptions. The successful team leaders I have worked with, however, see their primary responsibility as engendering the commitment of the

Table 9.2. Differences Between Management Paradigms

Control paradigm	Commitment paradigm
Elicits compliance.	Engenders commitment.
Believes supervision is necessary.	Believes education is necessary.
Focuses on hierarchy.	Focuses on customers.
Has bias for functional organizations.	Bias for cross-functional organizations.
Manages by policy.	Manages by principle.
Favors audit and enforcement processes.	Favor Learning Processes.
Believes in selective information sharing.	Believes in open information sharing.
Believes bosses should make decisions.	Believes workers should make decisions.
Emphasis on means.	Emphasis on ends.
Encourages hard work.	Encourages balanced work/ personal life.
Rewards conservative improvement.	Rewards continuous improvement.
Encourages agreement.	Encourages thoughtful disagreement.

work force rather than eliciting their compliance. They do this by teaching, coaching, and leading team members so that the workers' own self-control can replace the externally imposed controls of traditional supervision. The differences between the control management paradigm and the commitment management paradigm can be seen in Table 9.2.

The Pervasive Influence of the Control Paradigm

Most of us have been heavily influenced by the control management paradigm because it is the most prevalent operating paradigm of management in modern organizations of all kinds. Many of today's supervisors grew up in families where parents were bosses who set rules, made the decisions for the family, determined chores, allocated resources, and administered punishments. They went to school where teachers were bosses who made assignments, ran the classroom activities, determined grades, and decided when students could go to the bathroom. In the military they had bosses who, because of their rank, could issue orders that were to be followed precisely and without question. Churches and community organizations they were associated with were run by bylaws, commandments, and rules of conduct. Governments created vast bureaucracies to regulate and enforce national, state, and local laws. In the workplace there were clear chain of command hierarchies, with every higher level of management responsible for the work of those below them. These workplaces were also permeated with laws, rules, regulations, contracts, and procedures.

Is it any wonder that so many of us see our roles as controling subordinates? I am not suggesting that the control paradigm is bad. In some situations it may be entirely appropriate. But it has clearly influenced contemporary management thinking because it has been so pervasive. It would be difficult to imagine a single supervisor who has not been immersed in the ocean of control paradigm examples that have washed over modern cultures.

The Language and Structure of Control

Even the language of many business organizations makes this paradigm explicit. Interestingly, the title "supervisor" sounds like "look over (the shoulder)" or "more important (than workers)." The title of senior financial people in the organization isn't "communicator," but "controller." Certain staff people are normally "auditors" rather than "teachers," and senior managers are often promoted to being "directors," rather than "facilitators" of particular groups. Instead of a "chief learning officer," we have "chief executive officers." We use these titles simply because they are logical extensions of our thinking.

There is additional evidence of the control paradigm at work. The traditional way to describe an organization, for example, is with an organization chart. This way of structuring organizations is so prevalent that software is now available that automatically draws a triangle-shaped chart of boxes and lines representing the cascading links in the management chain of command. Each level of the triangle has more authority and responsibility than the level below it. The boss is at the top of the pyramid, various levels of sub-bosses and their reports are sandwiched in the middle, and the base of the pyramid is composed of the people who do the work. What better example is there of control paradigm thinking? These organization structures are put in place not to allow for easy communication and coordination of activities, as is often posited, but to provide an authorization path for decisions.

There is, of course, additional evidence of control paradigm thinking. We sometimes share information, for example, on a "need to know" basis. This selective information sharing usually follows hierarchical lines because senior managers "need to know" while others apparently do not. Ironically, the people who must implement something often do not have access to the information necessary for effective implementation.

Clear class distinctions are implied in the reporting relationships described as "subordinates" and "superiors." Pay systems are set up to reward people for rank. This causes an interesting pay delivery pattern. Imagine you are an anthropologist 200 years in the future who comes upon the pay plan of a major current American company. What conclusions would you draw from the ancient artifact of a company of the twentieth century? Would you find it curious that the people who actually designed, built, or delivered the products and services of the corporation were among the lowest paid people in the operation? Would that be supportive of the written corporate statements you find that say that quality and customer focus are the primary goals of the operation? Would you wonder why such a corporation reserved its lowest rewards for the people who actually touched the product and worked with customers? Would you wonder what was really important in that operation? Is it really customers and quality they value, or is it control?

Results vs. Control

This reminds me of another issue that deeply concerns me. I have heard people say that certain supervisors at all different levels of the operation cannot support empowerment because they are just too results oriented. This is plain and simply untrue. This kind of management resistance comes because these supervisors are *not* results oriented. To be more precise, they value control more than results. Perhaps you know supervisors like this. They will not empower people because that is too "touchy feely," but they will spend thousands of dollars on consulting, training programs, or equipment that people know will not produce sustainable results. They will gladly waste precious time, energy, and money tangled in senseless bureaucratic red tape and protocols, but they would not think of "wasting time" in meetings to share information or decision making responsibilities with others. Is that being results oriented? No, it's being control oriented.

Contrary to popular belief, in order for SDWTs to work, we need more leaders who are results oriented, not fewer. We need more leaders who will put company profitability over personal profitability. We need more leaders who will put satisfying customers over maintaining management policies. We need less control paradigm thinking.

And it isn't just supervisors with this control management paradigm in their heads. One of the major transition obstacles organizations face is to help team members accept responsibility for solving problems and making decisions, which were traditionally seen as the job of management. There is something comforting in knowing that someone else is responsible for solving your problems. Some team members are uncomfortable picking up "management responsibilities."

SDWTs Require Commitment Paradigm

Does this kind of thinking and its manifestations in the workplace block effective SDWTs? Yes. Says Frank Merlotti, retired chief executive of Steelcase, "We tried to remove anything that got in the way of people communicating, discussing ideas. We wanted to get rid of the top-down thing."[10] Lots of organizations are following suit. Many of the artifacts of a workplace culture based on the control paradigm rather than on the commitment one are disappearing. In fact, quickly becoming obsolete in the SDWT workplace are:

- The traditional concepts of rank and privilege (parking places, office differences, executive perks, etc.).

- Status-laden organization responsibilities, described in "up" terms (higher, "more important," etc.) and "down" terms "lower," "less important," etc.).

- The typical business language that infers superiority and inferiority depending on job titles.

- And many of the other "we" vs. "them" distinctions of the classical operation.

There is an old saying that "the eyes are the window of the soul." Similarly, language is the window of paradigm and assumption. Successful team leaders, for example, don't say, "I did this." They say "We did this" or "The team did this." They don't say, "He works for me," or "She reports to me." They say, "We work together." They don't talk about "my employees" as though the managers were benevolent slave owners; they talk about "the teams" they work with. These kinds of statements reflect their internal conviction that they are working with the team as partners, not as superiors. Management titles are changed to reflect facilitative rather than directive responsibilities. More common than manager, foreman, or supervisor, for example, is leader, counselor, or advisor.

Team leaders use different metaphors as well. Traditional supervisors think about their jobs as a mechanical process. You can tell by the analogies and metaphors they use to describe their roles. For example, I have heard numerous supervisors talk about "driving" or "steering" or "jump starting" the organization they manage. This implies a mechanical view of managers as the people in the drivers seat of the organizational vehicle. Those who think this way believe that they are solely responsible for making things happen. Cars, unlike people, are not self-starting and self-steering. Team leaders tend to use metaphors that are more organic. They talk, for example, about the importance of helping to "grow" or "nurture" the organization. Their language doesn't imply a mechanistic or superior relationship with others. It suggests a developmental or teaching focus.

Summary

The invisible elements of the self-directed team leader role (like values, assumptions, and paradigms) can help or hinder the leader. Certain common beliefs about workers, for example, can actually limit the team leader's ability to be effective. Theory X assumptions, in particular, severely inhibit team leader success in the empowered workplace. If we believe people need to be supervised, for example, we will find ways (excuses) to supervise them. This creates a basic incompatibility in the work system between the SDWT concept (the stated value) and the management process (the demonstrated value).

For many of us, other invisible things need to change personally and organizationally if SDWTs are to succeed. Most organizations are loaded with the artifacts (language, structures, policies, etc.) of the prevailing control paradigm. Though most supervisors have been immersed in the control paradigm (the brother of Theory X assumptions) for years, successful team leaders change themselves and their operations to manifest a different paradigm. That mind set, the commitment paradigm, may be the crucial discriminating factor between successful and unsuccessful leaders of SDWTs. Although certainly some individuals and organizations require no significant changes to demonstrate to others in the workplace that their values are consistent with SDWTs, that is not true for everyone. What are those values?

In the next chapter we'll discuss some of the more specific nontraditional values and beliefs that seem to characterize successful team leaders.

Endnotes

1. James Fallow, *More Like Us: Making America Great Again* (Boston: Houghton Mifflin Company, 1989, p. 13. Used by permission.

2. Paul Fussell, *The Great War and Modern Memory* (New York: Oxford University Press, 1975), p. 13. Used by permission.

3. *Holy Bible*, King James Version, Proverbs 23:7.

4. Ricardo Semler, "Managing Without Managers," *Harvard Business Review* (September–October 1989), pp. 77. Italics added.

5. Ibid., p. 79.

6. Larry Hirschhorn, *Managing in the New Team Environment* (Reading, Mass.: Addison Wesley O.D. Series, 1991).

7. Thomas S. Kuhn, *The Structure of Scientific Revolutions* (Chicago: University of Chicago Press, 1970).

8. Joel Barker, *Discovering the Future: The Business of Paradigms*, Burnsville, Minn. Charthouse, videocassette, © 1990.

9. Richard Walton, "From Control to Commitment in the Workplace," *Harvard Business Review* (March–April 1985).

10. John Greenwald, "Is Mr. Nice Guy Back?" *Time* (January 27, 1992), p. 43.

10

The Values and Assumptions of Team Leaders

Lessons from the Trenches

If you really believe in quality, when you cut through everything, it's empowering your people, and it's empowering your people that leads to teams.[1]

JAMIE HOUGHTON,
CEO of Corning

Over the last decade or so I have talked to hundreds of team leaders in self-directed workplaces about their roles in these organizations. They represented over 45 different sites of more than 20 different North American companies, including American Transtech, A.E. Staley, Best Foods, Boeing, Colgate Palmolive, Cummins Engine, Digital, Esso, Gaines Pet Food, General Electric, General Motors, Nabisco, Northern Telecom, Procter and Gamble, Rockwell, Rohm and Haas, Shell, Signetics, Tektronix, and Xerox. These team leaders came from sites ranging from two decades of experience with self-directed work teams to those that were still in the planning stages prior to opening or to redesigning facilities. Twelve of these sites are unionized, five are nonmanufacturing organizations, and 25 are redesigns of existing organizations. Those discussions contain numerous illustrations of how a lot of leaders describe what they care about: the invisible elements of their role. It has been difficult, in fact, to identify visible characteristics that characterize these team leaders in self-directed workplaces. But I have been impressed by the commonality in their stated values, assumptions, and paradigms about how to work with others.

Published Value Statements

Consider some published value statements. The following examples are from the president of a high tech firm and from a manufacturing management team, respectively (Tables 10.1 and 10.2).

Values Must Be Demonstrated

As we mentioned in the last chapter, the importance of these value declarations, of course, is not the selection of the wording (although in both cases great effort was put into getting the appropriate message across). Rather, the power comes from the *demonstration* of the values by the culture team leaders and management team leaders. No Plexiglass entombed shrines are helpful here. Also mentioned in discussions with team members in the manufacturing area were the get-togethers that the leaders had with their teams after the presentation of these values. Team members were impressed with the unusual candor of the team leaders when they "opened up" and expressed sincere, heartfelt convictions about what was really important in their businesses. It was an unusual departure from the way the team leaders had talked to them before.

The statements in Tables 10.1 and 10.2 illustrate some of the things

Table 10.1. Example of a Culture Team Leader's (CEO's) Values

Customer service (our obligation to society and the basis of our legitimacy

Dignity of each individual (the human quality of our company culture)

Knowledge seeking (the basis for valid thinking and behavior)

Competence (the delivery of knowledge and skill)

Continuing improvement (the road to competitive advantage)

Personal initiative, commitment, and accountability (the essence of self-respect and sense of self-worth)

Work as an integral part of our lives (a fulfilling and quality part)

Desire to develop and grow (the pursuit of a sense of self-worth and the ability to contribute and progress)

Responsibility and substance in work (the highest order of productivity—evidence of trust and respect)

Quality (a universal and lasting value)

Table 10.2. Example of a Manufacturing Management Team's Values

Meeting customer needs is our obsession. Their needs drive our actions.
Our work should create wealth for customers, stakeholders, and employees.
We balance short-term business needs with long-term business strategy.
Everyone is a business partner.
We eliminate artificial barriers so that each individual can make their maximum
contribution.
We take courageous actions.
We add value and eliminate waste.
We keep things simple and use common sense.
We are antibureaucratic. We manage systems, policies, and methods and are not
managed by them.
We are quick, flexible, and responsive.

that which team leaders think are important in the self-directed work-place. Although values are usually unique to each workplace, I have noticed some strong common denominators. In this chapter we will concentrate on three very common concerns of successful team leaders on which there is near universal agreement:

1. The importance of managing by vision.

2. The need to focus on customers.

3. The necessity to institutionalize continuous improvement.

These values seem to have a strong driving influence on culture, management and operations team leaders alike. Let's consider them in more detail.

Manage by Vision

One thing team leaders talk about is the value of vision to give teams a sense of purpose and direction. This was clearly important in Kodak's 13 Room. With a clear future vision in place, team leaders can lessen their reliance on policies and procedures based on the control paradigm to coordinate the work force. A common technique used to start SDWTs, in fact, is to jointly create exciting visions of what the team or teams could be like in the future. Apple Computer's new plant in Fountain, Colorado, for example, has teams of new employees go through an orientation training program. Part of the orientation includes drawing a large newsprint-sized picture of their vision of the ideal plant. These hand-drawn pictures are then framed and placed in the hallway leading from the entrance to the production area. They usually have pictures of smiling customers and productive teams of people working together. Some are on rocket ships soaring to great uncharted heights. One is of a rock band featuring Jimmy Bilodeau, the plant manager, as the lead singer. With these kinds of compelling visions in place, people have something to look forward to. It gives them a sense of purpose that is bigger than themselves and helps them to rise above the daily problems they encounter.

A Cummins Engine operations team leader says of vision, "It's critical that you have a vision. You take three steps forward and two steps back, but you keep focusing on the vision." Chuck Frost, a vice president of Tektronix, summarizes another common value of team leaders: "We encourage the expression of diverse points of view, and we expect consistency and focus to come from common values and vision, not from rules." Says operations team leader Susan Payne at Tektronix, "I have a vision of where we are going and some values I try to manage by. That way, I can lead the team without having to rely on a bunch of rules which would unnecessarily restrict their ability to manage our business."

Create Organizational Alignment Through Vision

Charles Eberle, a former culture team leader from P&G, describes the most effective team leaders as follows:

> They are purposeful—that is, they are able to articulate a clear vision of where they want to get. And they remain consistently dedicated to getting there. They truly believe they can create what they want. They enroll others in their vision [and] they create a voluntary alignment of those around them.[2]

He suggests, in fact, that these visions are often grounded in a fairly common set of Theory Y assumptions:

> The assumptions that have driven all of P&G's organization designs are: 1) That people want to be responsible, 2) That they are capable of directing themselves, 3) That they can work collaboratively, in alignment... [with] common goals, and 4) That ultimately the majority of improvements or innovations come from individuals whose personal interests are congruent with those of the organization.[3]

Vision Inspires and Clarifies

One management team leader had his vision made into a 35 mm slide, which he shares with his plant regularly. It says simply, "[I intend] to manage the best high density circuit board business in the world." His vision is known as the primary goal of the factory: world leadership. An operations team leader at P&G has another, more microlevel vision for his team of 14. He explains:

> I have a picture of an ideal basketball team in my head that I compare to the production team. When I see people not passing to each other or I see somebody taking all the shots I know we have to work on teamwork. When we're not using the backboard we need to work on skills. When only part of the team can get rebounds we have to do cross-training.

At Digital, people recognize the importance of the vision as a clarifying vehicle: "We need pictures which spark new dreams and hopes or rekindle old ones reluctantly given up as unattainable," it says in a book they published to document the startup of one facility. "Pictures of how it would be if it were right. Pictures which excite, energize and inspire." One plant manager put it very succinctly: "What motivates people is a vision of themselves in the future."

Vision Helps Teams Self-Correct

This vision of what they could be helps the team gauge progress, and it helps team leaders know when to intervene and when to stay out of the way. The danger, of course, requires no explanation setting an unrealistic expectation for how quickly the team will reach the desired future can take all the air out of the tires. It does not matter if you're on the right road if your tires are all flat. When done well, however, vision provides many of the benefits of the traditional tools of the hierarchy (coordination, clarity, consistency, etc.), without restricting autonomy and creativity. Team leaders help teams self-correct by asking them, "Are we doing things that will help us accomplish the vision?" If the team supports the vision, it is a simple and powerful intervention.

Focus on Customers

Another common conviction held by the team leaders I've talked with is the absolute necessity of focusing on customers. One culture team leader has several posters in the office that quote him. They read: "If you think there is anything more important than customers, you're wrong." This level of concern is not atypical. Says a vice president of an electronics company: "Employee understanding of their customer's needs is paramount to our business success. We want employees to be motivated by a personal commitment to satisfying those needs."

A team leader at the Cummins Engine plant in Jamestown, New York, gives an example of this philosophy in action: "I saw a letter from a customer to the plant manager," he said. "The letter said the person was very upset with a product (backlog)." He then explained that the plant had been implementing just-in-time (an inventory, waste, and cycle time reduction process) and that the implementation had caused some temporary difficulties in accounting for the product going to customers. "I took the memo," he continued, "and made 35 copies. I called a team meeting and we talked about the implications." The results? "The backlog was made up in four weeks," he observed matter of factly, "and the same scheduler wrote a thank you letter. We also shared that with the team."

Like vision, maintaining the customer focus helps team members remember the overall purpose of the operation. Although it may not engender the inspiration of a well crafted vision, its pragmatism may be even more compelling. Everybody knows that customers pay the bills. Team leaders report that maintaining that customer focus value really helps people make the right operational decisions on a day-to-day basis much more effectively than rules or regulations ever will.

Everymanager Speaks

I would like to take the liberty of paraphrasing a number of these team leaders. For argument's sake, allow me to combine their voices in the first person voice of a fictional character called *Everymanager*. This is in the spirit of a medieval morality play, called Everyman, in which the character is representative of no one in particular, but lots of people in general. Similarly, *Everymanager* captures the essence and passion of our discussions about SDWT values.

> *Says* Everymanager:
> I have a sense of urgency about meeting customer needs. I really believe that serving the customer is the thing that gives us a reason to exist as an organization. This service gives our work meaning and focus. If we can help them to be successful, we will be successful too. I just don't believe in separating people from the consequence of their work. I continuously share customer data with the teams through frequent business information sharing, sharply focused customer visits, and joint improvement projects with customers. I can't expect people in the organization to be as concerned about satisfying customers as I am unless they have first-hand access to customer information and interaction. Nobody can get committed to something they don't understand or can't influence.

Institutionalize Continuous Improvement of Results

These team leaders are very results oriented and firmly grounded in doing what is right from a business perspective. They are committed to the ends and not the means, or, as one company officer said, there is "concentration on business outcomes rather than [on] activities."

These team leaders are also more interested in getting continuous improvement than in getting the temporary benefits that come from reaching short-term objectives. They believe that incremental improvement is not good enough to create a competitive advantage and that this kind of ongoing improvement comes only from workplaces where learning is valued. Eberle advises others to: "create open systems, open to learning and evolution and geared to continuous improvement. [Create] an emphasis on learning, from internal and external sources along with the freedom and ability to challenge the status quo."[4] In describing these workplaces he adds, "In other words, a spirit of inquiry pervades the organization, top to bottom. Questions are valued as much as answers."[5]

Don't Just Raise the Bar

These leaders recognize that continuous improvement is not simply a process of raising the bar after every high jump. That makes team members feel like nothing they do is ever good enough. Team leaders see continuous improvement instead as the continuous acquisition and application of knowledge to the task. They know that learning is the key to improvement, not artificially imposed higher standards from management.[6] Rather than raise the bar, they raise the person. Building their skills, knowledge, and abilities is almost as good as making the athlete taller. Then, when the team members easily clear the bar of last month's accomplishments, it is they, not the team leader, who say, "We can do better. Raise the bar!" The only self-sustaining continuous improvement processes are self-generated. By people searching for ways to apply their new learning.

Continuous Learning Is a Social Process

Team leaders also know that learning is a social group process even though most of us are preoccupied with individual learning. After all, we were taught in school that working with others is called "cheating." John

Seeley Brown, the chief engineer of the Xerox Research Center in Palo Alto, for example, tells the story of how he was asked to develop a training package for Xerox maintenance people. He accepted the task on the condition that he could research the learning process of the maintenance teams.

What did he and his research team find? They found that the original request for a training video would have done little good. The maintenance people learned best from telling stories at coffee breaks. Technicians would informally tell stories about a problem and how they solved it, or about how a technician up north that they heard about through the grapevine finally figured out a sticky situation, and so forth. The best maintenance people knew the most different stories.

Ironically, traditional supervisors were suggesting at the same time that breaks be shortened to improve productivity. Brown recommended against that controling gesture. He also suggested that, instead of a training video, they equip maintenance people with headsets so they could talk to other technicians when they were out alone on a call. The maintenance technology to be shared was a "distributed social mind" that Brown helped technicians tap into with the headsets. The program was such a success that when corporate funds for the headsets dried up, the maintenance people used their goal sharing money to purchase them from Brown's group.

SDWTs Are Not a Quick Fix

These team leaders acknowledge the evolutionary nature of a workplace characterized by learning, and they understand that it is a continual effort. The late Ross Silberstein, formerly the Vice President and Director of Manufacturing for the Automotive Aftermarket Division of Sherwin-Williams Company, said of his experience at the Richmond, Kentucky facility:

> This is a different way of life, it is not a quick fix. There is no program or formula. We have been working for 12 years and we're still working on it. We thought it was like a jigsaw puzzle and someday we would find the last piece, but there is no last piece.

Continues Everymanager:
I believe that the best way to get continuous improvement of results is by getting the team members' self-generated commitment. It is not by getting them to comply with my way of doing things. As long as we do what is morally and ethically right, it is the result that counts, not whether we get there using my way or not. I also believe that everyone has good ideas. Sometimes the best improvement ideas come from unexpected sources.

We don't accept or reject ideas because of who they come from. Even if improvement ideas sound a little crazy at first, I encourage teams to try out suggestions they believe will improve our business.

Continuous improvement comes from the continuous acquisition and application of knowledge to the task. You can't improve what you don't understand. I support and reward getting and applying knowledge. I also remove barriers to learning. I serve as a constant conscience to our teams to learn how to learn from ourselves and from others. This means that everyone is both a teacher and a learner. It also results not only in continuous improvement of our output, but also in the quality of our thought processes.

Attributed Values

We have talked about a few team leader values that seem to be common in the SDWT environment. It is also important to recognize, however, that there are two kinds of values: individual values and organizational values. Most of our discussion so far has been about the individual values of team leaders. But team members frequently attribute the perceived organizational values to their leaders. That is, if an organization seems to value traditional hierarchical things like supervisory controls, then the team leader is automatically assumed to value the same things whether that is true or not. Thus team leaders need to do more than demonstrate their individual values in the workplace. They often need to modify the perceived organizational values as well. This, of course, is no easy task.

Summary

Lots of successful team leaders share common perspectives about workers and the workplace. These values include things like the importance of managing by vision, focusing on customers, and institutionalizing continuous improvement. These particular values are becoming more common in successful workplaces whether they use SDWTs or not. In the next chapter we'll discuss some of the more unusual values that differentiate team leaders from many traditional supervisors.

Endnotes

1. Brian Dumaine, "Who Needs a Boss?" *Fortune* (May 7, 1990), p. 52. © 1990 by The Time Inc. Magazine Company. All rights reserved. Used by permission.

2. Charles Eberle, "Competitiveness, Commitment and Leadership," a speech delivered at the Ecology of Work Conference, 1987.

3. Ibid.

4. Op. cit.

5. Ibid.

6. Peter Senge, *The Fifth Discipline: The Art & Practice of the Learning Organization* (New York: Doubleday/Currency, 1990).

11

Team Leaders Value Teamwork, Authenticity, Development, and Barrier Busting

*On a day-to-day basis, my passion comes
from backing people's efforts, getting them
what they need to do the job, educating them,
and working with them as a member of the team.*[1]

BILL EATON,
Levi Strauss executive committee

Let's continue the discussion started in the last chapter about the values of team leaders. In this chapter we will focus on four more key values including:

1. A belief in the importance of teamwork.

2. A belief that work is life.

3. A belief in the aggressive development of team members.

4. A conviction that the role of management is to eliminate the barriers to team performance.

The Importance of Teamwork

Chuck Frost, a vice president of Tektronix, explains, "We will seek to form partnerships and teams to expand the potential of the organization beyond that of its individual members." Other team leaders frequently mention this same value. Team leaders value team work. Corning even calls their SDWT effort "partnership" to emphasize the importance of this value.

Minimize Status Differences to Help Create Teams

Leaders don't want anyone (including themselves) to be perceived as better or as more important than anybody else. This gets in the way of team work. In the workplace this often means exorcizing even the subtle evidences of position-based status. Things like office locations or access to information are often changed to create an environment of greater equality.

One organization felt they had made some progress in creating a team-oriented atmosphere by making all of their identification badges look the same. Previously, the large operation used certain colors for management badges and other colors for nonmanagement badges as a constant subtle reminder that there were differences between these two classes of people. Operators soon reminded them, however, that they hadn't gone far enough. Managers didn't act any differently. And with some degree of understandable cynicism they explained to management that they could plainly see that each badge also had an employee number on it. Management numbers had three digits in them and employee numbers had four digits in them. The difference was still there. People saw through what they believed was only a half-hearted attempt at window dressing. They needed more.

Mammoth Salary Differentials Get in the Way of Teamwork

Team leaders stress the importance of minimizing the differences between classes—even the sensitive ones. While differences in salary packages, for example, are not unusual in SDWT environments, some culture team leaders like the owners of Ben and Jerry's Ice Cream believe that the ratio of these differences should be no more than 7 to 10 times from the lowest paid employee to the highest paid one. When team members read accounts in their Sunday paper that CEOs commonly earn as much as 160 times more than workers, they are unlikely to feel like real business partners.[2] Huge management bonuses and stock options cause the same problem.

No one suggests that everyone should be paid exactly the same, but the "partnership" has to be felt. For example, ask some United Auto Workers how they felt about efforts in their industry to create teams in the 1980s when managers were getting fat bonuses at the same time that workers were being laid off. I don't think they felt much like partners. Nor did the job security guarantees negotiated into later contracts create the feeling. Workers were, of course, happy that they were getting almost their regular amount of pay to stay home when the plants didn't have enough work to keep them busy. But this well intended attempt to shore up eroding relationships between management and the workers only tended to emphasize the workers' differences from management (who received no such guarantees).

Get Rid of We/They Distinctions

Team leaders want everyone to feel like members of the team. There are few we/they distinctions in these operations. It's not management vs. nonmanagement, or office vs. operations, or this department/shift vs. that department/shift, or men vs. women, or black vs. white, etc. The emphasis is on multiplying the effort of people working together as teams, not on dividing them into factions based on job type, education, or race. Eberle notes that in these organizations there is "a focus on teamwork, including a blurring of the boundaries between levels of the hierarchy—and fewer levels to start with. Virtually the opposite of the military structures and style of most of our organizations."[3] He goes on to say that, as full team members, people are treated as partners, not as subordinates, and that these teams are characterized by "leveraging the synergy and options that come from diversity of human resources, i.e., the rich variety of perspectives provided by differences in background, age, gender, race, and ethnicity."[4]

Promote Diversity

Team leaders believe that the diversity of the team membership plays a significant role in team effectiveness. Highly homogeneous teams tend to be much more susceptible to groupthink, a disease of terminal consistency. I have worked with management teams, for example, where every member was a middle aged white male from the U.S. with an MBA and an engineering undergraduate degree. No wonder they tended to come up with the same solutions all the time. These teams are less effective in exploring the multiple alternatives available in decision making and problem solving. Multiple options are more obvious to groups with a diversity of race, gender, age, cultural and educational backgrounds. This diversity often lengthens and complicates the group processes in the short run. But it makes the group more effective over the long haul *if* teams learn how to resolve deadlock situations without resorting to conflict reducing tendencies like voting.

> *Says* Everymanager:
> Everyone has something important to contribute. We need a variety of perspectives, experiences, and skills to be successful. Although I, for example, play a different role in the team than other team members, I am no more or less important than anybody else. We are all part of the team. Inappropriate symbols of status separate people and get in the way of the work to be done. I value contribution, not titles. I respect people regardless of their background, salary level, education, or appearance.

Show That Work Is Part of Life

Although it is not as commonly expressed as the values already mentioned, a number of team leaders talk about the importance of not separating work from the rest of our lives. They are amazed, for example, that people who run homes, churches, and even communities have been asked in the past to check their minds at the door when they come to work. Alan Cheney, formerly an internal consultant at Texas Instruments, put it this way: "One of the great revelations of recent years is that the same people who have been required to 'leave their brains at the gate' and perform narrowly-defined, often repetitive tasks for eight hours on the job, were spending the remainder of the day at family activities, hobbies, or outside businesses that often required just the opposite."[5] They chafe at suggestions that people only put up with work so that they can afford to do what they want to do after work. They see that as a problem with the way work is designed, not as a natural outcome of a having a job. Some believe work should be fun. Many are offended when they hear arguments that it is okay to treat someone one way at work but another way at home.

Concern About Life Balance

They also are concerned about people's life outside the workplace. One management team leader has talked often in his factory, for example, about what he calls the "social cost" of high performance workplaces: the self-imposed cost of extra time sometimes required of people in these SDWT organizations, which would normally be spent with the family or used in pursuit of personal hobbies. I counseled with one team member, in fact, whose dedication to a project he was working on had nearly destroyed his already unstable marriage. His excitement about his work swung like a pendulum from one end of the commitment arc to the opposite extreme. He had to make some changes to bring the pendulum back into balance (a problem normally reserved to managers and highly paid staff members in traditional organizations). Team leaders believe in a healthy balance between the personal and the professional aspects of life.

Be Authentic

Most of all, these team leaders talk about being themselves, about being the same kind of person at work that they are at home. Says John Homan, retired vice president of A.E. Staley, "[You] can't be phoney or flim flam." Being authentic, they say, is what gives them the energy to carry on.

> Everymanager *notes:*
> I believe that work is life. Without integrity at work we don't have integrity in our lives. Without health at work we are not healthy. Work is a part of life, not something separate from it. The distinction between the work person and the family person is unhealthy and artificial. With more than 40 hours a week at work, we don't just work to "make a living"; we also spend a considerable amount of time living at work. I believe that we tend to underestimate the limits of human potential. Look at what we do at home. We can make good decisions about how to make the most effective use of limited resources. We can do a variety of difficult tasks if we know how and if they need to be done. We can do things that really make a difference in other people's lives. We enjoy a challenge. We can cooperate with others to accomplish more than what we can accomplish by ourselves. Given the opportunity, resources, and assistance, I believe we can do these things at work too.

Develop People

One of the most common convictions repeated by team leaders is the importance of developing people. We heard this repeatedly from the Kodak team leaders who were singularly preoccupied with "developing capability." Others emphasize it just as strongly. I have heard some say that the whole job of the team leader is to create a learning organization. This responsibility is mentioned by several leaders in high commitment workplaces. Lyman Ketchum, who was the plant manager for the Topeka Pet Food Plant remembers, "The new system had a snowball effect. The more time we spent developing people the better results we got." Posted just inside the entrance of the Forest Grove Etched Circuit Board Plant (they call it F-1) at Tektronix is a sign that declares simply: "What we are really doing here at F-1 is developing people. Our business performance will be the measure of how well we do that."

People Appreciate Rather Than
Depreciate Over Time

One manager at Tektronix adds, "The fundamental purpose of my job as General Manager is to prepare the people who work with me for the future. I have a personal responsibility for the future standard of living of all these people." This sentiment is not as unusual as it may appear. Another senior manager describes the Procter and Gamble organization like this: "There is far less bureaucracy and overhead burden, even though the investment in communications and training, at the front end and ongoing, is two to three times... [what] you would find in a typical industrial organization."[6] Why all the preparation, training, and communications? Maureen Key, a former plant manager of the Plastics facility at Tektronix answers:

> Because your ongoing success as a business is directly correlated to the capability of the work force. Human beings, like any other asset, need to be maintained. But unlike other assets, human beings are a developable resource which can appreciate instead of depreciate over time. So the primary responsibility of managers is to build that resource to develop the capability of their team members to understand the business and to respond appropriately.

Says Everymanager:

> I know I've done my job well when the teams don't need me to "manage" them because they are able to "manage" themselves. I believe that management is part of everyone's job, not a separate function. To add value to this business I have to do something besides tell other people what to do. I give people what they need to be successful as business partners.
>
> Another thing I believe is that constructive confrontation is okay. Even though it may be uncomfortable for me and other team members, I know that it is better to get things out in the open and resolved than to allow them to fester and hinder our effectiveness. This is an important part of development. Disagreements spring from the kind of commitment to the business that I want to foster. People will defend (sometimes passionately) the things they care about. The time it takes to work through these discussions, like the time it takes to talk about business, is just part of the investment required to make this stuff work.

Eliminate Barriers to Success

Some team leaders at P&G refer to themselves as "barrier busters" because they recognize the primary importance of removing the things that get in the way of the success of their teams. Like the cowcatchers on locomotives, they clear the track of impediments that would slow the progress of their charge. These team leaders have a definite bias to action and are loathe to sit and watch teams struggle with unnecessary obstacles.

Team leaders in these workplaces see themselves as support to the teams. They believe that a primary responsibility of theirs is to "grease the skids" for effective decision making and implementation of plans. They sometimes report, in fact, that they work for the teams.

Team Leaders Work for the Teams

When I was working for Tektronix as an internal consultant, a colleague and I received an unexpected invitation to spend some time with the CEO. As we sat down to discuss leadership in empowered workplaces, he gave what we thought was a simple and eloquent critique of classic organization charts. "The problem," he began, "is that people aren't shaped like boxes and that the triangle is wrong side up." He went on to explain that he would often draw the triangle with the point at the bottom to help culture team leaders understand that they supported the teams and not the other way around. This view of work is fairly common in these businesses. Leaders work for workers and not the other way around. Lamented the late Pat Haggerty, one of the founders of Texas Instruments, "There is probably no greater waste in industry today than that of willing employees prevented by insensitive leadership from applying their energies and ambitions in the interest of the companies for which they work."[7]

> *Everymanager:*
> I aggressively strive to eliminate barriers to team success. I actively challenge the artificial barriers to individual growth and contribution. Although I am careful to understand the reasoning behind them first, I attempt to alter inappropriately restrictive thinking, practices, policies, or procedures. I know that I can influence things that hinder the business, no matter how immovable they may appear.

I have a bias for action. I institute the actions needed to carry out my beliefs. If something doesn't work I'll try something else. I don't sit around and wait for things to happen. I recognize that convictions must be acted upon to achieve results. We identify very specifically the skills, processes, and systems required to turn convictions and ideas into actions that will add value for our customers. We assess the state of our organization against these needs. Then we prepare and agree to concise action plans with target dates. Implementing the action plans assures that people have the necessary skills to carry out the roles they have accepted. We also are assured of having useful work descriptions, information systems, reward systems, decision support processes, and other elements needed to carry out our convictions.

Summary

A number of values are commonly expressed by leaders of SDWTs: (1) a belief in the importance of teamwork, (2) a belief that work is part of life, (3) a belief in the development of team members, and (4) a conviction that the role of management is to eliminate the barriers to team performance. What is the conclusion of my discussions with these team leaders? It probably boils down to this: When team leaders live these kinds of values in the workplace, it builds trust and respect in the work force, and it forms the foundation on which their new role can be constructed. Without similar values supervisors are not likely to enjoy their roles, nor are they likely to succeed with self-directed work teams.

In the next chapter we will begin to describe the team leader role, which is based on the values we have reviewed.

Endnotes

1. Brian Dumaine, "The Bureaucracy Busters," *Fortune* (June 17, 1991), p. 34. © 1991 by The Time Inc. Magazine Company. All rights reserved. Used by permission.

2. A cover story in the June 23, 1991 *Parade* magazine (a Sunday supplemental magazine to many major U.S. newspapers) announced a pay disparity between workers and CEOs as being as great as 160 times.

3. Charles Eberle, "Competitiveness, Commitment and Leadership," a speech delivered at the Ecology of Work Conference, 1987.

4. Ibid.

5. Alan Cheney," "Self-Managed Work Teams," *Executive Excellence*, February 1991, p. 12. Used by permission of author.

6. Eberle, op. cit.

7. Cheney, p. 12.

PART 4

The Role of the Team Leader

12

The Supervisor vs. the Team Leader

Sheep Herders and Shepherds

But of a good leader, who talks little,
When his work is done, his aim fulfilled,
They will all say, "We did this ourselves."
LAO-TZU, *(about 550 B.C.)*

A favorite story of mine illustrates some of the primary differences between the role of the traditional supervisor (at all levels of the organization) and the role of the team leader.

When I was in high school, my family moved to a large farm house in central Utah. The house had been finished in 1900 by a sheep baron who had proudly displayed blown-up photographs of his prize-winning long-haired sheep throughout the home. The photos were large, measuring nearly 36 inches tall by 48 inches wide. They were made to look even larger through the use of thick wood plank frames painted jet black. Some of them were watermarked or otherwise damaged, and all of them looked like the sheep were posed with the same unsmiling formality of most turn-of-the-century photographs (see Fig. 12.1). Partly because of the pictures' value as a conversation starter, but also because they were an integral part of the history of the home, my mother and father kept some of the photos in their original locations on the staircase walls of the second story.

Figure 12.1

Probably because of the pictures, I started paying attention to tidbits I heard here and there about raising sheep. I found out, for example, about the importance of sheepdogs. During the long grazing drives into the rugged Utah mountains, sheep owners would use sheepdogs to circle around the flocks to keep them all together and heading in the right direction. Some called the better dogs "sheep herders," a title normally reserved for human beings, to designate their extraordinary skill in controling the livestock by barking and nipping at the legs of the sheep.

When the sheep wouldn't move, these sheep herders would get them going. When the sheep were heading in the wrong direction, the sheep herders would get them turned around. When an errant lamb strayed from the other sheep, the sheep herders were there to drive it back into the safety of the flock.

That summer I went to Israel for six weeks with a touring group of boy scouts. One day, when I was looking out the window of the old tour bus, I saw a small flock of sheep in the dusty hills by the roadside. The flock was accompanied by a lone shepherd carrying a staff and dressed in long desert robes. The shepherd, seemingly oblivious to the sheep in his charge, turned his back to the flock and walked briskly away. He didn't even glance backward. I thought his action was irresponsible. Without sheep herding dogs to keep the flock from scattering, it appeared that he was abandoning the sheep. But I was surprised to see that the sheep were not wandering aimlessly, but that they were following him. For some reason these sheep did not need their heels nipped to be moved. They simply walked along with the shepherd until they were out of my line of sight. This was inconsistent with my paradigm of sheep herding, but it was a tremendous learning experience about shepherding.

Sheep Herding vs. Shepherding Management

This story can be related to the two different management roles (shepherd versus sheepherder, see Table 12.1). Now people, of course, aren't like animals. Supervisors don't act like trained dogs obediently coercing dim-witted sheep. Nor do team members mindlessly comply with the manipulative force imposed on them. Nevertheless, there are some parallels.

Sheep Herders Drive Subordinate Flocks

The traditional approach to management, for example, is a lot like sheep herding. It often puts the supervisor in the role of regulating, enforcing, or directing subordinates. Supervisors in this role (regardless of their level in the organization) concentrate on driving the subordinate flock in some predetermined direction. They monitor the work performance carefully and take appropriate corrective action when their flock veers off course. They become skilled in barking and heel nipping techniques, like performance reviews, layoffs, and more subtle organizational censures. While they become quite proficient at moving sheep, they tend to create flocks that are compliant, complacent, and dependent on the sheep herder.

Table 12.1. Sheep Herders vs. Shepherds

	Sheep herder	Shepherd
Technique	Directing	Developing
Work focus	The fock itself	The flock's surroundings
Location	Behind the flock	In front of the flock
Purpose	Move sheep	Create shepherds
Methodology	Barking and heel nipping	Clearing the path
Result	Creates dependance	Creates self-reliance

Shepherds Lead and Develop

Shepherds, however, have more of a developmental responsibility than a directive one. They assume a position in front of the flock as a leader and an example, rather than behind the flock as a driver and director. They also spend considerably more time and energy analyzing the environment surrounding the sheep to anticipate dangers and opportunities than sheep herders do. The analogy breaks down somewhat, of course, because the sheep in Israel were very dependant on the shepherd. Even though his tactics were noncoercive and they followed his lead willingly, the sheep were incapable of surviving without him. In SDWTs, however, shepherds actually create other shepherds, fully capable of leading both themselves and other team members successfully.[1] Although they may not know many of the skills required to be self-directing when they join the organization, the SDWT shepherd makes sure they get them over time.

Problems with Sheep Herding

The problem with the sheep herding role of supervision is that, while it certainly can get the job done, it just does not fit with self-directed work teams. While skilled sheep herding may have been not only acceptable, but actually admired by traditional supervisors and work force alike, emerging work teams now see this way of managing as at best redundant or at worst as inconsistent with their own newly expanded responsibilities to regulate their own work flow and processes.

Sheep herder supervisors unintentionally create organizational cultures characterized by low risk taking and low initiative. Since direction, rewards, and punishments come from the sheep herder, subordinates (whether they are operators or vice presidents) rapidly learn that the way to prosper is to wait to see what the boss wants to do and then do that. They wait for directions, move only tentatively when the path is unclear, or stampede obediently wherever they think the boss wants them to go (whether the direction is right or not). The desirable culture for SDWTs, of course, is very different from this one. People take direction from the work itself, and rewards are seen as coming from customers, not bosses.

Shepherds Live in Traditional Organizations Too

Just because supervisors work in traditional organizations, however, they don't necessarily have to act like sheep herders. Excellent supervisors in traditional organizations have often mastered shepherding skills even though it may have been difficult for them to use them. Janice Klein, who has published extensive research about supervising SDWT organizations writes that "... [I] believe that many managers in control systems also hold to the same paradigm [as successful managers in empowered workplaces] even though their work environment may limit their ability to act on those beliefs."[2] Her research with Pamela Posey shows that the supervisors who are perceived to be the "stars" in traditional systems act like shepherds, not sheep herders, and they are generally skilled in "working the system" (sometimes working around the system) to use self-regulating techniques with employees even though they may not be encouraged or rewarded by their superiors for doing so.[3]

While successful supervisors in traditional organizations have often acted this way, even though it was inconsistent with the hierarchical and bureaucratic structures of their traditional organizations, SDWTs require the shepherding role from team leaders to make the work design completely functional. If only a select few act this way, while others continue the sheep herding role commonly observed in organizations today, the SDWT effort won't work.

Summary

Although excellent supervisors have often managed in nontraditional ways in traditional work systems, most supervisors have been trained and reinforced for acting more like sheep herders than shepherds. SDWTs need their leaders to be shepherds, people who lead, take risks, and develop other shepherds, not sheep herders who drive sheep with work rules and procedures.

In the next several chapters we will flesh out the specifics of the team leader role in more detail.

Endnotes

1. See Charles Manz and Henry Sims, "Superleadership: Beyond the Myth of Heroic Leadership," *Organizational Dynamics* (Spring 1991), p. 18, for more information on this important topic of developing team members into leaders.

2. Janice Klein, personal correspondence, 1987. Parenthetical notations added.

3. Pamela Posey, "Excellence in First Line Supervision," Harvard Business School doctoral dissertation, 1985, Janice Klein and Pamela Posey, "Good Supervisors Are Good Supervisors—Anywhere," *Harvard Business Review* (November–December 1986).

13
The Role of the Team Leader

It seemed to her [Ayla, a newcomer to the tribe] that it was more difficult to lead a group of people who believed everyone . . . had the right to speak out and be listened to. . . . It could become very loud and noisy when everyone had an opinion and did not hesitate to make it known, but Talut [the leader] never allowed it to go beyond certain bounds. Though he was certainly strong enough to have forced his will on people, he chose to lead by consensus and accommodation instead. He had certain sanctions and beliefs to call upon, and techniques of his own to get attention, but it took a different kind of strength to persuade rather than coerce. Talut gained respect by giving respect.[1]

JEAN M. AUEL,
The Mammoth Hunters

It took me a while to figure out how to really "shepherd" at the soap plant in Lima, Ohio. And I had some difficulty when I attempted to explain what I was learning to the frequent P&G visitors who toured the plant to observe our SDWTs. During the visits, for example, it was usually the technicians (hourly employees) who gave presentations about major projects they were managing, goals they had set and accomplished, teammates they had hired, equipment they had purchased, or cost savings measures they had implemented. In the traditional plants those were things, the visitors noted, which would be said and done by staff professionals, managers, or supervisors, but not by "workers."

"If the technicians do all that," they would ask, "then what do you do?"

I hated that question. At the time I didn't have a good way to explain the critical role of the team leader. This chapter is a belated attempt to respond to the query, "what do team leaders do?" It focuses on the general role and responsibilities of a team leader by comparing a traditional supervisory job description with one for a team leader. We will also look at the team leader as a boundary manager, and then conclude with seven important competency clusters for SDWT leadership.

Team Leader
"Job Description"

What is the role of a team leader? Pamela Posey and Janice Klein have done much of the pioneering work on this question, especially for the operations team leader. They have found that many of the behaviors of team leaders and successful supervisors are the same. Three consistent attributes, for example, are associated with the most successful leaders in both traditional and empowered organizations:

1. The ability to create strong mutual respect between the workers and the leader.

2. Assuring that the job gets done.

3. Providing leadership in getting problems solved.[2]

However, in addition to these attributes, SDWTs require some other things from their leadership as well. One distinguishing characteristic is the focus of their activities. A team leader's "job description" usually differs from the traditional supervisor because it focuses less on tasks and more on relationships. It also emphasizes fewer one-to-one interactions with employees and more team development, as shown in the example of a first level job description in Table 13.1.

These job descriptions change because the role of the team leader expands beyond the role of the supervisor. While the supervisor is responsible for the performance of the day-to-day work, the role of the team leader expands to include responsibilities that go beyond the immediate accomplishment of the task. They work more as a work process architect than as a work operations monitor. Thus the primary target of their work expands from tasks (the work) to relationships (things that affect how the work gets done), and from individuals (a smaller part of the work unit) to teams (a larger part of the work unit).

Table 13.1. Examples of First Level Job Descriptions

Supervisor	Team leader
1. Plan, organize, direct, control.	1. Ensure resources are available for team to produce on-time, quality product and/or services.
2. Meet cost, quality, and delivery objectives.	2. Develop team maturity—coach and counsel.
3. Manage daily problems.	3. Represent team in organization-wide activities.
4. Coordinate activities and resources.	4. Train and lead team in problem solving.
5. Plan and implement improvements.	5. Motivate team to achieve goals.
6. Administer safety, housekeeping, and communications programs.	6. Assume responsibility for indirect tasks.

SOURCE: Adapted from Pamela Posey and Janice Klein, "Traditional versus New Work System Supervision: Is There a Difference?" *Revitalizing Manufacturing: Text and Cases* (Homewood, Ill.: Irwin, 1990).

The Boundary Manager

One of the best ways to describe the overall team leader role is as a "boundary manager." As you can see in Fig. 13.1, the large circle in this figure represents the "team boundary." The boundary is simply the make-believe line that differentiates the team from the environment

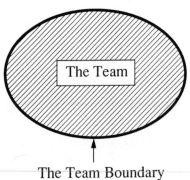

The Team's Enviroment

(All the things outside of the team itself)

The Team

The Team Boundary

Figure 13.1. The team boundary.

surrounding it. The team leader manages that boundary. What does that mean? Let's review a little organization theory to establish a common point of reference, and then we'll answer that question.

SDWTs Are Open Systems

Figure 13.2 adds some things to the picture of the team we looked at earlier. Team members must take "inputs" (like raw materials or information) of some sort and transform them into desirable "outputs" (like products or services). To do this they add value to the inputs (assemble, organize, edit, etc.). This is called the *transformation* or *throughput* part of the operation. Fig. 13.3 shows that outside the organization boundary is the environment (customers, competitors, other teams, etc.). Social scientists call this way of looking at organizations the *open system theory*.[3]

An information systems (IS) team, for example, may be responsible for turning data into useful information. They collect, compile, and program the data into computers. These bits of raw data are thus organized into useful reports, which are distributed to their customers. According to the open system model; the raw data is the input. The throughput process is the series of tasks that transforms the raw data into a delivered report. And the report is the output. The customer must feel that the report meets a need that is equal to or greater than what they must pay to get it from the IS team. If the information system team does this better than the alternatives for providing this service, then they are successful. If they don't, they won't survive in the long run.

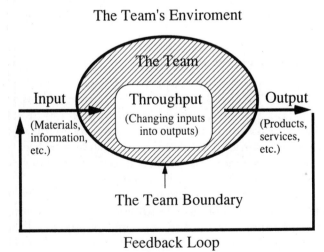

The Team's Enviroment

Feedback Loop
(Feedback from environment about outputs)

Figure 13.2. The team as an open system.

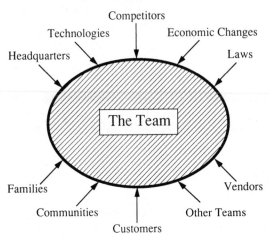

Figure 13.3. The team environment.

SDWTs Manage Inside the Boundary

Now let's get back to the original question: What does it mean to be a boundary manager? Traditional supervision usually focuses attention on the transforming process or throughput portion of the team's responsibilities. In this example that would include supervising activities such as the compiling of data and the accurate entering of that data into the computers. Supervising the day-to-day throughput operations of the team, however, is largely done by team members themselves in self-directed work team settings.

Team Leaders Manage the Boundary

This allows the team leader to focus on the environment surrounding the team, much as the shepherd looks beyond the flock itself and into the fields, which hold potential danger and/or opportunity. Rather than spending her primary energy on the throughput process, the team leader focuses more attention on boundary issues, such as interface problems with other teams, customer and vendor interactions, dealing with other corporate groups, assessing competitors and market opportunities, working legal or community issues of importance, forecasting new technologies, building communication bridges with other groups, forging important alliances, bringing training and development opportunities into the team, and so forth (see Fig. 13.4). Those are the things at the boundary of the organization represented by the circle. As a boundary manager, the

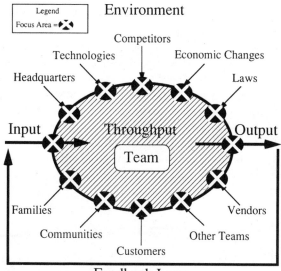

Figure 13.4. The boundary manager focus areas.

team leader manages these elements in the team's environment in a way that positively affects the team's ability to be successful.

One way to further describe the boundary manager's role is to look at sample boundary management responsibilities. The primary role of the boundary manager, of course, is to help the team adapt successfully to the environment. To do this she is an organization designer, an infrastructure builder, and a cross-organization collaborator. Each of these aspects of the boundary manager's role is a departure from the traditional role of supervisors at every level of the organization.

Boundary Management Is a Nontraditional Role

SDWTs won't function properly if supervisors at any level continue to work inappropriately inside the team boundary. Ralph Stayer, CEO of Johnsonville Foods, for example, tells a story of how he couldn't get the quality of the company's product to be as high as he wanted it until he stopped managing throughput and left that to the teams. Johnsonville is a producer of high quality sausage. As the CEO, Stayer continued tasting the sausages on a regular basis to demonstrate his personal commitment and concern for quality. The teams didn't assume full responsibility for product quality, however, until he stopped tasting the sausage and turned that task over to them. Rejects dropped from 5 percent to five-tenths of 1 percent when the teams fully assumed the responsibility of throughput management.[4]

Supervisors "Taste the Sausage"

There are lots of ways that supervisors "taste the sausage" and hinder SDWT development. Most do it through information requests (reports) and by expressing concerns about throughput problems they see. When the team itself requires this kind of information to monitor their throughput, it is *essential* to take the time to compile some facts and data. But when the information gathering is mandated by supervisors and is for the sole benefit of the supervisors, it actually causes more problems than it solves. In many circumstances, people have discovered that the process of filling out status reports for management, for example, costs *significantly* more in lost time and salaries than the value of any improvements that came out of the process. Team leaders avoid this trap.

In today's fast paced world, these kinds of imposed supervising processes on the throughput take too long to be useful anyhow. Team leaders don't bottleneck the teams by making them wait to take action until the team leader is in the loop. That defeats the purpose of self-directed work teams. But this isn't easy for many of us. Laments a controller at Tektronix, "What you've got (in a SDWT) is a manager who doesn't know what is going on." We aren't used to that. Most of us really enjoy being in the thick of things. Team leaders can be partly consoled by the fact that, by the time they hear about it, it's probably too late anyway.

Supervisors Work *In* the System; Team Leaders Work *On* the System

Boundary managers don't taste sausage. That's not their role. While supervisors at every management level usually work *in* the system, team leaders work *on* the system instead. That means working on things that affect the ability of the organization to be successful. One way to do this is as an organization designer. Team leaders believe that team members are already doing the best they can within the constraints of the system they are working within. So they focus on improving, or redesigning, the system. This virtually always requires working across the boundary (see Table 13.2).

Bill Synder, a former operations team leader at American Transtech, for example, acted as a effective organization designer and saw dramatic improvement in a SDWT. The labor cost per unit went from $180 to $100, quality remained consistently high, throughput improved by 100

Table 13.2. Examples of Boundary Manager Tasks

Hosting customer visits
Introducing team members to key external contacts
Buffering the team from corporate pressure
Sponsoring joint vendor/team projects
Bringing in information from headquarters
Evaluating market trends
Anticipating technology shifts
Building communication linkages
Bringing in customer feedback
Forging alliance
Solving problems between teams
Bringing in technical training from the community college
Inviting vendors to provide training on the equipment they sold the team
Getting resources for the team from other parts of the company
Brokering team members out into community service activities
Bringing in concerned citizens to discuss community problems
Evaluating competitive offerings for similar products and services

---

percent, and employee morale soared—all in the first six months of his tenure. What did he do?

> I provided feedback on all the goals once a week. I expected them to explain variances. I arranged for the marketing person to collect customer feedback and read it out at the weekly meeting. I arranged for team members to get technical training and apprenticeship opportunities. I initiated the development of a reward system that enabled team members to earn weekly cash bonuses based on team and organization performance. In short, I didn't do, I designed. The design elements helped us all to succeed.[5]

Organization Design

Synder "didn't do" the traditional supervisory tasks of telling people how to accomplish the significant improvements they achieved together; that is working *in* the system as a supervisor. Instead, he worked *on* the system. He brought in marketing information and technical training from the environment, so that people could be informed and skillful. He also changed the team bonus. By doing these things he designed system improvements. Though organization designers don't often do the design work themselves (they usually involve others in the spirit of empowerment), they do ensure that it gets done. And they ensure that it gets done in a way that incorporates open systems thinking. This is more difficult than it sounds. The general tendency for organizations is to make improvements based only on their needs and wants. The boundary manager knows that other elements outside the teams must be considered for effective organizational improvement. Anyone, for example, who has ignored customer needs during this process has done so at some peril to the operation.

The extent to which team leaders can act as a boundary manager, of course, depends on the maturity level of the team. Some teams still need a lot of help to learn how to manage the throughput of the operation. This needs to be done before the team leader can take on the new responsibilities of boundary management. Many of the full responsibilities of boundary managers, in fact, don't come until later. They evolve as the team gradually develops the skills and experience to monitor the throughput process themselves.

Infrastructure Building

Boundary managers help with this maturation process (which is detailed in later chapters). One way they do this is to ensure that effective infrastructures are in place to support SDWTs. This is a key part of the organization designer's responsibilities as well. The infrastructures help the teams manage throughput, and they can form an institutionalized way for team members to stay focused on the needs of the environment. As Snyder recalls:

> ...a timely information system... [provided] quality and profitability results on a daily or weekly basis. As long as the system measured the right things, and as long as the results were good, I could focus my attention elsewhere (unless the team asked for help). Certain peers were rankled by my confidence and freedom, and would warn me that the teams were "fooling around" and "taking advantage" of me in my absence. Those same teams were lowering their costs by 40% and achieving higher quality results than they had in years. I wasn't worried, and I told my peers that they shouldn't be either.[6]

Substitutes for Hierarchy

These kinds of infrastructures are important for effective team operation. Ed Lawler, a prolific management writer and employee involvement expert, calls these "substitutes for hierarchy."[7] Absent these systems the teams would be thrown into chaos, not competitiveness. Like it or not, hierarchy and bureaucracy have performed an important coordination function in most organizations that must still be performed somehow in the SDWT workplace. Boeing and McDonnell Douglas have both reported problems when hierarchical controls (management authorizations, policies, procedures, etc.) were withdrawn from teams prematurely without anything to replace for the clarity and direction that those controls provided. Boundary managers act as organization designers to ensure that teams have these substitutions for hierarchy in place.

Cross-Organization Collaboration

Boundary managers do other things as well. Rosabeth Moss Kanter, author and business school professor, describes this new role as managing channels of influence, networking horizontally, and managing external relations—or in her words, "brokering interfaces instead of presiding over empires."[8] What does this look like? Whereas supervisors focus on optimizing their own departments or sections, for example, team leaders (as boundary managers) are much more interested in optimizing the whole operation, even if that means suboptimizing their part of it. They act as cross-organization collaborators rather than empire builders because their knowledge of the environment shows them that collaboration is essential to survival. For more examples of how a boundary management approach differs from a traditional supervisory approach, see Table 13.3.

Seven Competencies of Boundary Managers

Thus the overall role of the SDWT leader is to be a boundary manager. This includes not only being an organization designer, infrastructure builder, and cross-organization collaborator, but a lot of other responsibilities as well. Boundary managers, for example, often play the role of translator, as they try to help team members comprehend the fuzzy and chaotic reality of the outside world. They also block certain disruptions from entering the team, shielding it from inappropriate distractions or unnecessary confusion. But as diverse as these different team leader responsibilities appear, all of them seem to require a common set of personal competencies.

A number of generic attributes are important for effective team leaders, such as a passionate commitment to get good results, a clear understanding of what it takes to be successful, excellent communication abilities, and a strong interpersonal and technical skill base consistent with the organization's culture. Some specific behaviors exhibited by successful SDWT leaders I know, however, include some other things as well. They:

Table 13.3. Differences in Approach Between a Supervisor and a Boundary Manager

Sample situation	Traditional supervisor approach	Boundary manager approach
Orienting new team members	Focuses on clarifying the new job description, specific job tasks, rules, procedures, and policies pertaining to her department.	Focuses on customer requirements, vendor issues, quality standards, ethics, and interface issues with other teams.
Problem with another group	Works on solving his department's part of the problem. Reminds the other group to solve their part of the problem.	Brings the groups together and facilitates a joint problem solving process.
Lack of skill in operation	Ensures that good technical training is completed.	Brokers in business training, interpersonal training, and technical training from her network of corporate and community resources.
Problem within the group	Engages in active problem solving, which may or may not involve other department employees. Focuses on getting the problem solved as quickly as possible.	Provides relevant resources or information from external sources so that the group can solve their problem themselves. Focuses on accomplishing the purpose of the team rather than just fixing things that are broken.

1. Articulate a vision for the organization.
2. Manage by principle rather than by policy.
3. Effectively coach individuals and teams.
4. Understand and communicate business information.
5. Aggressively eliminate barriers to team effectiveness.
6. Actively facilitate and develop team members.
7. Focus on the customer's perspective.

These behaviors can be developed into seven competency clusters, which further clarify the required skills for a successful team leader (see Figure 13.5):

1. Leader
2. Living Example
3. Coach
4. Business Analyzer
5. Barrier Buster
6. Facilitator
7. Customer Advocate

What do these clusters mean?

1. The *Leader* unleashes energy and enthusiasm by creating a vision that others find inspiring and motivating.[9]
2. The *Living Example* serves as a role model for others by "walking the talk" and demonstrating the desired behaviors of team members and leaders.
3. The *Coach* teaches others and helps them develop to their potential, maintains an appropriate authority balance, and ensures accountability in others.
4. The *Business Analyzer* understands the big picture and is able to translate changes in the business environment to opportunities for the organization.

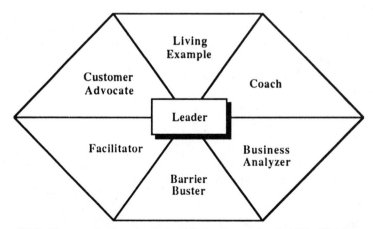

Figure 13.5. The team leader role. (*Belgard•Fisher•Rayner Inc. © 1989. All rights reserved. Used by permission.*)

5. The *Barrier Buster* opens doors and runs interference for the team, challenges the status quo, and breaks down artificial barriers to the team's performance.

6. The *Facilitator* brings together the necessary tools, information, and resources for the team to get the job done, and facilitates group efforts.

7. The *Customer Advocate* develops and maintains close customer ties, articulates customer needs, and keeps priorities in focus with the desires and expectations of the customers.

Summary

There are a number of role similarities, of course, between successful supervisors and successful team leaders. But leading SDWTs requires some special perspectives and competencies. Team leaders are boundary managers who act as organization designers, infrastructure builders, and cross-organization collaborators. They don't "taste the sausage."

While supervisors work *in* the system, team leaders work *on* the system. As boundary managers, team leaders perform responsibilities at the interface between the team and the team's environment. This allows them to help the teams stay focused on the big picture instead of becoming mired in the day-to-day throughput tasks for which the SDWTs now have primary responsibility. It also allows team leaders to get needed resources and information from outside the team.

We have found that successful boundary managers have a number of general attributes and skills. They have highly developed competencies in the areas of leadership, modeling, coaching, business analysis, barrier busting, facilitation and customer advocacy. Without skills in these areas, team leaders are not likely to be successful boundary managers.

Because of their importance to the team leader, each of these seven competencies will be described in more detail in the next few chapters.

Endnotes

1. Jean Auel, *The Mammoth Hunters* (New York: Bantam, 1983), p. 423. © 1983 by Bantam Books. Used by permission. This novel is a fictional story about a woman's (Ayla) adventures in a prehistoric tribe. The author, Jean Auel, worked at Tektronix prior to completing her series of books about Ayla. Parenthetical notations added.

2. Pamela Posey and Janice Klein, "Traditional versus New Work System Supervision: Is There a Difference?" in Janice Klein, *Revitalizing Manufacturing: Text and Cases* (Homewood, Ill.: Irwin, 1990).

3. David Hanna, *Designing Organizations for High Performance* (Reading, Mass.: Addison-Wesley O.D. Series, 1988). Dave does a nice job explaining open systems theory in this book. The original concept is usually attributed to Ludwig von Bertalanffy, "The Theory of Open Systems in Physics and Biology," *Science*, 111, 1950, pp. 23–28.

4. Ralph Stayer, "How I learned to Let My workers Lead," *Harvard Business Review* (November–December 1990).

5. William Synder, "The First-Line Manager in Innovating Organization," unpublished paper, University of Southern California, p. 16–17. Used by permission of author.

6. Ibid., p. 39. Bracketed word added. Used by permission.

7. Edward Lawler, "Substitutes for Hierarchy," *Organizational Dynamics*, Summer 1988.

8. Rosabeth Moss Kanter, "The New Managerial Work," *Harvard Business Review* (November–December 1989).

9. These descriptions and the "Team Leader Role" model are used by permission. © 1989 by BFR, Inc. All rights reserved.

14

Essential Competencies for Team Leaders

Leader, Example, and Coach

All coaching is, is taking a player where he can't take himself.

BILL McCARTNEY,
Defensive Coordinator
San Francisco '49ers Super Bowl Season

A running critique of large organizations is that they are typically over-managed and underled. While in a traditional operation this is unfortunate, in a SDWT it can be disastrous. SDWTs need leadership to be successful. In this chapter we will review the first three competencies of team leaders: (1) leadership, (2) modeling, and (3) coaching.

Acting Like a Leader

Nothing has been studied so thoroughly or written about so consistently as leadership. What is a leader? Two leadership characteristics are particularly important to the SDWT boundary manager: (1) they are masters of change, and (2) they are visionaries.

134

Leaders as Change Agents

Leaders are masters of change. They are so committed to continuous improvement that they constantly challenge the status quo. They empower those around them to do what is "right" rather than allowing them to succumb to the momentum of the "way we usually do things around here." The team leader has the skills required to make these changes in a way that minimizes counterproductive disruptions, motivates people to achieve, and creates the support of enough followers to accomplish an honest modification of the culture. Tichy and Ulrich call this unique bag of skills needed to move a lumbering organization in a new direction *transformational leadership*,[1] a term that captures the scope and significance of this characteristic. Simply stated, leaders create big, sustainable change. One of the primary ways they effect change is through vision, the second important element of leadership.

Vision: Gotta Have One

Leaders are visionaries. In fact, as mentioned in the earlier chapters on team leader values, managing by vision is one of the key characteristics of a team leader. Vision is a leadership tool. Like a hammer, it can drive a nail or smash a thumb. But when it is used effectively it makes a big difference.

One Apple computer plant manager describes Steve Jobs, cofounder of Apple, as such a visionary: "Steve had his problems," he said, "but I can still remember how he could inspire and motivate us with his vision. He would get us together and tell us that Apple products were going to *change the world*. He made that happen." Think of what Apple accomplished in those early days of the company. I was working as an intern with IBM in 1979 when good IBMers were laughing at this upstart little company with its toy computers. I remember being in meetings when senior managers declared that microcomputers would never replace mainframes in the office. They were wrong. Job's vision motivated people enough to break the office technology paradigm and change the world.

Jobs himself said of his role with the Macintosh design team:

> The greatest people are self-managing; they don't need to be managed. Once they know what to do they'll figure out how to do it . . . what they need is a common vision and that's what leadership is . . . leadership is having a vision, being able to articulate that so that people around you can understand it and getting a consensus on [it].[2]

How Have Leaders Influenced You?

Think of leaders who have inspired and motivated you to do your best. How did they do it? Chances are that they believed in you, they were honest and trustworthy, and they had a vision that you believed in. Although they are often controversial, great leaders bring about great change with these visions. Dr. Martin Luther King inspired millions with his "I have a dream" speech of little black children and little white children living in harmony. Ghandi moved millions with his vision of nonviolent change. Walensa changed a nation through a vision of worker solidarity. Gorbachev dismantled the former Soviet Union with his vision of *glasnost* and *perestroika*. Kennedy focused the unchanneled creativity of a nation on putting a man on the moon.

This kind of vision is important for any human organization, and it is certainly a useful tool for operational, management, and culture team leaders. Whether the team is a Fortune 100 company or a small group of office workers, a good team leader has a vision of what that team could accomplish that will allow her to provide clarity of direction and values. The vision must be concise enough to be focusing but broad enough to allow the creative autonomy necessary to accomplish it. Phil Rittenhouse, while a plant manager at Corning, had an unusual and compelling vision for his plant. He was vacationing in India with his family one year. He found, hand-scrawled on a monument a paragraph described what the graffiti writer thought was required to help India achieve its own economic and spiritual potential. Rittenhouse modified it somewhat and presented it as his vision of the factory. "[The factory] will be made of what we are. As we are big so will [the factory] be. We want to enjoy success. We want jobs and fair rewards. We want people who are going to stand up for what they think is right and not submit humbly to wrong. We challenge ourselves to do big things. We cannot command success, but success often comes to those who dare to act." The vision captured the attention of the plant. It was also so different from the traditional mission and objective statements that they were used to, that it clearly signaled a departure from the norm.

Nested Vision

Since every team leader uses vision as a tool to motivate and focus team members, there is a risk of a serious problem. If multiple visions empower multiple teams to head in lots of different (read "inconsistent") directions, an organization can be ripped apart.

A concept that is useful to coordinate multiple visions is called *nested visions*. If the vision of culture team leaders is broad enough, then the vision of management team leaders can fit inside of it. If the vision of management team leaders is not too restrictive, then the vision of operations team leaders will fit inside it as well. Thus the visions nest inside of one another. Like Russian Matreshka dolls, the smaller visions fit inside larger and larger visions. Each is completely whole and developed, but each is consistent with the size and shape of the others it fits within. This process also makes it more likely that the visions will become shared visions in the operation because there is consistency in the visions' messages.

Shared Vision

Just having a vision isn't good enough. Obviously, if the vision isn't (1) communicated and (2) agreed to, then it won't make any difference at all. Leaders know this. Shared vision is the only vision that drives the nail home. How do you create shared vision?

Sometimes just articulating a well crafted picture of the future is enough to create shared commitment to achieving it. This seems to work especially well for leaders who have a certain amount of charisma and who are trusted by team members. Many team leaders, however, prefer an alternative process that enrolls the team members in the modification/creation of the vision. How? Some share their vision in an informal setting and then invite others to modify it to the extent required for them to support it. Others use a joint visioning process, in which they work with the team to create the vision together from scratch.

A Joint Visioning Process Example

Let me give you an example to illustrate both a joint visioning process and the nested vision concept. In one large, progressive organization, company representatives were commissioned by culture team leaders to jointly create a company-wide vision for empowerment. The representatives included consultants and people from manufacturing and distribution units, non-manufacturing units, the union, and management. After some discussion, the company-wide vision was written as a mission statement (see Fig. 14.1).

The involvement process automatically made the vision a shared vision. And the vision they came up with was of secondary importance to the fact that they created it together. The magic wasn't the document itself, but what happened in the room leading up to the development of the document. As individuals personally and collectively committed to the vision, they created implicit agreements to help each other change the culture. As you can see in Fig. 14.2, an informations systems division of the same company came up with their own unique vision of empowerment, which though more specific than the corporate one, is still consistent with the

---

Mission

Create a sense of urgency to change the environment across the entire company to unleash and focus the full potential of all employees in our drive to serve the customer and to be the best in the world in every one of our plants and businesses.

Employees will be provided with all the information to understand their business (customers, suppliers, and products) and to focus on our competitors as the common adversary.

All employes will be the best trained, most flexible, productive, and secure in their areas of employment.

All employees will be trained and empowered to make operational decisions across a very broad range of tasks for which they and their work groups will be responsible.

Every unit will develop and implement a plan to continuously design or redesign their operations to ensure that we beat our competition.

All employees will participate and share in the success and financial prosperity of the business.

Figure 14.1. Sample of a company-wide vision of empowerment.

broad direction. You can also see that the division vision leaves plenty of room for individual teams to create clear and motivating visions of their own. Interestingly, in both of these vision documents the participants choose to include some statements of their values as well. As they have taken action towards operationalizing the statements on these sheets of paper, they have started to make significant progress towards creating empowered work teams.

Being a Living Example

The second competency cluster for the team leader is being a living example. Team leaders model the behaviors they demand from others. They also embody and symbolize the vision of the organization. It is hard to overstate the importance of this part of the team leader's role, as evidenced by the Kodak team leaders and others. Team leaders simply must walk the talk, or in the words of some Boeing managers, they must at least "stumble the mumble." Team leaders understand that the eloquence of their example is far more powerful than their words.

Vision

Information Services will be an organization in which employes are vested with both the responsibility and authority to deliver total customer service.

Principles of Empowerment

In order to achieve our empowerment vision, Information Services subscribes to the following operating principles:

An integrated, well communicated division direction guides each individual's actions such that a sense of commitment, dedication, and power exists within each employee.

An openness exists throughout the organization which facilitates communication, minimizes bureaucracy, and speeds decision making.

Responsibility for the success of the empowerment effort rests with all I/S employees. Responsibility for creating an empowered environment rests with the I/S management team.

Increased responsibility, authority, and accountability reside at the action initiation or customer interface points within the organization.

Coaching, mentoring, and collaboration skills are emphasized and are the dominant organizational style.

Processes are simplified to allow broader involvement in direction and priority setting.

Continuous improvement is expected and is measured by a periodic Empowerment Survey.

Figure 14.2. Sample of a division-wide vision of empowerment.

Alexander the Great is said to have won the commitment of his soldiers by risking his own life along side them. He was the first man to charge the Theban Sacred Band at Chaeronea and plunged so often into the thickest of the battle that his soldiers, fearful of losing him, begged him to go to the rear.[3] He was also the first to scale the walls of the Mallians. The ladders broke after he and two others had leapt into the city and found themselves alone among the enemy. He collapsed from loss of blood just as his armies broke into the city and saved his life. On one occasion to calm a potential mass sedition, he presented himself to his army and asked which of them could show more scars than he "whose body bore the marks of every weapon used in war."[4] He led by example. An old saw about the difference between leaders and managers in the Civil War said that you could tell which they were from their position relative to the charging troops. Leaders were in front. Managers shouted direction and encouragement from behind.

People simply do not care what team leaders say, they care about what they do. The best team leaders I know don't talk about how they value employee input, they solicit it. They don't give speeches about the importance of customers, they visit them. They don't pontificate about quality, they shut down work when the operations are just slightly out of spec. And they empower (by example) the team members to do the same things.

Team Leaders Aren't Above the Law

Team leaders don't hold themselves above the law. They realize that a double standard causes distrust and looks hypocritical to people. If sound business reasons dictate the need for certain policies, they adhere to them. If money expenditures require authorization, they go through the same process as the team does for approval. If vacations need to be coordinated they coordinate their vacations too. Any policy that applies to the team member applies to the team leader as well. If it is silly for team leaders to conform to any of the policies, then it is silly for team members to conform to them. Team leaders often, in fact, find themselves eliminating these kinds of practices and policies in their role of barrier buster. Team leaders, in short, practice what they preach.

John Adamoli, the Vice President of the Martin Marietta Astronautics group, for example, wanted to do two things. He wanted to demonstrate that his role was to support the organization, not boss it around, and he also wanted to emphasize the importance of cross-training for the newly empowered project teams. Instead of just having a meeting to tell this to people he took off his suit, went down to the production floor, and had employees teach him how to weld.

Team Leaders Put the Message in Their Behavior

That's the way the best do it. Stew Leonard is a culture team leader for the huge, remarkable grocery store of the same name headquartered in Connecticut. He doesn't just talk about continuous improvement, he takes his team of managers in the company van on field trips to competitor's stores. He asks every participant to come up with "just one new idea."

He actually got the idea of doing this when he was visiting Wal Mart's late chief executive, Sam Walton. He went with Walton up and down the aisles of a Wal Mart store. The Wal Mart chain carries some products that are similar to those carried by Stew Leonard's. Leonard learned a lot by following Walton around. Walton commented the whole time, for example, about this great end display, or that great aisle arrangement as he walked on through the store. Leonard asked a Wal Mart vice president if Walton was always like this. The VP replied that Walton could find something good in every store he had ever visited. Each time he visited an operation he modeled the behaviors of positive reinforcement and continuous improvement by always looking for new ideas to share with his other stores. Sam Walton asked Leonard, in fact, if he had any new ideas for Wal Mart now that he had seen a Wal Mart store. "Sure," replied the savvy Leonard aware of how Walton was expanding across the United States, "please don't open a store in Connecticut."

Managing by Principle Rather Than by Policy

One of the most important skills for walking the talk is managing by principle rather than by policy. No other activity better symbolizes the difference between traditional organizations and self-directed work teams than backing off from rules and regulations and trusting people to do what is right. Team leaders manage by principle rather than by edict because they want to develop an entrepreneurial spirit, often called "ownership" in others. Traditional, nonparticipative systems typically are managed through policies and procedures, which can be two-edged swords. While rules ensure consistency and control of the business, an undesirable side effect is that they also restrict creativity, flexibility, trust, and commitment, which are keystone attributes of competitive organizations.

While some rules are necessary, of course, a reliance on them as a vehicle of management often leads to memorized answers and rigid solutions. Managing by principles, however, allows enough flexibility to respond appropriately to the ever changing needs of the business in ways that both address the needs effectively and that maximize individuals' commitment to business results.

Few things are as demonstrative of this team leader characteristic as when the leader makes a visible alteration of a well-known written or unwritten rule. For example, when Boyle of Honeywell wrote a you-don't-have-to-wear-a-tie-when-it's-hot memo to his division,[5] he sent a message that *principles* like maintaining a professional image with customers (the reason for the dress code) were more important than rules like everyone needs to wear a tie to work. If this is done enough, people remember that the principle, not the policy, is important. Eventually they will feel free to challenge policies that unintentionally inhibit organization effectiveness rather than mindlessly complying to something that doesn't make sense.

Managing by principle is more difficult than managing by policy. At the Lima plant we managed by three particularly important principles:

- Do what is right.
- Get results.
- Do it together.

Are these kinds of principles more vague than policies would be? Are they subject to individual interpretation? Do they apply differently in one set of circumstances than they might in another? The answer to all of these questions is yes. That is why they are difficult to use. It is also why they work. On many an occasion team members would say, "Hey, wait a minute, what we are doing now is what is cheap or easy but not what is right." Or "We should do something different than what we are planning now, I don't think it will get good results." Or, "Hold it, we are making a decision that affects another team, we should make this decision together." In virtually every situation these kinds of discussions led to results that were far superior to what would have occurred if employees were simply complying with a management rule.

Coaching Teams

The third competency of team leaders is coaching. Coaches recognize that they need to develop individual players on the team and help the team learn how to work together effectively. Like the other competencies of team leaders, coaching is important in any organization. The reason it is especially important in an empowered work system, however, is that everyone plays a much larger role in running the business. Decisions are made at the point where action is taken on the decision. Responsibilities are given to those who are most directly affected by the consequences. Business direction is influenced by those who need to implement it. The rule of thumb is that people are given as much responsibility, authority and autonomy as they can handle. The amount they can handle, of course, depends on how effectively they have been developed and will therefore change over time.

Many one-on-one performance coaching skills are readily transferable from traditional organizations to SDWTs. But coaches in these team-based operations also need to be proficient in working with the whole team as a unit. Coaches need to help team members build their skills.

Although people need a number of particular technical and social skills, a few fundamental areas require special coaching attention. Team leaders develop teams that:

1. Produce good results.

2. Exhibit teamwork (working together effectively).

3. Demonstrate self-sufficiency (producing and maintaining a high level of results with little external influence).

4. Communicate effectively (keeping everyone well informed).

These focus areas form a foundation upon which the more specific skills tailored to the operation can be built.

One of the most difficult and most important skills to build into a team is the skill of learning how to learn. This thinking skill is critical to continuous improvement and self-direction. How do we coach it? One way is by asking questions instead of giving solutions.

Socratic Coaching

Allowing team members to build inner skull muscle tone is more important than any other development activity. Coaches refrain from judgment statements like, "That won't work." Instead, they ask questions like, "What is the problem you want to solve?" or "How will you know when you have solved it?" or "What information did you base this conclusion on?" Socratic coaching is a skill not to be undervalued in the SDWT environment. If done well, it teaches, strengthens, and empowers.

Relying on this technique too much, of course, can cause serious problems. Coaches that continually ask team members, "What do you think?" frequently lose their effectiveness when people eventually stop coming to them for advice. Better questions focus on where information can be found or on teaching particular thinking processes that help people make good decisions. There was one division manager at P&G, for example, who had a reputation for always asking, "What other solutions did you consider and why did you reject them?" After the second or third interaction with this management team leader, operations team leaders began to understand that he was teaching us to think through things carefully and not always settle for the first satisfactory solution.

High Expectations

Coaches also recognize that there is a time and a place to be tough. When I think back on people who have been great coaches in my life, they have always had very high expectations of me. And they let me know when I wasn't performing to my level of capability. They did this in the right way, of course, by sharing good data and clear examples with me. Delivering feedback is an important coaching skill. And there are more effective and less effective ways of doing it.

Performance Appraisals Are a Lousy Way to Coach

Traditional performance appraisals are undoubtedly one of the least effective coaching techniques. They are depressing, nonsupportive, artificial, and untimely. I can just imagine what would happen if we applied this technique to professional basketball teams. Would the NBA work better if coaches gave each player a thoroughly documented performance review at the end of each season? I don't think so. What team members need is ongoing effective feedback during the game. Several team leaders I work with regularly share customer and peer feedback with teams to let them know whether they are on track or off track. Professional sports teams use videos of their games to help players self-review performance, and orchestras listen to their tapes for the same reason. Similarly, charts, graphs, and project reviews can help teams monitor their progress against performance goals and objectives, while internal and external customer visits can offer some real-time feedback that is more likely to motivate than discourage.

Summary

Effective coaching is a key competency for the team leader. Running practices and giving good feedback is a helpful way to build the capability of team members individually and collectively. Although the traditional method of formal performance reviews is not likely to help, one method of effective development is Socratic coaching. If used effectively, questions help the team member learn and improve. Another important competency for the team leader is walking the talk. What we say as team leaders doesn't matter as much as what we do. Successful team leaders carefully consider whether their actions set the right example or not. They manage by principle rather than by policy because they realize that this approach provides clarity without unnecessary restriction. Team leaders, of course, also demonstrate leadership skills. In particular, they are visionaries and change agents. They know how to coalesce people around a shared vision that is nested with the organizational leadership. These three competencies—leadership, modeling, and coaching—are important parts of the team leader role.

In the next chapter we will review the final four competency clusters of the team leader role: business analysis, facilitating, barrier busting, and customer advocacy.

Endnotes

1. Noel Tichy and David Ulrich, "The Leadership Challenge—A Call for the Transformational Leader," *Sloan Management Review* (Fall 1984), pp. 59–68.

2. J. Natham and S. Tyler, *In Search of Excellence*, film based on the book by Peters and Waterman (1984).

3. Will Durant, *The Life of Greece* (New York: Simon & Schuster, 1939), p. 541.

4. Ibid., p. 550

5. R. J. Boyle, "Designing the Energetic Organization: How a Honeywell Unit Stimulated Change and Innovation," *Management Review* (August 1983), pp. 20–25.

15

The Business Analyzer, Barrier Buster, Facilitator, and Customer Advocate

You can't get people to focus only on the bottom line. You have to give them an objective like "satisfy the customer" that everyone can relate to.[1]

PAUL ALLAIRE,
CEO of Xerox

In this chapter we will consider the last four competencies of the team leader in more detail. They are:

1. Business analysis

2. Barrier busting

3. Facilitating

4. Customer advocacy

With this discussion we will finish the review of the seven competency clusters that make up the role of the SDWT leader.

Analyzing Business

More than anything else, business analysis is the process of gathering and then disseminating business information. While it is true that the effective team leader must be skilled in the process of evaluating and analyzing, the most common inadequacy associated with this competency cluster isn't whether the analysis itself is good or bad. It is whether that analysis is shared with the team effectively or not.

Let me explain. My fourth grade teacher first taught me the importance of sharing information. Mrs. Anderton was a very large woman who wore a thimble on the middle finger of her right hand to plunk on the foreheads of errant students (I was on the business end of that thimble more than once). She suggested one day that "democracy would not work." After a dramatic pause that captured my attention as a young patriot (willing to risk even the thimble for a developing belief in democracy), she continued. "Unless people are informed," she said.

Democracy without information is nothing more than uninformed mobocracy. "I am a firm believer in the people," said Abraham Lincoln. "If given the truth, they can be depended upon to meet any national crisis. The great point is to bring them the real facts."[2] Bringing them the facts, however, is the key. Timely, accurate information is what drives effective democracy. It is the engine fuel. You might as well have a few people making good decisions autocratically than a lot of people making stupid ones democratically. There is nothing good about that.

Empowerment Without Business Information Is a Sham

Similarly, empowerment without information is a condescending and manipulative sham. Teams cannot work towards self-direction without understanding their businesses *well*. I already mentioned that Corning has been using the word "partnership" to describe their SDWT work. I like the word because it helps people be honest about the effort by asking a simple question. "Am I treating others (and am I being treated) like a business partner?"

Would you join a business partnership if your soon-to-be partner told you that, although you would have equal access to decision making, he was not going to be able to share all the business information with you? Would you placidly accept his reasoning that it is just too time consuming or expensive to do this? What if he said that he wanted to wait until he had all the facts before he shared them with you, or, worse, that he feared you wouldn't be able to understand the information anyway? I wouldn't be a partner in an operation like that.

We Need Better Information Systems

Team leaders cannot share good business information, of course, unless they have access to it. Unfortunately, many businesses are sadly lacking in information that can be used to manage the business at each team's level. At the same time they are inundated with reports and paperwork that quantify things for reporting up and out of the organization. Although these kinds of information are helpful for coordinating things across the organization, they add little value for self-directed work teams. My colleague, Steve Rayner, calls this the elevator model of information sharing. At the bottom floor, the data is shoveled in, and the doors close. When the elevator opens at the bottom floor again, there is a decision, not helpful information, in the elevator. As mentioned in earlier chapters, technology is available now to aid in the team information sharing and evaluating process, but we have to use it effectively.

What Kind of Information Do SDWTs Need?

What kinds of things do team leaders need to understand and then bring to the team members? Leaders need to have a good understanding of the business variables at the boundary of the team including specific facts and data relating to at least these eight topic areas:

1. *Customers/markets*: Who are they? What do they need from us?

2. *Technologies/technical*: What are the options? How do they affect us?

3. *Competition*: Who are they? How are we different from them?

4. *Environment*: How do we eliminate contaminants? Do activists affect us?

5. *Political/governmental*: What laws affect us? Are there community concerns that could affect us?

6. *Demographics*: What are the changing requirements of the work force?

7. *Suppliers*: Who are they? How do they affect our work and customers?

8. *Economics*: How is the economy? How does that affect us?

It is a sad commentary on businesses today that many team leaders cannot answer basic questions relating to these areas. Many times I have visited with team leaders at different levels of the organization who could not name end use customers of the products or services they provided. Others haven't known their competitors and their strengths and weaknesses. Many have been unaware of government regulations that affect them or of the new technologies that were available to help them accomplish their work more effectively. While answers to these questions are generally available in certain compartmentalized functional areas of the organization, they were not widely known.

There are, of course, some refreshing examples of leaders that do this well. After Bill Gates, the billionaire wunderkind founder of Microsoft, expressed concern that managers didn't know enough about their competitors, Jeff Raikes, then manager of the word processing business, got to know Pete Peterson, his counterpart at WordPerfect. He put a picture of Petersen's children on his desk and he continues to send them birthday cards each year. The pictures, of course, were only a symbol of the thoroughness of his investigation into the competition. Family photos do not substitute for good competitive information.

Institutionalized Methods for Joint Business Analysis

The bottom line is this: Business information needs to be to disseminated throughout the organization, and there needs to be institutionalized methods for regular discussion of these and other topics relating to the internal workings of the business. That is what creates a forum for joint business analysis. It is for this reason that many SDWTs in manufacturing settings have shift overlap meetings every day and why white collar teams meet several times a week. These meetings provide an opportunity for sharing real-time information. They also become the primary forum for ongoing skill training and for group problem solving and decision making activity. Where the supervisor relied on controls to coordinate and focus work activity, the team leader now relies on information instead.

Eliminating Barriers to High Performance

The second competency for team leaders is barrier busting. One of the quickest ways to make team members feel empowered is to identify and eliminate organizational barriers to their performance. Perhaps no activity is more energizing to a team than isolating a particularly restrictive policy or practice and working with the team leader to modify or eliminate it. It is true of both real and perceived barriers as well. Barrier busting builds trust in the team leader and credibility for the change effort.

One note of caution, however, is that this stuff cuts two ways. Unsuccessful efforts to make these kinds of changes will slow and stop the progress of empowerment. It is far better to build some momentum by biting off a few smaller projects that have a reasonable chance of success than by going after the big high risk one right out of the barrel.

Quality of Work Life Concerns

Early concerns identified by teams are often related to the quality of work life. When the sanitation department of New York City began their empowerment efforts several years ago, for example, workers were much more interested in putting in clear thermal curtains to keep the cold winter air out of their work areas than they were in improving technologies or cutting costs. But that came later. After the workers came to trust the team leaders who helped them improve the quality of their work life they then went after things like new cutting torch technology and painting techniques that eventually saved the city millions of dollars associated with maintaining the largest nonmilitary fleet of vehicles in the United States. Barrier busting team leaders made it happen by freeing up worker time and project resources to work on improvements (they created an R&D department), which were unavailable with the more restrictive work practices of the past.

Eliminate Unnecessary Policies

Barrier busting is tricky business. It needs to be handled in a way that doesn't disenfranchise key resources to the team. Blaming central staff groups for stupid policies, for example, often makes them unwilling to help the team later on when their expertise may be essential. Similarly, the clumsy dismantling of long-standing corporate artifacts can upset important senior leadership. [We used to call these CLMs (Career Limiting Moves) at Tektronix]. Nevertheless, when done with sensitivity and when supported with good business information, barrier busting can create enormous psychological and business gains. Even the little wins make a difference.

With the help of some team leaders, a small team of union executives at a P&G plant were able to change a policy relating to travel to nonunion plants and an unwritten rule about sharing profitability information inside the plant. Busting these barriers built up trust in the facility between management and the union that had eroded away over decades. In a Tektronix division, a management team leader helped eliminate a requirement that people report their time using a particular method that required very detailed record keeping. Sadly the team leader discovered that the reports generated from this time-consuming activity were compiled, distributed, and virtually ignored. The previously unchallenged policy was significantly simplified and resulted in a savings of thousands of employee hours a month. Moreover, it created a flurry of activity. When team members saw that management was willing to get rid of inhibiting practices, they surfaced a number of barriers that they had always thought were immovable. Although some were, in fact, barriers that resulted from legal requirements that could not be changed, a number of them were simplified. Production output increased, quality improved, and development speed increased.

Facilitating Skills

The third competency cluster is facilitating. Team leaders realize that people, like seed corn, will be productive only as long as they have the resources that are necessary. Although not all seeds are germinated, just like all team members aren't productive all the time, most will bear fruit in favorable conditions. Team leaders therefore facilitate higher crop yield by creating the favorable conditions. Fertilizing, administering pesticides and herbicides, irrigating, being responsive to destructive molds and diseases, harvesting, and so forth are the ways that farmers ensure that the seeds have the resources necessary to produce as much corn as they are internally capable of producing. Conversely, withholding resources can cause corn to wither and weaken. The unsuspecting team leader who, even unknowingly, withholds information, authority, autonomy, budget, training, or whatever resources are necessary to get the job done, lowers productivity even as she may be struggling so hard to "make" people be productive. Trying to make people productive is like a farmer "making" corn grow: It isn't effective.

We have already mentioned that team leaders believe that most people will do what is right. Therefore they focus most of their time and attention on how to provide the appropriate resources, experiences, and information needed to do the job successfully rather than on how to influence opinions. They enable people to be successful. They assume that most problems are the result of a lack of resources rather than of a desire to subvert the operation. Team leaders also understand that motivation is internally generated. They realize that while they need to *allow* people to be productive, they cannot *make* them productive. Hence the title "facilitator" rather than director.

How Do You Facilitate?

How does the team leader facilitate? The facilitator's ongoing objective, of course, is to actively solicit and channel the participation of others. This facilitation may take the direct form of asking for participation: "Jim, I know you have a lot of experience on this, what do you think we ought to do?" As team members become more comfortable with the participative process, it may take the form of requesting more thorough proposals that require a significant breadth and depth of organizational understanding.

Team leaders also actively focus on the development of others. That was the war cry we heard at Kodak's 13 Room so often: "Develop capability." Instead of taking over conversations and making the decisions, the team leader walks to the chart pad, grabs a pen, and starts asking people where we should go from here. Instead of doing things for the team that they could learn to do for themselves, the team leader teaches them how to do it. He becomes skilled at understanding the dynamics of a work group and knowing when and where to intervene. She develops expertise in teaching people processes that will help them solve problems and make decisions themselves instead of just giving them a solution or decision to implement. She takes advantage of every teaching moment that presents itself. When I had team members come to me to ask me to solve a problem I would say, "Sure!" and bring them along with me. After a while, they knew it made more sense just to go solve the problem themselves without dragging me into the middle of it.

Training

Training becomes a crucial element of the facilitator's responsibility, especially in the early stages of SDWT implementation. Most team leaders seriously underestimate the time commitment required to do this. Says Bob Condella, Director of the Administrative Center of Corning:

> The biggest mistake we made was that we did not train enough. People need a lot of help in the beginning. People need more help and more tools (than we thought). We spent about 10 percent of our time in training. But when I went out and benchmarked, companies were spending about 20 percent.

Training is an ongoing responsibility as well. Both Tektronix and General Electric found that, if you include all types of training (classroom, mentoring, cross-training, business meetings, team meetings, etc.), the ongoing requirement for training time is in the neighborhood of 10 to 20 percent of every person's work week. That is almost a whole day a week dedicated to learning. It is a far cry from the traditional organization's training record of 0.5 to 2 percent. Far-sighted companies like Motorola are already establishing goals for team member training, which help the organization understand that training is part of the work to be done, rather than something that takes people away from their work. And they are backing it up with resources as well. In 1987 they spent $44 million dollars for training, a 2.5 percent expenditure of annual payroll upgrading the skills of each of its 96,000 employees.[3] Although this amount was already more than twice the average training budget (as a percent of annual payroll) at the time, they were spending up to $60 million dollars a year by 1990 (plus an estimated $60 million in lost work time), "and everyone thought it was money well invested."[4] William Wiggenhorn, Motorola's corporate vice president for training and education and the president of Motorola University, acknowledges that the facilities that didn't reinforce the training had a negative return on investment. But plants that reinforced the training received a $33 return for every dollar spent including the cost of wages.[5] They expect these training budget increases to continue as empowerment requires further buttressing of basic skills and an expanding curriculum of business skills for employees on teams.

Career Development

Facilitating career development also takes on a new and important twist in the SDWT. In these flatter organizations, there are fewer and fewer opportunities for promotions. Therefore, lateral development takes on more importance than vertical development. That means that the team leader is responsible for ensuring that team members get experience across the operations, rather than just inside a traditional functional silo, or limited to one area of narrow technical expertise. This may come partly from classroom training, but it requires much more. Typically team leaders ensure that processes are in place that require the regular rotation of responsibilities to give team members actual experience in a wide variety of technical and leadership assignments across the team and then into other teams as well.

Customer Advocacy

The fourth competency of team leaders is customer advocacy. This a key part of boundary management. Customer advocacy is one of the main ways to help the team stay focused on the purpose of the organization. It helps the team keep the proper perspective and allows them to solve problems and make decisions with the bigger picture in mind. When the customer advocate does his job, we don't see as many dysfunctional internal squabbles that can cripple the productivity of a team. People know they can't afford much of that. We focus on quality, cost, and speed not because of upper management, but because of customers.

Stew Leonard, the grocery store manager, doesn't just say that customer feedback is important; he actively solicits and applies it. His suggestion boxes in the store are stuffed with hundreds of customer suggestions a month, which are typed and distributed to employees on a daily basis. A few results of these suggestions include fresh fish being taken out of the packaging and put on ice, and customers filling containers with strawberries and eggs themselves instead of purchasing them preboxed. The result? Sales have more than doubled for these items.

Team leaders take actions like these to reinforce the importance of keeping the focus on customers. They bring internal and external customers into team meetings to talk to the team members, and they coordinate site visits so that team members can see how selective customers actually use their products or services. There is no substitute for firsthand interaction. The "we have customers" concept in the abstract is not meaningful to anybody. Why do sales and service employees talk about customers so much? Because they deal with them on a day-to-day basis. They know when they are happy or unhappy, and they are typically rewarded for some measure of customer satisfaction. Everybody needs to feel like a salesperson does about customers. What does it take to make them feel that way? The same things: information, interaction, and rewards.

Team Leaders Develop Customer Empathy

Team members need to see customers as real people like themselves who want value for their money. They need to know their names and experience their problems. One steel mill, for example, reported that a visit to a nearby bicycle manufacturing company that used their steel helped employees have more empathy and enthusiasm for the importance of quality and delivery issues. Tektronix reported improved (more practical and user-friendly) designs and customer relations when engineering team members visited end users. One team leader brings in a different customer each month for a plant-wide assembly so that team members across the facility can hear from them on a regular basis. Many team leaders have had success with sit-down meetings with their teams and visitors from other teams who act as internal customers for their services. These meeting serve to clarify expectations, define deliverables, and resolve problems that may ultimately affect the cost or quality of a product to the end use customer.

Misusing Customer Advocacy

Aetna found an interesting problem with this customer advocacy process, however, that is worth mentioning. They found that too much emphasis on the demands of the *internal* customer (like another downstream department inside Aetna) was causing problems for the external customer. The teams, anxious to please the internal customers, were sometimes complying with requests for additional services that ended up increasing the cost to the final customer. Not good. They resolved the problem by eliminating the focus on internal customers and emphasizing end users. Although this may not be necessary in most organizations, the clear message is to make sure that all internal vendor/customer relationships are aligned so that they serve the final end user.

Some company teams talk about their management as their customer. This is the classic mistake of using the commitment paradigm vocabulary to reinforce the control paradigm organization. Bosses aren't customers and never will be. They work for customers just like everybody else.

The bottom line is that organizations exist to serve customers who pay for products and services. Companies who remember this are much more likely to be successful than those who get tangled up in the day-to-day work priorities. They can't continue to make decisions that improve their own work situation at the expense of the customer. American automakers are still paying for the popular perception that they traded off quality for production in the 1960s and 1970s. This is ironic because arguably General Motors was "born" when this group of small automakers decided that they could survive against the powerful production machine built by Henry Ford only by listening to customers and by offering them an alternative to black Model T cars. As another example, Burger King has carved out a piece of McDonalds market by letting customers have it their way.

Team leaders help team members establish work priorities by keeping the customer up front. This helps people made tradeoffs in favor of quality and service and, perhaps most importantly, provides a purpose for their work beyond just getting the job done. Team members with this understanding have a completely different orientation to their work than an autoworker who described his view of working prior to empowerment as "an eight-hour interruption of my leisure time."

Summary

The role of the team leader in an empowered organization setting is to act as a leader, living example, coach, business analyzer, barrier buster, facilitator, and customer advocate. In this chapter we reviewed the last four competencies of business analysis, barrier busting, facilitating, and customer advocacy. Customer advocacy focuses team members on the purpose of their existence, and helps them make good decisions. This requires, of course, that internal customers aren't emphasized to the detriment of the end user and that people don't see management as customers. Facilitating builds the ability of the team to be self-directed. Barrier busting enables them to break through the vestiges of traditional control-oriented bureaucracies. And business analysis gives them the real-time fuel for effective operation. Once again this assumes that operations have good information systems and institutionalized methods of sharing that information.

The team leader role is necessary for the ongoing effective operation of a self-sustaining team. It is important to understand that the role is an aggressive and proactive one, not the commonly misunderstood one of a milktoast passivist whose only responsibility is to "stay out the way."

More on this topic in the next chapter.

Endnotes

1. Brian Dumaine, "The Bureaucracy Busters," *Fortune* (June 17, 1991), p. 2. © 1991 by The Time Inc. Magazine Company. All rights reserved. Used by permission.

2. Abraham Lincoln in Roger Burns, *Abraham Lincoln* (Broomall Penn.: Chelsea House Publishers, 1986), p. 51.

3. Barbara Jean Gray, "Motorola's Workers Go Back to School," *Human Resource Executive* (November–December 1988), p. 33.

4. William Wiggenhorn, "Motorola U: When Training becomes an Education," *Harvard Business Review* (July–August 1990), p. 72.

5. Ibid., p. 75.

16

The Myth of the Marshmallow Manager

Perhaps if there has been one failing within our organization over the years, it is that we haven't tried to dispel the notion that our success comes out of a computer. It doesn't. It comes out of the sweat glands of our coaches and players.

TOM LANDRY,
*former Head Coach,
Dallas Cowboys*

Not long after I arrived at the P&G plant in Lima, Ohio, the team was having a problem with one of their peers. Thinking it the right thing to do, I encouraged them to resolve the issue themselves without involving me. I was reluctant to jump in and fix something that I thought was the responsibility of the "semiautonomous team." We called this way of managing "the concept," a characteristic of our business that we considered a competitive advantage. When I had been hired by a joint group of technicians and managers from the plant, in fact, the plant manager warned me that *the worst* thing I could do as a manager at Lima was to harm "the concept."

The team was normally responsible for handling most of the disciplinary problems with their peers. They dealt with absenteeism, job performance, and other issues primarily through peer pressure and by using systems they had developed to ensure fairness. But this particular issue was a personal and very complicated one that they could not solve. In fact the team finally convinced me that I should have solved that particular problem without their involvement at all. They needed me to handle the situation autocratically. At the time I was troubled because it seemed somehow inconsistent with the concept. But as I became more experienced in the operation, I discovered that at certain times an appropriate management intervention was not only acceptable, but required for SDWT effectiveness.

Team leadership is an art, not a science. As a result, no precise prescriptions are very useful to the team leader, who ultimately learns the role only through personal experience. But some general observations can accelerate the learning curve. One particular dilemma faced by team leaders, for example, is knowing when to intervene and when to not intervene in the SDWT. Generally speaking, team leaders intervene to generate support and clarity around vision and values as mentioned in earlier chapters. They also, as in the example of the personal problem with my team, intervene when teams are operating outside of their agreed-on responsibilities or skills. But for one reason or another, team leaders certainly will intervene. It is a primary value-adding responsibility of the leader. In this chapter I will show that team leadership is not passive, even though it sometimes appears that way. I will also introduce another one of the important skills of the team leader: setting boundary conditions. Using boundary conditions is another way that helps the team leader know when to intervene in the SDWT.

Team Leaders Are Neither Permissive Nor Passive

I have talked to other team leaders who had the same misconception about their responsibilities as when I first started with SDWTs. Team leadership is not an abdication of responsibility. It is a shared responsibility. And team leadership is neither passive nor permissive management. So why do some people mistakenly think that their primary responsibility as a team leader, in the words of one well-intended team leader, "Is to just stay the heck out of the way"?

If we watch effective team leaders work, it is easy to come away with the misconception that this role is a passive activity. Commitment-eliciting managers delegate a lot. They sometimes refuse to get involved in certain "management-type" decisions that they believe belong to the team. It may appear like gutless acquiescence or responsibility dodging to the casual observer. In fact to some observers these team leaders look like marshmallows—soft, squashy, and indecisive.

Marshmallow Managers

What do I mean by marshmallow managers? They are the supervisors who act sweet and sticky; they seldom take a stand under pressure, and they change their opinion easily to whatever is popular and noncontroversial. They can be operational, management, or culture team leaders who justify personal inactivity by saying, "That is the team's responsibility (not mine); they do whatever they want to do." It is often assumed erroneously that the switch from supervisor to team leader is a switch from "kick butt and take names" (in control) management to "going marshmallows" (out of control). Even if it looks that way to some, nothing could be further from the truth. Even shepherds carry a stick. Let's consider an example that demonstrates why the role might appear as though it is something it is not.

Why Team Leadership Sometimes Looks Passive

As one circuit board plant was starting up, the plant manager Gene Hendrickson chartered a large task force to make decisions about the design and operation of the cafeteria. The task force struggled for months, taking some of their precious production time to argue about the vendors, services, and facility layout of this cafeteria. External observers of this process (and, in fact, a few of the task force members) were baffled. Was this the way to engender commitment? Does participation mean that the team leader just lets go of decisions and lets people waffle around undirected for a while? Why spend hundreds of people hours deciding something so trivial that it could have been decided by a single supervisor in an afternoon?

What people did not understand was that this team leader had a vision for his organization that included a work force with the ability to make business plans and decisions. What appeared to some as unremitting chaos was a carefully orchestrated training process in business information gathering, evaluating alternatives, communicating with others, and sticking by tough, unpopular decisions. Since it was a process of guided self-discovery, however, instead of a three-day workshop or some other highly structured activity, people could not see what they went through as training until later. All they saw from him at the time was restraint, abeyance, and delegation.

The Role Can Look Confusing to Outsiders

Observers of this process could have been confused about the role of the team leader. It is pretty easy to see the seemingly passive actions of leaders in examples like this one and to assume that they are marshmallows. On the contrary, successful team leaders are usually people of passion who have values and trust, which allow them to be patient in the time-consuming development of team members.

In the plant cafeteria decision, people became, in fact, capable of making significant business decisions over time. Three years later a similar group from the plant created the business plan, a sophisticated piece of market evaluations and business strategies to direct the entire operations for the following 12 months. It was voted the second best business plan of the Tektronix businesses by the senior managers of the company (who were unaware that it was developed by a group of mostly nonexempt employees).

Team Leaders Aren't Marshmallows

A contrasting story, told in the same plant, is about the time that Hendrickson was trying to decentralize the plant engineering function. He had tried several times to encourage the engineers to relocate from their centralized office area to their respective production teams on the manufacturing floor. But his encouragement was to no avail. They just didn't want to move. They liked their offices away from the noisy work floor and appreciated the collegial opportunity to review technical problems with other nearby engineers.

Hendrickson, however, had a different vision for the plant. So he came in with a moving crew one weekend and physically muscled the engineers' desks out into the plant. His behavior was in the classic style of the autocratic manager. Without even consulting the engineering team members, he took action. Was his action consistent with the role of a SDWT leader? Was this effective boundary management or was he messing inappropriately with the operational duties of the team?

Ironically, most of the same engineers later declared that it was exactly the right thing to do at the time (even though they were very upset with him when he did it). Said one, "We never would have gone out there (to the production floor) if he wouldn't have forced us to. Now that we have seen the benefit of being right there when the problems happen we can see that it was a smart thing to do. I like it." Was this the action of a marshmallow? Hardly. Effective team leaders are just as strong and passionate and bullheaded as traditional supervisors. But they demonstrate their strength in fundamentally different ways.

Setting Boundary Conditions

Instead of controling specific team member activities, for example, team leaders clarify the boundary conditions within which team activities are performed. These boundaries include things like project cost, schedules, or customer requirements. That provides people the autonomy required to generate personal commitment instead of the robotic compliance that is generated by externally imposed controls (in much the same way as managing by principles does). It also obsoletes the requirements for most externally imposed controls like supervision, policies, and procedures. Team leaders are ferocious about these boundary conditions. They aren't marshmallows. Their ferocity comes from a knowledge that the survival of the team depends on their ability to meet these requirements. How do you use boundary conditions?

Let me give you an example. One company decided to redesign the manufacturing floor, and they wanted to empower employees to do this task. Traditionally, if employee input was sought at all, it would be highly restricted in conformance with numerous policies and procedures about equipment placement, power usage, mandated construction processes, management authorizations for spending capital, and so forth. In this case, however, team leaders wanted to complete this project in a manner that would be more consistent with the SDWT concept, which had been recently introduced in the operation. So they developed boundary conditions for the project instead. These boundaries included the following:

- A requirement that the new design enhance the production of quality products
- A project budget
- A time by which the project had to completed
- The need to incorporate technical resources from engineering into the design process if necessary
- A requirement that the team study just-in-time concepts and incorporate what they learn into the design

There were a few other minor boundaries, but that was about it. Team members felt they had lots of flexibility about how to accomplish the redesign task. They felt trusted to do what was right for the business.

They needed additional skills and support to be successful, of course, but the boundaries marked the field they were to play on.

Good Boundary Conditions Clarify

As team leaders clarify true business boundaries and hold the team accountable for them, team members are able to cut through the ambiguity of the workplace to accomplish things. Like the lines on a football field, they define what is in bounds and out of bounds; they enable team members to assess their progress, and they show them where the goal is located. Without these boundaries team members are likely to get frustrated and demotivated, but with them they can work together to create a series of winning plays.

These boundaries are much broader than directives. Directives, the tools of traditional supervision, dictate what is to done and how to do it. Boundary conditions simply clarify the key constraints that must be considered. They provide clarity without unnecessarily limiting the alternatives the team can choose to accomplish the work to be done. Sometimes they actually encourage people to do things differently. Like the fence surrounding parts of the Grand Canyon, they provide a feeling of security that allows people to explore options right up to the edge of the boundary. Absent these, we often keep away from the edge of our experience and knowledge, sticking to the tried and true things we have done before. They are much more safe, but they may not be what is needed.

The Natural Consequence of Being Unresponsive to Boundary Conditions

The fact of the matter is that boundaries exist whether we make them visible to team members or not. And they have natural consequences if they are not observed. If you are late to the market, you lose some market share. If you go over budget, you have to increase the price of the product to the customers and may thereby reduce sales. If you miss quality boundary conditions, customers may not purchase the product at all. There is little need for artificial punishment in a SDWT environment when boundaries are set well. The punishment is simply the natural consequence of not responding to the boundary. Team leaders help team members avoid the problems that result from walking blindly into these known barriers. Enough unknown problems will surface during any significant project to keep their attention without the needless frustration of crashing into walls that are foreseeable and avoidable.

Summary

Empowered teams don't need marshmallow managers; they need principled leadership that is clear, motivating, and firm. Marshmallows, in fact, are likely to get toasted in these environments, which require often heated, vision-directed assertiveness. Team leadership isn't permissive or passive management. It is true, however, that the role often requires constraint, patience, and delegation, things that are often misunderstood by outsiders who aren't familiar with the history and situation of the work group. This leadership is not a science; it is an art. As such, it is difficult to explain when to intervene aggressively and when to back off. Only experience teaches that. But team leaders do use some processes that help to focus the team and at the same time clarify when certain management interventions are appropriate.

They use boundary conditions, for example, as a way to help teams control themselves. And when the time is right (usually when boundary conditions, vision, values, or agreed operating norms are violated), they take strong unilateral action, which looks to some like a return to autocracy. While supervisory action that takes back control from the team should be avoided at all costs, appropriate management interventions that reinforce values are necessary. These actions strengthen rather than diminish the SDWT process.

In the next chapter we will discuss how the team leader changes boundaries over time to adjust to the maturity level of the team.

17

The Five Stages of Implementing Empowerment

When we were getting ready to start up the Richmond facility, I visited what we thought were the state-of-the-art plants operating like this. They all told me that one of the biggest mistakes they made was to give up too much too soon. People's ability to participate increases over time if they are developed properly, but given too much responsibility before they are prepared can cause some real problems.[1]

ROSS SILBERSTEIN,
*former VP and
Director of Manufacturing,
Sherwin-Williams
Automotive Aftermarket Division*

One of the difficulties of describing the role of the team leader comes from the fact that it is a moving target. So far we have talked about the different competencies of the team leader role as though the role were static. But the role actually evolves as the team matures. It is difficult at first, for example, to act like a boundary manager instead of a supervisor when the team is less mature. They require more assistance on elements inside the team boundary and will allow little time for the team leader to focus on the team's environment. Primary emphasis during the early stages of team maturity, for example, are on being a trainer, and then emphasis moves towards coaching as the team has more experience with the skills they have been taught. Leadership competencies become more crucial as the team matures and requires less intensive coaching.

Although a number of factors may prompt the use of different team leader competencies, none is more significant than the maturity level of the team. As mentioned in earlier chapters, the value set of the team leader is not situational. It provides the continuity and authenticity required for true SDWT leadership. But skills and role requirements will change with the maturity level of the team(s). For this reason, I would like to suggest a team maturity model that allows us to discuss how the team leader role changes over the typical life of the SDWT operation. We will consider the role prior to SDWT implementation and show how each successive stage of maturity has its own unique challenges. We will also begin to consider the tasks to be performed during the five stages. Later chapters will detail the tasks required for operations, management, and culture team leaders during the maturation process.

The Cycle of SDWT Maturity

This model of the typical evolution of self-directed work teams was devised for purposes of this discussion. Life, of course, is not as neatly segmented as any model. There are no boxes and arrows in the workplace, and perfectly clear lines don't separate one maturation step from the other. It is a lot messier than that. But this model does facilitate a useful discussion about how the team leader role evolves.

Self-directed work teams go through five identifiable stages during the evolutionary process (see Fig. 17.1):

1. Investigation

2. Preparation

3. Implementation

4. Transition

5. Maturation

As major empowerment changes are made, the team may continue to cycle through these stages multiple times. Some teams complete a full cycle of the maturation process in just a few months. Some take years. Some never complete the cycle at all because they get blocked at one of the

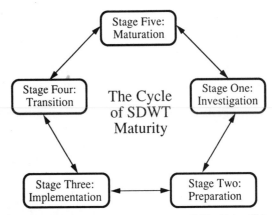

Figure 17.1. The cycle of SDWT maturity. (*Adapted from K. Kim Fisher, "Management Roles in the Implementation of Participative Management Systems," Human Resources Management, Fall 1986 © Copyright by John Wiley & Sons. Used by permission of author.*)

earlier stages. Critical events may also move teams backwards in the maturity cycle. Changing team membership, for example, always moves a mature team back to the transition stage where new responsibilities and operating contracts must be renegotiated.

The Five Stages of SDWT Implementation

During each of the five stages, team leaders need to play a different role in order to maximize the effectiveness of the organization. The five stages of self-directed work team system evolution are:[2]

Stage One. Investigation: In this stage the idea of either developing a new start-up self-directed work team or of changing an existing organization to more empowered work teams is explored. It typically involves a relatively small cadre of people and will produce a few "charismatics" who will champion the concept through the early stages of work system development.

Stage Two. Preparation: The organization goes through the planning/designing and preparation required to successfully transform the organization. This is the stage for generating and demonstrating organizational support for the champion's vision.

Stage Three. Implementation: The new work structures that are manifestations of the shift in the management paradigm are born. Changed or developed are the job design, work rules, developing formal statements of work ethics/values, policies and procedures, performance appraisal systems, team structures, pay and promotion policies, skill development practices, information passing mechanisms, etc.

Stage Four. Transition: This marks the "completion" of implementation and the beginning of adjusting to and becoming competent in the new work system. The work teams themselves are growing, so that they can take on the responsibilities required for maximum organizational effectiveness. Authority and autonomy transfer from team leaders to team members as skills warrant it.

Stage Five. Maturation: A key attribute of this "final" stage is, ironically, that even though the work systems are "completed" in the sense that they are fully functional, they continue from this stage forward to evolve and change. This is what Cherns calls incompleteness, or in other words, continuous improvement of the work unit.[3] Analogously, though adults are chronologically mature, they continue to learn and change in response to the things around them. Work units, like the human beings who work in them, are never finished.

Challenges During the Five Stages

Each stage, of course, has its special challenges. While many of these challenges overlap the stages and typify most change efforts, a few are especially characteristic of one of the five stages. The primary challenges for each stage are listed in Table 17.1.

Table 17.1. The Primary Challenges for Each Stage of the DSWT Maturity Cycle

Stage	Primary challenge
One: Investigation	Understanding it
Two: Preparation	Accepting it
Three: Implementation	Making it work
Four: Transition	Keeping at it
Five: Maturation	Keeping it continuously improving

SOURCE: Adapted from K. Kim Fisher, "Management Roles in the Implementation of Participative Management Systems," *Human Resource Management* (Fall 1986). © Copyright by John Wiley & Sons. Used by permission of author.

Stage One: Investigation Challenges

Challenge = Understanding It. When Procter and Gamble started up the Lima, Ohio soap plant in the late 1960s, only a handful of other organizations with similar "whole-scale" self-directed work teams existed. Predictably, upper management was disappointed that the behavior and results of the new organization did not meet their step level improvement expectations for this new type of plant for a full two years after startup. During this time people were going through the difficult and time-consuming process of learning new skills. Even though information about these kinds of "up-front investments" of whole scale attempts at self-directed work teams is now available, other organizations still encounter similar "disappointments." Like other major business transformations (mergers, technology shifts, market changes, etc.), starting self-directed work teams requires an investment. Understanding not only what self-directed work teams means, but also the costs and risks associated with this kind of transformation, minimizes downstream surprises.

Stage Two: Preparation Challenges

Challenge = Accepting It. During this stage acceptance for the transformation needs to build to critical mass. Trust is a necessary prerequisite to this acceptance.

In one organization in the mid-West United States, a survey indicated that a lack of "trust" between employees and management was the single biggest concern shared by members of the organization. Subsequent efforts to modify work systems to more self-directed ones were implemented more rapidly and with less resistance in areas where there was a higher perceived level of trust than in areas where there was a lower trust level. Lower trust areas quickly reached impasse as supervisors waited for nonmanagers to display the ability and interest to be involved in business decisions. Meanwhile, nonmanagement waited for supervisors to start including them. Nothing happened during the standoff. A lack of management change to participative behaviors, in fact, was frequently mentioned as the primary inhibitor to the implementation of work system modifications.

Working through the trust crises that often occur at Stage Two and then gaining the acceptance of the self-directed work team paradigm are the most typical and difficult challenge of preparation. Acceptance comes as people see, not hear about, the management paradigm shifting from supervision to team leadership. This shift needs to occur *prior* to the implementation of self-directed work teams.

Another major challenge of the preparation stage, of course, is to appropriately prepare for implementation. While team leaders should *diligently* avoid a planning trap that generates paper but little action, they will need to complete appropriate "prework" (reallocating resources, reevaluating business charters, thinking through alternative structures/ modifications, etc.) to make implementation successful.

Stage Three: Implementation Challenges

Challenge = Making It Work. Even with trust, excellent plans, information systems, and resources in place, actually implementing the new work system is tough. Quarterly stockholder reports cause many American and European companies to be overly concerned with short-term results. Thus, serious threats to the survival of self-directed work teams can occur when the implementation causes temporary disruption of the work flow. As the proverbial waters get rough, some team leaders may abandon ship and revert to autocratic management, or even worse, give up, go marshmallows, and turn everything over to ill prepared subordinates.

This is a stage of turmoil where all employees try to figure out the specifics and test the limits of the emerging system. A senior officer's concern at Honeywell that implementing participative management systems was much like wrestling with jellyfish is not uncommon for any employee as they explore new behaviors and try to make sense of this work evolution.[4]

While team members are often resistant to the concept of self-directed work teams at first (primarily during the preparation stage), the main resistance to the concept at this stage will usually come from supervisors for reasons that have already been described in earlier chapters. Transformation efforts in parts of Corning, Tektronix, Mead, Weyerhaeuser, Clark Equipment, and P&G have been slowed when supervisors at all levels were concerned by the perceived implications these changes had on their jobs. One internal consultant in a high-tech firm undergoing a transformation to self-directed work team work systems lamented:

> It took us a while to realize that you cannot assume that managers will fall in line and support this just because their bosses do. They need to buy into the new roles and let go of the old ones because *they* want to or it won't work. And there has to be something in it for them in order for them to be willing to let go.

Inordinate confusion about what kinds of things people will do in a self-directed work team system (or pretending that there will not be a sense of loss for the earlier roles) makes the mourning about the death of the previous management paradigm more difficult and painful than necessary. This can prolong implementation.

Stage Four: Transition Challenges

Challenge = Keeping At It.   A dilemma of the implementation cycle is that SDWTs perform successfully only when all the participants have the skills and information they need. This means that, even though team leaders start practicing empowering behavior in Stage Two, they are really not self-directed work team leaders until the management or non-management team members are fully prepared to participate successfully during Stage Four.

Making this skill and perspective transition usually takes tremendous time and energy. In the words of one manager of an organization in the transition stage:

> It is a gut-wrenching experience to watch people learn how to make business decisions when they haven't made them before. At first you'll have people who want to be a ballerina when they just don't have what it takes. A team will decide to not stay at work one afternoon in order to get more time off or something. You sometimes have to step in and stop it. And it gets tricky to intervene and head off poor group decisions while fostering the belief that you still want them to take risks and to participate.

A plant manager at Tektronix describes this common frustration of the transition stage like this:

> The best way to learn how to make [higher level] business decisions is by making them. People learn by making bad decisions, but it is hard to sit by and watch them making bad decisions when you could step in and fix things so easily yourself. But sometimes you need to let them fail. I do a quick risk analysis every time I watch people start to learn these things. Unless the likely negative outcome of their decisions really outweighs the positive learning experience they will have by falling on their faces a few times, I don't interfere. That is often a very difficult thing to do.

Stage Five: Maturation Challenges

Challenge = Keeping It Continuously Improving.   One of the biggest challenges of this stage is the successful perpetuation of an appropriate self-directed work team system. It is easy to "rest" after people make it through the transition stage, when they finally settle down into roles and responsibilities that they now have come to understand, accept, and become competent in. Unfortunately, in today's competitive and turbulent environment, to rest may mean to become stagnant and uncompetitive.

Another thorny challenge of this stage, of course, is to help people continue to grow and develop. People who have "grown up" in a self-directed work team environment hunger for additional opportunities. They want to be challenged as much as in the earlier years when they were learning a variety of nontraditional skills and participating in the "higher level" roles that they may not have been able/allowed to do in their earlier work experiences. As they progress through the new skills and roles, the reward systems often become obsolete. Since promotions are generally becoming less of an option as organizations become flatter, creative ways to meet this challenge are often necessary.

Leadership Tasks During the Maturation Process

Leadership responsibilities vary somewhat depending on the position of the team leader during the implementation and maturation process. Management leaders, for example, typically are the ones who champion the changes with implications beyond single teams.

An apocryphal story is told in the Northwest United States about a management team leader who wanted to make changes in the way people thought about their new responsibilities in the self-directed work team system. After gaining acceptance for a significantly reduced number of different job descriptions, he took the thick book of current job descriptions out into the parking lot, poured gasoline on it, and burned it to cinders to symbolize the death of some of the restrictive involvement barriers. While this kind of activity may be overly histrionic for many organizations, it evidences the passion for change often required of champions during the implementation stage.

Culture leaders provide broad boundary conditions for implementation and encourage the appropriate challenging of the status quo during Stage Three. They continue to emphasize values, key business focus areas, and essential organizational objectives. They find ways to recognize appropriate implementation activities. Having management and operations leaders address audiences of their peers about their successes to date, for example, reinforces the difficult behavior changes and makes letting go of comfortable habits and institutions more tolerable.

Summary

Although we have talked about the competencies of SDWT team leaders as though they all applied equally all the time, this role is not static. It evolves and changes depending on a number of variables. In this chapter I have highlighted the most important reason for team leader role evolution: the maturity level of the team. Different team leaders have different responsibilities during the maturation process, as we will see in the next few chapters.

We reviewed a five-stage SDWT implementation model, which helps to characterize this evolutionary process. During each of the five stages, team leaders face a unique set of challenges demanding different skills and behaviors. During the investigation stage, the primary challenge is understanding SDWTs and what is required for effective implementation of them. During the second stage, preparation, the challenge is accepting the new paradigm and practices. During implementation, the primary challenge is making the systems and processes work. During the fourth stage, transition, the challenge is sticking with it. And in the final stage of maturation, the challenge is continuous improvement.

This five-stage model is not intended to suggest that the SDWT maturation process is an orderly or linear procedure. It is not. The reality of life in these operations is messy and nonlinear. Teams don't always become more mature over time. Sometimes they actually become less mature as they spend more time together. But utilizing this maturity construct does provide a vehicle that allows us to discuss the important topic of the changing role.

In the next chapters we will continue this discussion in more detail.

Endnotes

1. From a personal interview with the late Ross Silberstein, former plant manager of the Sherwin-Williams facility in Richmond.

2. In earlier publications I have used slightly different names to describe the five stages. The original names for the stages were conception, incubation, implementation, transition, and maturity. I have modified them here to promote clarity. Also changed are earlier references to different team leaders. Culture leaders used to be called executive managers, management team leaders integrative managers, and operations team leaders interface managers. The terms used in the book are, I think, easier to remember and a little less hierarchical.

3. Albert Cherns, "The Principles of Sociotechnical Design," *Human Relations*, 29 (8), 1977, pp. 783-792.

4. R. J. Boyle, "Wrestling with Jellyfish," *Harvard Business Review* (January–February 1984), pp. 74–83.

18

Leadership Roles During the Early Stages of Team Maturity

The decisions take longer, and sometimes it takes longer to get things done. It's frustrating, because sometimes it takes people longer to see something that I'd like. But you can't say, "Well, okay, your 36 seconds are up. We're going on." You've got to take time to explain things. Sometimes you end up doing that several times.[1]

ROGER SMITH,
former CEO, General Motors

I used to have a picture on my desk that was torn from a magazine. It showed the outstretched hands of a midair acrobat several inches away from a flying trapeze. The caption read. "Timing is everything." Those words can also describe the team leader role during the cycle of SDWT maturity. What is appropriate in one stage may be disastrous in another one. Timing is everything.

During each of the five stages, team leaders need to play a different role in order to maximize the effectiveness of the organization. In this chapter we will explore the role of team leaders in the investigation, preparation, and implementation stages. We will also look at how operations, management, and culture team leaders generally play distinct roles during the early stages of the implementation process. Many of the team leader activities mentioned in this and in the following chapters have already been discussed earlier in the book. But they will be put in a kind of sequence that helps the team leader understand what behaviors are most appropriate during the various stages of implementation.

The operations team leader, for example, progresses through a series of roles that change subtly but distinctly in each of the stages. In the earlier stages they primarily coach and develop the work group members' technical skills (function-specific skills such as work technologies, business fundamentals, etc.) and self-management/regulation skills (group decision making, giving and accepting feedback, confrontation resolution, working in a multicultural group, etc.). In later stages, however, they spend a bigger proportion of their time managing external forces affecting the ability of the team to be successful (getting resources for projects, lobbying for participation in key corporate activities, monitoring competitor's activities in the marketplace, etc.). Similarly, management team leaders and culture team leaders have different roles at different stages. Playing the wrong role at the wrong time, of course, can have a very negative impact on the organization's effectiveness.

Investigation Roles

The leadership role at this stage is primarily performed by management and culture team leaders. Most of the successful transition efforts I know about are actually started by management team leaders rather than by culture team leaders. The most senior managers (presidents, vice presidents, etc.), in fact, are often only consulted rather than being seen as driving the change. But where culture leaders do become actively involved in at least managing the symbols of the change process, the transition is simplified and expedited considerably.

Here are some suggestions for culture leader activities during Stage one. Culture leaders can examine the organization's culture to determine whether it is compatible with the SDWT paradigm (see Table 18.1). Cultural modifications will probably be necessary for any significant progress towards self-directed work team maturity. But if SDWTs are fundamentally opposed to the basic assumptions forming the culture of the organization, change may require such dramatic measures that it will become a very unattractive alternative. It is better, of course, not to start than to abort the process midstream. Once started, SDWT methods create expectations for continuing involvement that, if later violated, can

Table 18.1. Culture Leadership Roles During Early Stages

Stage	Examples of culture leader's role
Stage One: Investigation	Assess compatibility of culture with SDWTs. Create culture bridges. Tie self-directed team evaluation to real business needs. Develop common vocabulary. Make self-directed team issues salient.
Stage Two: Preparation	Build trust. Provide opportunities for people to discuss SDWTs. Model appropriate behaviors. Show support for workplace evolution.
Stage Three: Implementation	Encourage appropriate deviation from the norm. Provide broad implementation parameters. Emphasize overarching values/business focus/objectives. Recognize success.

SOURCE: Adapted from K. Kim Fisher, "Management Roles in the Implementation of Participative Management Systems," *Human Resource Management* (Fall 1986). © Copyright by John Wiley & Sons. Used by permission of author.

create an environment of nearly violent distrust. It will be difficult if not impossible, to go down the self-directed work team road again with the same people.

Create Bridges to Span the Chasm Between Old and New Cultures

If the chasm between the existing culture and the self-directed work team paradigm is spannable, culture team leaders can minimize the predictable frustrations associated with culture shifts by providing culture bridges that somehow link the two. As an example, the late Howard Vollum, one of the founders of Tektronix, was being interviewed for the company paper when the interviewer observed, "It sounds like you might be in favor of the type of participative management being tried at [name of facility]. "Sure," Howard answered, "That's not new to [name of facility]. It was here at the start. Then we kind of got away from it. I think it's very important that we get back to it." These kinds of statements by respected leaders can make the journey more like coming home than like jumping off a cliff into an unknown abyss.

Demonstrate Support for the Change

Culture leaders also need to demonstrate appropriate support for the paradigm shift. People will watch for signals from culture leaders and act accordingly. One good way to do this is to raise the issue of SDWTs in important meetings and coaching sessions, and then to encourage management and operations champions to rise to the challenge of carrying the empowered organization towards maturity. How do you do this?

In one operation, for example, culture leaders hosted a two-day meeting for the 200 top managers of the company. During this "People Involvement" session, managers heard the convictions and broad expectations of senior management. Then representatives from each business group shared progress and ideas on self-directed work teams. These kinds of activities evidence the culture leader's desire to make change happen without necessarily dictating a specific course of action.

Create a Common Vocabulary to Facilitate Communication and Learning

It is also helpful for culture team leaders to provide a common vocabulary for key aspects of the self-directed work team cycle. This enables people to communicate about what otherwise may become a set of values, assumptions, and systems that become difficult to explain to others. Common vocabularies allow cross-fertilization of ideas and help to demystify self-directed work team concepts. Establishing some sort of management network can help to communicate and formalize this language.

Couple Team Design to Business Changes

During Stage One, management team leaders analyze the organization for the appropriateness of some sort of participative work system. They identify the costs and risks of moving forward, pass information to and gain commitment from the key people, and justify and empower resources to design the work system and the development or transformation process (see Table 18.2). It is particularly helpful for management leaders to determine the most appropriate timing for Stage Two and Stage Three now.

Several successfully transformed organizations have credited their success in part to coupling the implementation of self-directed work teams to other significant changes. New organization startups, new product introductions, new technologies, equipment or methodologies, or reorganiza-

Table 18.2. Management Leadership Roles During Early Stages

Stage	Examples of management leadership's role
Stage One: Investigation	Complete SDWT feasibility analysis. Support the real need for evolution. Champion SDWT concept. Line up commitment/resources for next stages. Determine appropriate timing for introduction.
Stage Two: Preparation	Build trust. Demystify SDWT/facilities clarification activities. Articulate vision. Model appropriate behaviors. Ensure training and development. Facilitate "implications for us" analysis. Ensure that good communication processes are in place. Provide necessary resources.
Stage Three: Implementation	Champion SDWTs. Recognize successes. Clarify roles/expectations.

SOURCE: Adapted from K. Kim Fisher, "Management Roles in the Implementation of Participative Management Systems," *Human Resource Management* (Fall 1986). © Copyright by John Wiley & Sons. Used by permission of author.

tions, etc. are all ideal times to make self-directed work teams happen. After all, self-directed work teams are a way of doing things rather than things to do. They are a means to the end of organizational effectiveness, not an end in themselves. Buying a new facility, introducing a new product or reorienting the organization to focus on customers *in a self-directed work team way* is a much more appropriate focus than implementing self-directed work teams for their own sake.

Preparation Roles

This is the first stage of widespread management involvement. Preparation is a period for discussion and clarification of self-directed work teams. Culture leaders train management leaders, management leaders train operations team leaders, and operations leaders train nonmanagers in the fundamentals of self-directed work teams. People discuss the implications of moving towards self-directed work team maturity for themselves individually and for them as teams. Employment continuity discussions are often required to build trust and allay the fears of hidden agendas.

Create a Common Vision to Facilitate Change

This stage produces organizational acceptance for the change. Management and operations team leaders, therefore, need to make self-directed work teams "real" by articulating their vision for the self-directed work team future in their organization (see Table 18.3). In a 200-person manufacturing organization of a division within a large electronics company, the manufacturing manager decided that he wanted to learn more about sociotechnical systems. After he attended a few seminars on the subject and discussed it with some experienced external and internal resources, he wanted to implement a "high performance system" in conjunction with division plans to change to a Just-in-Time manufacturing process.

He determined that the time was right for the transformation. This type of self-directed work system would build naturally on a fairly recent organizational change, which split functional groups into product-oriented work teams. It was also consistent with the just-in-time technology, which required teams to be more flexible and more involved with certain production decisions. He felt the basic division and company values were congruent with participatory work alternatives.

Table 18.3. Operations Leadership Roles During Early Stages

Stage	Examples of operations leader's role
Stage One: Investigation	Study SDWTs.
Stage Two: Preparation	Give input to work system design/values and transformation plans.
	Learn team leader behaviors.
	Model team leader behaviors.
	Share information with teams.
	Implement technology changes.
	Make SDWT real for teams.
	Feedback facilitating/inhibiting factors for implementation preparation.
Stage Three: Implementation	Implement transformation plan.
	Ensure team training and development (technical and SDWT skills).
	Get resources for training and development.
	Champion operations changes.
	Institutionalize information-passing mechanisms.

SOURCE: Adapted from K. Kim Fisher, "Management Roles in the Implementation of Participative Management Systems," *Human Resource Management* (Fall 1986). © Copyright by John Wiley & Sons. Used by permission of author.

Concurrently with his discussions with his management, he began sharing his ideas of what the organization would be like in the future. These discussions came to be known as "Jerry's vision." This vision was clear enough that people could picture what the business would be like and how they would act differently in it. It was referred to frequently during the preparation and implementation stages as a focus and a justification for their work.

Share Business Information and Line Up Resources

During Stage Two, management leaders ensure that all appropriate information is provided to effect implementation. They see that the right people are involved in the process and that sufficient resources are allocated to produce the desired results. It is often appropriate to bring in external consultants or internal subject matter experts to minimize the "reinvention of the wheel" and to help the organization avoid some of the common roadblocks that get in the way of these of efforts.

Make Technology and Operating Principle Changes

Technology changes that facilitate the work system implementation (automation of boring, repetitive jobs, introduction of new products/ services, or relocation of equipment of decentralized areas, etc.) are spearheaded during this stage by operations leaders in a way that is consistent and illustrative of the self-directed work team paradigm. Principles or values that guide the organization and define appropriate behaviors are developed and agreed to throughout the organization.

Implementation Roles

The operations leader plays a number of important roles during the implementation stage. Establishing and then maintaining forums for on-going information passing and training becomes pivotal. At the very least they will need time for the discussion of business information. While these meetings will be frustrating and ineffective at first, they can become the forum for group decision making as teams are coached in their appropriate use by their operations leader. Without this information, teams are incapable of doing the operations analysis and redesign that is the hallmark of this stage. Team leaders actively facilitate these processes, often with the help of other internal and external consultants. They deal with the elements of the implementation as they arise. Rather than trying to anticipate all the interelated aspects of the SDWT process, they are sensitive to the needs of the team, and they help them work on the things that need to be worked on when they need to be worked on. Generally speaking, they work on reward systems last to ensure that the pay design and delivery mechanisms support the organizational design.

Begin Appropriate Training and Development

This phase requires intensive training in the technical areas of the new or recently changed jobs. Operations leaders also coordinate training in SDWT technologies and skill building in group decision making, problem solving, etc. The operations leader focuses on the development of new teams so that they will be able to be self-regulating and manage their part of the business effectively during the latter stages. One warning is that these development activities are best placed just prior to when team members actually use what they learn. Giving the teams skills training much before they need it is a waste of time. Most people already know more than what they are allowed to do anyway.

Summary

Team leader roles change during the cycle of SDWT maturity. During the investigation stage, for example, culture leaders can do a number of things to clarify what SDWTs are and to empower people to move towards them. They build bridges between the old and the new culture. They demonstrate their active support of SDWTs and create a common vocabulary to facilitate learning. They couple the SDWT initiative to real business needs and changes, but they don't actively participate in developing the specifics. Other people are empowered to do that. It is during the preparation stage that management and culture team leaders create a common vision that guides and motivates team members. All team leaders work to clarify the SDWT concept and to eliminate misconceptions and fear during this stage. They line up resources and make appropriate preparations for implementation. And they facilitate technology and operating principle changes to grease the skids for SDWTs. The implementation stage requires team leaders to create ongoing forums for information passing and training. The actual implementation of appropriate team structures and systems is facilitated by team leaders at this stage.

If the appropriate preparation work has been done, this stage can be fairly straightforward. But it is never simple. Most agree that this stage feels as though you are always going two steps forward and one step back. Since the process is always tailored to the operation, it contains large blocks of unique and unpredictable activities. It is messy, invigorating, and tiring. But in this stage the team leaders begin to see some of the early results of the self-directed teams. These emerging work systems, however, require careful nurturing and development after the implementation process.

In the next chapter we will review the changing role of team leaders in the transition and maturation stages of team maturity.

Endnote

1. "The Painful Reeducation of a Company Man," *Business Month* (October 1989), p. 78. Reprinted with permission, *Business Month* magazine. Copyright © 1989 by Goldhirsh Group, Inc., 38 Commercial Wharf, Boston, MA 02110.

19

Leadership Roles During the Later Stages of Team Maturity

Forget structures invented by the guys at the top. You've got to let the task form the organization.[1]

RAYMOND GILMARTIN,
CEO of Becton Dickinson

Once SDWTs are implemented successfully in Stage Three, the role of the team leaders changes again. In this Chapter, we will discuss the evolving role of team leaders in the later parts of the maturation cycle. In the early stages of the cycle is reviewed, the culture leaders play a predominant role. While culture team leaders offer ongoing support and input through the cycle of self-directed work team (see Table 19.1), the primary roles in Stages Four and Five are played by the management and operations team leaders.

Transition Roles

Transition is an uncomfortable stage, during which organizations often know what they are supposed to do but they have not yet become skilled enough to do it. Expectations for involvement precede the skills required to be successfully involved. People who are still learning make mistakes.

Table 19.1. Culture Leadership Roles During Later Stages

Stage	Examples of culture leader's role
Stage Four: Transition	Support appropriate work. Transfer authority and autonomy to business teams as skills expand.
Stage Five: Maturation	Provide development opportunities.

SOURCE: Adapted from K. Kim Fisher, "Management Roles in the Implementation of Participative Management Systems," *Human Resource Management* (Fall 1986). © Copyright by John Wiley & Sons. Used by permission of author.

Managing Skepticism

Early in Stage Four management leaders find themselves continually encouraging skill development and risk taking. They spend significant time nursing the skinned knees of those who have tried and failed, but who must get up and try some more. These mistakes fuel the fires of those people who never really thought that self-directed work teams would work. Management leaders continue to patiently answer the challenges of these remaining skeptics who observe the shortfalls of the transitioning system (see Table 19.2).

Protecting the New Team

Later in transition, management leaders often find themselves in an umbrellalike protection role of defending the organization from the acid rain influence of well meaning observers who see people struggling with the development of new skills and perspectives. These outsiders encour-

Table 19.2. Management Leadership Roles During Later Stages

Stage	Examples of management leader's role
Stage Four: Transition	Encourage skill building and risk taking. Transfer authority and autonomy to teams as skills expand. Help people learn from mistakes. Provide protection from outside forces.
Stage Five: Maturation	Facilitate continuous improvement. Lead system-wide changes. Provide skill development opportunities. Deal with destructive behavior.

SOURCE: Adapted from K. Kim Fisher, "Management Roles in the Implementation of Participative Management Systems," *Human Resource Management* (Fall 1986). © Copyright by John Wiley & Sons. Used by permission of author.

age the organization to revert to the more predictable and less painful roles of the recent past. The management leader holds off the pressure until members of the organization have the skills in place to be successful. This is particularly difficult when the host organization, of which the transitioning group is a part, still has one foot firmly set in the established culture.

When the Lima P&G plant was starting up, for example, it initially received a lot of pressure to revert to a traditionally managed operation. Why? The results during the first two years of operation were poorer than expected. The division manager, however, was convinced that the results would improve dramatically as the plant personnel became more experienced. He finally convinced corporate management to be patient and allow the facility to progress along the learning curve without pressure to abort the process and return to the management practices of traditional P&G locations. As predicted, results improved dramatically in the third year when the training investment began to pay returns. Had the experiment been stopped during the first two years, the plant would never have had the 30 to 50 percent improvements over the traditional plants it has sustained since its third year of operation. The division manager saved the SDWTs, which, without his direct intervention, would have surely been dissolved prematurely.

Operations leaders serve as trainers early in Stage Four, and then they make the transition into a resource role as the teams become more self-sufficient (see Table 19.3). They transfer authority and autonomy to others when people have the skills and information to use it successfully. During this stage operations leaders begin to change their primary focus from developing their subordinates' skills to managing forces outside of their team(s). Changing behaviors from an "inward" to an "outward" focus is difficult. It is not unusual for both leaders and their teams to experience some frustration as the teams are weaned from the leader and as the management role starts to focus on boundaries.

Maturation Roles

At maturation the organization has reached the minimum acceptable level of SDWT performance. People in the organization have become competent and more comfortable in the system. Artificial barriers are continuously challenged and changed as they become issues. People develop closer ties to their internal and external customers. Management leaders assess the organization periodically for behavioral congruence with the values on which the system is built. They deal appropriately with aberrance from those values.

Table 19.3. Operations Leadership Roles During Later Stages

Stage	Examples of operations leader's role
Stage Four: Transition	Assess team member skill development. Transfer authority and autonomy to teams as skills expand. Change from internal to external focus. Continue skill training/feedback.
Stage Five: Maturation	Assess need for resources for teams. Get resources/be a resource. Provide skill development opportunities as needed. Assess external environment. Funnel data to teams. Deal with destructive behavior. Manage external interfaces. Facilitate continuous improvement of team. Facilitate appropriate work system evolution.

SOURCE: Adapted from K. Kim Fisher, "Management Roles in the Implementation of Participative Management Systems," *Human Resource Management* (Fall 1986). © Copyright by John Wiley & Sons. Used by permission of author.

Although the team leader obviously needs to spend time facilitating the effectiveness of the group (particularly as new people rotate into the group), the operations leader's role shifts from trainer to environment scanner. In this stage, the team leader becomes a fully functional boundary manager. She looks at the external environment to note business trends and opportunities that need to be relayed back to the group. The leader, for example, may discover important projects being developed in other areas of the company that affect the operation. She will want to get one of the team members involved early in the project to ensure that the team's input is considered. At other times the operations leader may find herself protecting the teams' "turf" when staff members or other managers want to usurp decisions that should be made by the team.

Facilitating Continuous Improvement

In this stage, the team leader determines how to best help the established maturing team. This is an art form. As the team is maturing the team leader changes his approach to the team so that it corresponds to their changing needs. How do you know when they are maturing? Typically the types of business and interpersonal tasks they are able to complete successfully act as the best indicator. One clue is how they respond to the requirements for increased responsibility and ownership. Ernie Turner, an operations team leader at Tektronix, describes the typical evolution during the maturation stage as follows:

> At first, the team comes to you and says, "Here's a problem, what are you going to do about it?" Later they come to you and say, "Here is a problem and here are some of the things we think can be done about it." Still later they say, "Here is a problem and here is what we think we should do." Eventually they say, "There was a problem and here is what we did."

There is great satisfaction in seeing the team develop to this level of capability. When they reach this point, however, continued assistance is often necessary to keep the team growing. Tasks, once thought impossible, become more routine. The primary roles played by both the management and operations leaders at this stage, therefore, are encouraging continuous improvement and warding off organizational stagnation. As people develop higher level skills they need to be presented with increasingly difficult challenges.

Summary

One of the challenges of being a team leader is the responsibility of playing the appropriate role as the team matures. Team leaders normally progress from coaching and training roles in the early stages to facilitative and leadership roles as the team matures. Full boundary management responsibilities are assumed only in the later stages, after the team has been well prepared to handle the responsibilities of work-directed, rather than supervisor-directed assignments. In the later stages of the five-stage cycle of SDWT maturation, operations and management team leaders help the teams through the transition to full maturity. They manage skepticism and pressure from the people who see the normal mistakes that accompany transition and that try to force the SDWT backwards to more comfortable traditional roles. As the team reaches maturity, team leaders help them to continuously improve. These responsibilities are difficult but necessary for team leaders at all parts of the organization.

In the next chapter, we'll go into more detail about specific tasks that might do this. We will consider a story that illustrates three typical days in a team leader's work week as the team reaches maturity.

Endnote

1. Brian Dumaine, "The Bureaucracy Busters," *Fortune* (June 17, 1991), p. 26. © 1991 by The Time Inc. Magazine Company. All rights reserved. Used by permission.

PART 5
The Team Leader Workout

20

Three Days in the Life of a Team Leader

*You cannot do to your people what was done
to you. You have to be a facilitator or coach
and, by the way, we're still going to hold you
accountable for the bottom line.*

PAUL ALLAIRE,
CEO of Xerox

Let's look at a few days in the life of a team leader. He is a hypothetical operations team leader of a team nearing maturity.

Monday 7:00 A.M.: Team Meeting

Cindy, one of the team members, grabs a pen and walks up to the chart pad to get the meeting organized. The team has shift overlap meetings at which the team members, called "associates," review the previous shift's activities and share business information. She writes down three agenda items: computer problem, vacation coverage, and customer feedback. The team decides to wait on the computer discussion because it will require advice from a technical expert from another team. After a short and emotional discussion about vacation coverage, three team members give their report on last week's visit to a customer site in a neighboring town. As they are starting to leave the meeting, the team leader asks who is going to contact the technical expert for the computer problem discussion. A team member volunteers and says he will have the person here sometime this week.

7:25 A.M.: Unplanned Feedback

The team leader catches Cindy walking out of the team meeting and congratulates her for stepping up to the chartpad and facilitating (she had

189

been uncomfortable getting up in front of people until very recently). Recalling the computer discussion, the team leader asks if Cindy wants to know a simple technique to make sure that things don't fall through the cracks in meetings. She says yes. "It helps me to think of the 3 w's," the leader replies. "Facilitators can ask the question, *'who* will do *what* by *when?'* " Cindy agrees that could work and thanks him for the idea.

7:30 A.M.: Area Walkthrough

As he is walking through the work area, the team leader sees what he thinks may be a problem. Two members of the team are arguing about something. "Can I help?" he asks. "No," says Tom, "We'll work it out." The team leader walks through the area, chats with the associates, delivers reports to some people, and gets invited to play in a softball game for charity.

8:05 A.M.: Business Coordination Meeting

All the team leaders meet together with associate representatives for what used to be the facility manager's staff meeting. Cross-facility issues are discussed that require coordination across multiple teams including staffing, quality problems, training issues, an emerging pay concern, and some general information from headquarters. The facilitation of the meeting is rotated every week, and the team leader's turn is coming up next Monday.

10:15 A.M.: Working at the Desk

The team leader squeezes in some time to get back to his desk to pick up voice mail messages, return phone calls, and do some project work. He calls back a staff manager from headquarters who tells him that they need some up-to-date information about the budget. When the team leader tells the staff person that he will transfer him to the team's budget coordinator, the staff manager is confused. "Aren't you the manager?" he asks. For the millionth time in the last two years the team leader politely explains the team concept and then tells him that Rita, an associate, has more up-to-date information than the team leader does, because she authorizes and tracks the team's spending on a day-to-day basis. He makes a couple of more calls, jots down some notes on his pad about the compensation project he has been working on, and arranges for a sales rep to give a brief presentation at next Monday's business coordination meeting.

11:00 A.M.: Drop in on Human Resources

On his way to the cafeteria the team leader drops by the HR cubicles to see if Bill is there. Bill, a former supervisor, has been helping the teams on their training needs. The team leader wants to take Bill up on his suggestion to do some training on hiring laws and skills. The team is going to start interviewing soon for an opening. "When could you do the training?" the team leader asks. Bill suggests that it be just before the team has their first interview and says that he could be available either this Thursday morning or next Monday afternoon.

11:08 A.M.: Problems

The team leader hears his name paged on the intercom system and goes to the phone to call the team's work area. Tom answers and tells him that he better come over and help settle an argument. In the workplace to greet him are Tom and Joe, who have both been assigned to the supplier quality improvement project. Tom speaks first and says, "Joe thinks we need to take a trip down to see this vendor, but I don't think it will be worth it. Besides that I am still behind in my work, and I don't think it is fair to ask the team to cover for me again since I was just on the customer visit last week." Joe impatiently interjects, "Well, I think we need to do what is best for the business." The team leader asks Joe why he thinks a visit would be best for the business. "Because," he replies, "this stuff has been causing us problems for three weeks. If we can see their processes and get face to face with these guys I think we can resolve the material problem." "Well," says the team leader, "what is this problem costing us?" Joe picks up some reports and does a series of calculations that take a couple of minutes, checking periodically with Tom to see if he is doing the math correctly. "It is more than I thought," he says. "Looks like we're losing about two thousand a week." "What do you think Tom?" asks the team leader. "Jeez," says Tom, "That's really serious. I guess we better do something." Joe commits to working on it with the team over lunch and getting something set up with the supplier ASAP.

11:35 A.M.: Lunch with Team Leaders

The team leader apologizes for being late and then walks over to the refrigerator to get his lunch box. He enjoys these periodic lunches with other team leaders. Today they have a speaker from the university talking about some new technologies that may be appropriate for their business some day. Most of the time they just get together and blow off a little steam or talk about how things are going with their teams.

12:30 P.M.: Working at the Desk

The team leader returns to his desk to make arrangements for a coaching session and for project reviews later in the week. The phone rings and he answers it. It is Joe telling him that the team can cover either Joe or Tom (but not both) to go to the vendor right now. The vendor has also been contacted about a meeting tomorrow morning. They will do it. The team leader says that he feels like a couple of them probably ought to go on the visit and he volunteers to pick up a company car and drive them down. "Good," says Joe, "pick me up at 6:30." "How about I meet you at Bob Evans for breakfast at 6:00," counters the team leader. "OK by me," says Joe.

1:00 P.M.: Safety Meeting

A close call precipitates a meeting sponsored by the safety committee. Everyone is required to attend one of the three scheduled sessions to review the incident.

2:00 P.M.: Area Walkthrough

The team leader walks back through the area to see how things are going. Two or three people see him and ask him questions or request help. Things seem to be running pretty smoothly. He leaves several copies of the professor's handouts about a promising new technology on the break room table with a note that says he will be happy to review this with team members if they are interested. The associates start coming in for the break.

2:30 P.M.: Break Room Talk

Several team members are talking about a problem they had this morning. They isolated the problem, corrected it, and got up and running with only a short break in production. "I remember when we used to just call maintenance and then come in here and park it until things were fixed," says Cindy. "Yep," adds Joe. "Things have sure changed around here." The team leader agrees. He thinks back to a time only a few years ago when the same people had the same problem. But back then it was the supervisor's job to solve problems and make decisions. By the time he lined up the maintenance people, got the thing fixed, and rounded up the operators to get them back to work, they lost half a day. Today they were down for 20 minutes, and he didn't even know about it until it was all over.

2:40 P.M.: Area Walkthrough

The team leader walks back to the work area with several team members and sees Rita updating the whiteboard with the team goals on it. "How's it going?" he asks. "OK," she replies, "but we're never going to meet this cost reduction goal without some new software." "Can you cost-justify it?" he asks. "I dunno," says Rita, "but I'll run the numbers and let you know."

3:30 P.M.: Team Meeting

After the associates complete the pass-down information to second shift, the team leader reviews the options for the hiring training. The group agrees to the Thursday time slot, and they spend the rest of the meeting figuring out how to cover for the associates who will be on the interview team. As they are leaving Cindy realizes that no one has said they would close the loop with Bill about the training. "Wait a sec," she says "who will talk to Bill and when can they get it done?" The team leader flashes her a thumbs up signal as Tom says he'll drop by HR on his way out tonight.

4:00 P.M.: Working at the Desk

The team leader walks back to his desk (a cubicle smack in the middle of the production area) and reviews voice mail. Nothing urgent. He sits down and works on the compensation project and a speech he has to give tomorrow, interrupted only twice by calls. "Amazing," he thinks to himself at one point, "45 minutes straight without an interruption."

5:30 P.M.: Return Home

After dinner the team leader goes into the garage and picks up a woodworking project he started a few weeks ago. He is soon lost in the sound of the table saw. Turning his work around in his hands a couple of hours later he says to himself, "Boy it's nice to watch something progress so quickly." He wishes his work was more like that sometimes. "That's life," he chuckles as he walks into the house.

Tuesday 6:00 A.M.: Breakfast and Travel to Supplier

After a quick breakfast Joe and the team leader get in the company car. During the two and one-half hour drive, they plan their approach to the supplier problem. They go over the data Joe prepared yesterday afternoon and brainstorm ideas for structuring the meeting to eliminate fault finding and to focus on resolving the problems. The team leader asks Joe what he wants to accomplish during the meeting and how he will know if the meeting is successful. Together they generate some "indicators of success." Joe also talks about his family, and the two compare notes about raising teenagers. They decide that resolving supplier problems are a whole lot easier than raising teens.

9:00 A.M.: Supplier Meeting

The supplier meeting begins with a tour of the facility. After the tour they sit down with the supplier and Joe presents the data about the quality problems. After a two-hour conversation they are nowhere. Joe is getting frustrated. "Well, something has changed in the last few weeks," he reiterates. "If nothing else, I know that the bags you ship the material in have changed from a clear color to a purple color." The team leader didn't know that. "That's right," said the supplier. "We did have a new stretch-wrap machine installed in the packaging department that just came on line six weeks ago, but I don't see what that would have to do with product quality." The team leader and Joe ask if they can see the packaging department. When they arrive, Joe asks the operator if he has noticed anything recently that might account for their problems. "Maybe," replies the operator, "this new film is a different gage and it has more static electricity. We also use more heat to seal the package now." The team leader and Joe ask if they can take home some product before it is wrapped and after it is wrapped to see if there is a difference when it is used in their process. "Sure," say the suppliers, "let us know how it works out." They know it is a long shot but it is all they have to go on for now.

1:00 P.M.: Drive Back to Work

On the way home they critique the meeting and share their disappointment that they didn't get the issue resolved. "I did learn some things though," says Joe. "They have one of the same pieces of equipment that we do, but they set theirs up different than ours. I'm going to talk to the team about trying it that way when we get back." The team leader spends the rest of the trip talking with Joe about his work. Joe confides in the team leader that he doesn't get along very well with Tom. When the team leader asks if it interferes with work, Joe answers, "Yea, sometimes." They talk for nearly an hour about how to give feedback to somebody you work with every day to minimize the possibility of getting a negative reaction. "Or," says the team leader, "you can ignore it and hope it gets better by itself." "Slim chance of that," says Joe. "Slim chance," echoes the team leader.

3:30 P.M.: Team Meeting

Joe and the team leader get back just in time for the afternoon team meeting with first and second shift. They share their experience with the vendor and show everyone the wrapped and unwrapped product. Joe proposes an experiment when they set up second shift production tonight, and the team members agree. He also tells them about the different setup the vendor uses on their RR7 machine. The team finishes the pass-down, and John tells everyone that the technical person will be in tomorrow morning's meeting to work the computer problem.

4:00 P.M.: Working at Home

After the team meeting the team leader drives home to finish his speech for the City Club dinner and spend a little time with his wife and kids.

6:30 P.M.: City Club Dinner

On behalf of the company, the team leader accepts an award for "Corporate Citizen of the Month." He says a few words, thanks the City Club, and has a great dinner with his wife. He is glad that the work of the facility to improve their image in the community has been recognized, and he is flattered that the Business Coordination Team asked him to go and represent them at this dinner. The bronze plaque will make a nice addition to the "Wall of Fame," a growing collection of awards recognizing the many accomplishments of the facility.

Wednesday 7:00 A.M.: Team Meeting

John facilitates the meeting so that the pass-down from graveyard to day can be done as quickly as possible, allowing most of the team meeting to work on the computer problem. Mary, the technical person, works with the team on brainstorming several possible causes for the intermittent hardware malfunction and they narrow it down to two probable causes. The team agrees to collect specific facts and data on the computer's performance until Friday when Mary will come back to the work area and help troubleshoot. They will use the quality problem solving tools they learned recently. Joe also excitedly reports that second shift called him last night to let him know that the experiment showed that there was a definite difference between the vendor material that had been wrapped and the material that had not been wrapped. He says he will call the vendor later today.

7:20 A.M.: Area Walkthrough

During the walkthrough Rita stops the team leader and hands him several sheets of paper. "What's this?" he asks. "The cost justification for the software," she answers, "it pays out in three months with a rate of return of over 40 percent." "Sounds pretty good," says the team leader. He remembers when the operators wouldn't even know the meaning of those words, let alone be able to do the calculations. "Let's move forward on this. How do you want me to help?" "Grease the skids, will ya?" requests Rita. "Ever since those guys on the mid-West customer team went on that software buying frenzy a year ago, it's been hard to get requisition signatures for this kind of stuff. Headquarters wants to authorize all personal computers and software."

9:00 A.M.: Working at the Desk

The team leader makes phone calls to get information for the marketing analysis project he is working on. He also calls his daughter to tell her that he'll swing by to say hello on his way to the dentist.

10:00 A.M.: Dentist Appointment

The team leader feels a little guilty about not being at work—but not that guilty. He enjoys the brief chat with his daughter and the ride to the dentist. He does not enjoy his time at the dentist's office, however. Some things never change.

11:45 A.M.: Lunch with the Boss

The team leader meets his boss, Jane, in the cafeteria. "How's it going?" she asks. "Okay," he replies, "but I could use some help on a couple of things. You got a minute?" "Sure," she says. He sits down at her table and reviews the week's activities so far and then sees Rita come into the room. "Rita come join us if you can," he requests. Rita and the team leader review the idea for new software with Jane. "You know," says Jane, "that un-budgeted software purchases are a political hot potato right now." The team leader and Rita nod. "What will it take to get your support for this purchase?" asks the team leader. "Rock solid cost justification," answers Jane. The team leader pulls out the sheets Rita gave him earlier and together they walk through the analysis. "Looks good to me," says Jane, "go for it Rita." He writes a note to himself to work with Jane to get this new policy from headquarters eliminated. He remembered when challenging corporate policies was a CLM (Career Limiting Move). Now it was ex-pected.

12:30 P.M.: Coaching Discussion

John has requested a "coaching session" with the team leader. In prepara-tion for the discussion, John asked the other team members to give him some feedback on his performance. This information has been compiled and summarized by the team leader. Their discussion includes a review of the peer feedback and some observations that the team leader has already shared with John. The team leader makes a special point to reinforce John for doing a good job of arranging for the team discussion with Mary, the technical expert.

1:30 P.M.: Market/Competitive Analysis

A cross-facility project group has been working for some time to complete a market analysis to be used to update all the teams. The team leader will purchase competitive products and put up a display for people to look at and play with. Nobody use to do this kind of thing before, but the teams found market and competitive data very helpful to them now. The project team meets to review everyone's assignments and to do a dry run of a presentation they will do for the monthly facility-wide meeting next Fri-day. It is still a little rough, but all the pertinent information is there.

2:30 P.M.: Break Room Discussions

The team leader passes by the break room and is waved in by Joe and Cindy. "We tried Joe's idea and it cut setup time on the RR7 by 13 minutes," they explain nearly in unison. The team leader feels proud of his team. "I'm bringing the donuts tomorrow," he says. "How about we bring in Jane for the afternoon meeting and we tell her about the success-ful setup and the vendor test? Looks like your meeting, Joe. Let's brag a little." Joe is beaming so brightly that it looks like his face will catch on fire. "Okay" he says, "but I want Cindy and the second shift guys to do the talk with me too. It was a team effort you know."

2:40 P.M.: Doing Some Work

On his way into the work area he sees team members buzzing like angry yellowjackets. "The !**#!* computer dumped last weeks invoices," shouts John, "We need everybody we can free up to reinput them before the mail deadline at 4:00." The team leader fights back the urge to take over and control the crisis. It looks like John is doing fine. "I'm free," says the team leader. "Have a sit-down at terminal two," says John as he exits the room,

"I'll go get the technician and some more team members." The team leader sits down at terminal two and Tom sits down at terminal one. Before long the three remaining terminals are filled with Rita, Paul, and Mary, the technician. Although the team leader doesn't have the speed or accuracy of the other team members, he holds his own and the data is all entered before the deadline. Just barely before the deadline. "Not bad," says Cindy as she walks in and reviews the team leader's work, "but keep your day job." Her voice is tinged with grudging respect. The four of them missed the team meeting. Cindy brings them up to speed on what was covered.

4:00 P.M.: Team-to-Team Conflict Resolution Meeting

The team leader arranged some time ago to have Bill, from HR, facilitate a conflict resolution meeting between the team and one of the second shift teams down the hall. Bill runs them through an organized process that gives them each a way to say what they need from the other team to meet their mutual goals of providing top flight service and products to their customers. They finish the meeting with work to do, and though they are far from being best friends, the session helps to take the personalities out of their disagreements and focus both teams on getting the work done.

5:45 P.M.: Return Home

Going back into the garage, the team leader picks up his woodworking project. To himself he reviews the last few days in his head. "You know," he thinks, "even though we have a long way to go, we are really making some progress as a team." He looks at the accomplishments and commitment of team members and he feels good. They are doing a lot of the things that only he or the staff people would have done before. And even though the transition was pretty hard on him, he feels as though he is getting the hang of this team leader thing. It took him several months to learn how to ask questions to get the team members to think through problems themselves, rather than just telling them what they should do. He liked getting rid of vacation and overtime scheduling chores. But it nearly killed him to turn over the budgeting and work scheduling tasks that he really liked and was good at. Especially when he didn't know what he was supposed to do instead. But he had to admit that he felt darn good about what was happening now. He liked the coaching and development of team members. It was a lot tougher to do his job than it used to be, but he wouldn't want to go back to the combative workplace of pre-SDWTs. "Yep," he whispered out loud, "things are pretty good." Then he turned on the saw and went to work on the block of wood in his hands.

Summary

Thus ends three days in the life of a team leader. But getting to the point where team leaders skills come naturally isn't easy. Preparing to be a team leader is like preparing to run a marathon. Just as the marathon athletes condition themselves for the long run, less experienced team leaders can build up stamina and speed through a transition training program. In the next chapter, this process is described.

Endnote

1. Brian Dumaine, "The Bureaucracy Busters," *Fortune* (June 17, 1991) p. 34. © 1991 by The Time Inc. Magazine Company. All rights reserved. Used by permission.

21

A Weekly Activity Guide for Team Leaders

We're never going to outdiscipline the Japanese on quality. To win, we need to find ways to capture the creative and innovative spirit of the American worker. That's the real organizational challenge.[1]

PAUL ALLAIRE,
CEO Xerox,
Baldrige award winner, 1989

Marathon runners start their training programs with short runs that condition the athlete for longer runs. After runners develop stamina they then work on speed. In this Chapter you will find a similar development schedule for team leaders. While some supervisors and managers are able to transition immediately into self-directed work team settings, most of us benefit from a staged development approach that, like training for a marathon, builds up competence and confidence over time. This is especially true for new team leaders who are transferred into mature, established SDWTs.

Short Runs

Team leaders can do a number of things immediately which, like the short runs, will begin to develop stamina. Two important things team leaders can do during the early part of their development process are to spend specific blocks of time with the work group and to engage in personal education activities. The team block time should be time to be with the team as they work ("hanging around" time as one team leader calls it), which allows the team leader to be available for spontaneous team interaction and support. Consider the following short run schedule for specific recommendations for a workout for the first four weeks (see Table 21.1).

Communication Skills

One of the especially important skills to strengthen during this time is increased communication effectiveness. If team leaders build this skill early, it serves them well throughout their careers in SDWT settings.

In traditional organizations, employee attitude surveys frequently and predictably say that communications are poor. In many of those same organizations, however, management reports that they communicate fairly well. How can this disparity exist? It is because management assesses themselves on effort and intent, while employees assess business communication on results. "How much do I know about what is going on?" they ask themselves, with the nearly inevitable reply being "not much." In SDWT organizations, effective team leaders close the gap between their intentions to communicate and the perceptions of team members about the effectiveness of business communication. This requires patience and

Table 21.1. The Shorter Run Workout (Weeks 1–4)

Monday	Tuesday	Wednesday	Thursday	Friday
Schedule non-meeting time to be in the work area (1 hour).	Read some team leadership materials (1 hour).	Schedule non-meeting time to be in the work area (1 hour).	Read some team leadership materials (1 hour).	Schedule non-meeting time to be in the work area (1 hour).
Gather some relevant business information (30 minutes).	Share relevant business information with team (15 minutes).	Gather some relevant business information (30 minutes).	Share relevant business information with team (15 minutes).	Gather some relevant business information (30 minutes).

Special Activity:

At some time during the month, get training on SDWT basics and then visit a SDWT site (3–5 days).

tenacity. One culture team leader from Shell laments that this process can be tedious. "We gave the vision presentation more than 100 times," he said, "Remarkably, there were still people who said they didn't know what the vision was!"

Communication Topics

What do team leaders communicate about? The answer is anything that you would share with a full business partner. Topics like timely and ongoing quality, financial, and goal achievement status are a must on the communication "to do" list. The list also includes information about customers, the market, products, services, other team responsibilities and accomplishments, etc. Unfortunately, most of this data doesn't exist in the traditional management information system. Team leaders have to go out, get it, and then format it it so that it is easy to understand. That is why this activity is called a "workout." It is often a whole lot harder than it looks.

This information is not communicated well in memos. It requires face-to-face, question-and-answer types of active interaction. Dry, one-way delivery of the information is not a whole lot better than no information at all. How do team leaders communicate this kind of information to team members? One particularly important communication forum is the team meeting.

Team Meetings

Teams typically have some sort of team meeting every day. Without meetings, the team has no institutionalized forum for information sharing, problem solving, and decision making. Because these meetings are typically ineffective and frustrating at first, team leaders are often tempted to work to eliminate them in lieu of more pressing business concerns. This can be very shortsighted. While there certainly is no hard and fast rule on the required frequency of these meetings, it is not uncommon to have short operational meetings daily (every shift overlap for multiple shift operations) with more extended meetings for project work as needed. Figures 21.1 and 21.2 are examples of operational team meeting agendas for a production facility team, and a office professional team, respectively. In both cases the same agenda is used daily and the meeting length varies from 15 to 30 minutes a day.

Core Group Agenda
(Production Example)

Quality Report (Get results of daily monitoring/quality audit results weekly/customer feedback from quarterly reports or special visits.)

Finance/Throughput/Waste Results (Highlight key cost leverages.)

Round Robin (Briefly review projects/problems from yesterday/last shift.)

Coverage/Job Assignments (Team decides who will do what today.)

Special Announcements (make announcements regarding current topics.)

Figure 21.1. Team meeting agenda example (production).

Meetings as a Substitute for Hierarchy

These meetings are used to coordinate many of the tasks that would be done by a traditional supervisor (work assignments, firefighting, paperwork, vacation and overtime scheduling, etc.), and they are also used as a real-time opportunity to provide information, training, and coaching (see Table 21.2). One Shell manager suggests that "the biggest mistake companies make [in the transition to SDWTs] is to change the role of the supervisor before the team has effective processes that will substitute for [the administrative service provided by] the traditional supervisor."

Ops Meeting Agenda
(Office Team Example)

Schedule and Calendar review (Who will be where when?)

Client Status (Nail down project progress/review action items/customer feedback and requirements/who needs help/who is available to help.)

Office Issues/Follow-Up (Team decides who does what today and highlights upcoming issues requiring coordination.)

Figure 21.2. Team meeting agenda example (office).

Table 21.2. Possible Meeting Topics

External customer requirements	Organization values
Internal customer requirements	Professional ethics
Emerging technologies	Goal status
Budget review	Information from other teams
Vendor information	Legislation review
Project updates	Information from headquarters
Staffing issues	Team effectiveness assessment
Work assignments	Role clarification
Capacity review	Planning
Work flow and process update	Community issues
Competition updates	Safety information
Problem solving activities	Customer feedback
Market trend information	International concerns
New product/service review	Work charts and graphs review
Profitability review	Quality review
Process simplification	Etc.

This is true. The move to SDWTs is not an elimination of supervisory tasks, but is instead a structured transfer of many of those tasks to the team members. These supervisory tasks in successful SDWTs can be assumed only by teams who have institutionalized processes and methods for organizing and prioritizing them. A team, for example, with the responsibility to manage the cross-training of its members is more likely to be successful if it has a process (charts, assignment algorithm, etc.) with which to accomplish this responsibility than if it does not. Even though mature teams often appear as though they are "making it up as they go," they virtually always start with a structured process which, after it becomes a habit, provides a mental map for action even though it may be invisible to the outside observer.

My team in Lima, for example, made job rotation and coverage assignments according to a formula that had been established and continually renegotiated for years. It included agreements for new employees to always start their assignment as a "maker," which was the core work process around which each of the other four jobs (unloader, analyst, boilerhouse, and maintenance) revolved. They then rotated to other roles as they became available. Similarly, team members who had not been makers for a long period of time were usually assigned by the team to cover for maker's vacations so that they could refresh their skills in the core work technology. Someone who was unaware of this prioritization methodology might assume that the team simply picked rotation assignments at random. But when they come to understand the unspoken rationale behind the decisions, they see the pattern of decisions created by a methodology that had become internalized and institutionalized by the team.

Longer Runs

The short run workout develops basic skills and work habits that are strengthened in the longer run workout. In this series of development activities, team leaders spend more time working with the team in nontraditional ways (as illustrated in the examples in Table 21.3), continuing many of the short run efforts and adding some new exercises to increase stamina. In this workout for the second month, team leaders build an action-oriented team training and development focus on the established base of solid information passing established in the first month's workout. Team leaders also practice coaching, empowerment, example setting, and customer advocacy skills.

An important part of this workout is to begin facilitating team member training. Table 21.4 presents some examples of the kind of training topics to consider for team development.

Caution: Although teams often require a great deal of training and development activities to prepare them to be effective as an SDWT, clustering all of the training together and delivering it to the team in great training extravaganzas is giving them a drink from a fire hose. It is too much to assimilate effectively. It is better to spread the activities out over time and to schedule them so that they occur just prior to an opportunity for them to apply the new skills they have developed. Team leaders pace the training in social, technical, and business skills appropriately. After all, SDWT members spend about 20 percent of their time in some sort of training activities, in contrast to the traditional employee training time commitment of 2 to 3 percent. That is an order of magnitude difference in training time, which corresponds to the increased responsibilities of self-regulating groups and the increasing need for up-to-date skills and information.

The Speed Workout

After stamina is developed in the first two workouts, team leaders work on speed. In this third workout, more difficult skills—like soliciting personal performance feedback, barrier busting, networking and defining boundary conditions—are emphasized (see Table 21.5). Elements from the earlier workouts continue to be reinforced. These activities tend to

Table 21.3. The Longer Run Workout (Weeks 5 to 8)

Monday	Tuesday	Wednesday	Thursday	Friday
Identify team training needs and make some helpful training happen (1–4 hours, sometimes during the week).	In a one-on-one coaching conversation, empower a team member to do something big (30 minutes).	Find a way to be a good example of something you have told the team is important. Walk your talk (15 minutes to 3 hours).	In a team coaching conversation, empower the team to do something big (30 minutes).	Schedule time to be in the work area (1 hour).
Schedule time to be in the work area (1 hour).	Help the team establish or review their success indicators and operational guidelines (1 hour to establish; 15 minutes to review progress).	Schedule time to be in the work area (1 hour).	Talk with another team leader and get at least one good idea (30 minutes).	Gather some relevant business information (30 minutes).
Gather some relevant business information (30 minutes).	Share relevant business information with team (15 minutes).	Gather some relevant business information (30 minutes).	Share relevant business information with team (15 minutes).	

Special Activities:

At some time during the month, get training on team leader skills, such as setting boundary conditions, facilitating, barrier busting, and managing by principle. Practice the skills you learn. (3–5 days)

Develop and share your personal vision of greatness for your team. (half day)

Take some team members with you on a customer visit, or have a customer come in and speak to the team. (1 hour to 2 days)

help the team progress towards maturity and effectiveness more rapidly as the team leader helps them focus their efforts and cut through impediments to improving their work processes.

Table 21.4. Examples of Team Training Topics

Social skills	Technical skills	Business skills
Giving feedback	Using quality tools	Setting/tracking goals
Receiving feedback	Operating equipment	Understanding economics
Making decisions	Maintaining equipment	Using financial ratios
Solving problems	Troubleshooting	Planning
Leading	Analyzing work flow	Managing projects
Facilitating groups	Redesigning work flow	Identifying customer needs
Coaching	Selecting equipment	Working with vendors
Interviewing	Integrating technologies	Working with the public
Making presentations	Using core technologies	Providing customer service
Resolving conflicts	Developing new products	Understanding competitors
Working as a team	Doing the work	Analyzing markets

Running the Marathon

After all the preparations, of course, the important thing for the team leader athlete is to run the marathon. Continuing to run them helps the team leader to stay in shape. This particular series of races requires both speed and endurance, and with each new event comes new learnings as well as the satisfaction of knowing you finished.

Summary

Like a runner preparing for a marathon, the team leader can build stamina and speed by going through team leader workouts consisting of (1) short runs, (2) longer runs, and (3) speed runs. These workouts help team leaders build their own competence and confidence. Short run exercises emphasize communication skill building and personal role education. The longer runs build on this foundation and focus on developing team members and on practicing the team leader skills of coaching, empowerment, example setting, and customer advocacy. The speed workout emphasizes all of the earlier competencies and provides practice time for receiving feedback, barrier busting, networking, and setting boundary conditions. Although these workouts certainly aren't very comprehensive, they can provide some experience in many of the essential tasks of team leadership.

This chapter focused on some ideas for building team leader competencies. But even more important than *skill* building is *will* building. To

Table 21.5. The Speed Workout (Weeks 9 to 12)

Monday	Tuesday	Wednesday	Thursday	Friday
Schedule non-meeting time to be in the work area (1 hour).	Identify a barrier to the team's effectiveness and work to eliminate it (1 hour).	Ask the team how you can help them, and do what they request (1 hour).	Talk with other team leaders at your level and get at least one good improvement idea (30 minutes).	Identify a barrier to the team's effectiveness and start to eliminate it (1 hour).
Gather some relevant business information (30 minutes).	In a one-on-one coaching conversation, empower a team member to do something big (30 minutes).	Schedule time to be in the work area (1 hour).	Ask the team how you can help them, and do what they request (1 hours).	Schedule time to be in the work area (1 hour).
Identify team training needs and make some helpful training happen (1–4 hours sometime during the week).	Share relevant business information with team (15 minutes).	Gather relevant business information (30 minutes).	In a team coaching conversation, empower the team to do something big (30 minutes). Share relevant business information (15 minutes).	Gather relevant business information (30 minutes).

Special Activities:

At some time during the month commission the team members to manage a major improvement project with clearly defined boundary conditions. (2 hours to 2 days)

Take some team members with you on another customer visit or have another customer come in and speak to the team. (1 hour to 2 days)

complete this change team leaders have to want to do something different. Skills alone won't help. I would argue, in fact, that many traditional supervisors already have the skills to be team leaders, but they just don't have the desire to use them. Later in the book we focus on this important issue. We will address the question, "What does it take to help supervisors really change to team leaders?" But first we will review a common problem faced by most team leaders in the early stages of SDWT development.

In the next chapter we consider some alternatives for working with the traditional employees who don't want to act like team members. This Chapter attempts to answer the difficult question, "What do you do when people resist the change to SDWTs?"

Endnote

1. Brian Dumaine, "The Bureaucracy Busters," *Fortune* (June 17, 1991), p. 34. © 1991 by The Time Inc. Magazine Company. All rights reserved. Used by permission.

PART 6

Common Problems and Uncommon Solutions

22

When Team Members Resist the Change to a Self-Directed Work Team

The economy is simply too important to be left in the hands of a few at the top of that [corporate] ladder. To solve our problems, we need reconciliation, cooperation, and the broad participation of all parties to the economic enterprise: workers, consumers, unions, the state and federal governments. Working together, we just might make a difference.[1]

CHRISTOPHER MEEK, WARNER WOODWORTH,
W. GIBB DYER, JR.

Overall, supervisors are typically more resistant to the implementation of self-directed work teams than team members themselves are. But the earliest and most vocal concerns about these work systems come from individuals on the team.

It is not unusual for a work team in a factory, for example, to resist assuming responsibilities that are new to them. Workers may demand more pay for doing "management" work. They may see multiskilling as deskilling. They may believe that SDWTs are a union busting strategy or a method for eliminating seniority and protective job rules and classifications. Office workers or staff professionals may protest the time away from their projects to work on team tasks or express discomfort about the new ambiguity that comes with group decision making and problem solving." I liked it better when the director just told me what to do. That was quicker and simpler," they say, questioning the sanity of other team members who seem to enjoy the additional responsibilities and worries of the new assignments required of a business partner. Teams of managers, newly empowered to assume strategic responsibilities previously reserved for senior management, may fear failure or be uncomfortable with the career risks associated with open feedback to upper management.

All these concerns, of course, are perfectly normal during the early stages of transition. They must be resolved, however, to the satisfaction of the critical mass of the team members for the implementation to be successful. Working through these concerns keeps the implementation process honest. It provides a living example of how the work culture will function in the future. How do you do it?

Change Model

A clear pattern is associated with successful individual change efforts. The elements of this pattern of successful transition can be visualized as a four-faceted diamond (see Fig. 22.1). What are the four key components necessary for someone to change roles? People require:

1. *Clarity*: A clear picture of the emerging role and how it differs from the classic role of a worker.

Figure 22.1. Role change diamond model.

2. *Felt need*: A personal desire to change to the new role.

3. *Support*: The organizational encouragement to create and sustain this personal role change.

4. *Self-awareness*: The ability to assess one's impact on others and make necessary "midcourse corrections."

Each of these facets is essential to the transition.

Even when a team member wants to change, is organizationally supported, and is aware of how she affects others, for example, she will have little success without a clear understanding of what the new role entails. You can't get on the right train if you don't know where the trains are going. Each of the four facets deserves some specific attention.

Clarity

The first facet of effective role change is clarity about the emerging role. Even when the team members have been compeled to action with an exciting vision of the organization of the future, they need specific clarity about how that new organization will affect them personally on a day-to-day basis. "What will I do in the future that is different from what I do today?" is a question that must be answered to the satisfaction of the team members. Many of the effective role transitions in Apple, Corning, IBM, and numerous other companies have used a training process to help with the clarification task. There are common methods for accomplishing this work.

Using Simulations to Clarify the New Role

One of the most effective techniques is to begin with a simulation that demonstrates the difference between traditional roles and team member roles. These simulations are normally separated into two activities. In the first activity the participants create a product or deliver a service using traditional work roles. This part of the simulation takes from two to eight hours and it graphically (and sometimes humorously) demonstrates the inefficiencies inherent in a traditional job-focused work system. Team members see how traditional work structures create the, "That's not my job" syndrome, how compartmentalized departments restrict information flow, and how manager-dominated problem solving and decision making slow down a business. The best of these simulations further demonstrate how these traditional operations affect quality, profitability, and morale.

The second part of the simulation then allows the team to redesign the workplace to better meet the customer needs. Taking from two to eight hours, this part of the simulation demonstrates how teams can create a sense of "ownership" for the product or service, which is not possible with traditional job roles. Instead of being assigned traditional job descriptions, which focus each individual on a narrow set of job responsibilities, the work tasks are managed and assigned by the team as a whole. People share responsibility for meeting the customer needs, and they make decisions and solve problems jointly as a team rather than bottlenecking everything through the supervisor. It is a commonsense approach to getting the work done, driven by the customer and the work itself rather than by the supervisor, rules, or regulations. It also shows dramatic improvements in business indicators of effectiveness.

Explain the New Team Member Competencies

In addition to this kind of general awareness training for team members, organization-specific training on the roles and responsibilities is required. Visits to other SDWT sites can be a helpful way for team members to better understand these roles. But each organization has specific tasks that are unique to the SDWT members in their own operation. How can you deal with that? Consider the following general description of the role of a team member, which explains the essential competencies to be explained to members of a SDWT (see Fig. 22.2).[2] Using this model as a start, team members can construct the specific tasks and assignments for each pie segment themselves to provide additional clarity for their emerging role.

- *Customer advocate*: Strives to better meet the needs of the customer.
- *Trainer*: Trains others in job/skill areas continually shares knowledge with others.
- *Resource*: Has a diverse and ever expanding set of skills continually broadens knowledge base.
- *Skilled worker*: Demonstrates all the necessary skills and knowledge to perform the job well continually strives to improve skill sets and assure total quality.

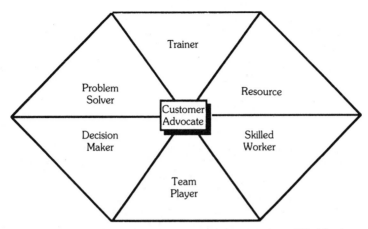

Figure 22.2. The team member role. (*Belgard•Fisher•Rayner, Inc.* © *1989. All rights reserved. Used by permission.*)

- *Team player*: Demonstrates good interpersonal skills; supports other team members.

- *Decision maker*: Provides input and makes decisions on issues that dirtectly impact the work area.

- *Problem solver*: Understands and utilizes problem solving techniques to regularly identify and solve problems.

SDWT Role Descriptions Differ Significantly from Traditional Job Descriptions

It is important to help people understand how this kind of a role description differs from a traditional job description. Where a traditional job description is focused on separate individuals getting certain tasks done, for example, this role description is focused on each team member sharing responsibility for getting the work of the team done. Team member responsibilities also include the planning, administratation, and execution of tasks, instead of just the execution of tasks as in a traditional work system. A traditional job description is activity driven ("do clean up, graphics, quality checks, and anything else required by your manager"), whereas the team member role is purpose driven ("do what makes sense to satisfy customers").

SDWT Members Make Up Their Own "To Do" Lists

Traditional organizations write job descriptions that are organized like discrete "to do" lists. SDWTs, on the other hand, use more purpose-oriented words like "role" when describing responsibilities. Job descriptions, if they exist at all, are so generic that they are nearly meaningless.

One company charged new employees to "find things that need to done and do them" in lieu of a specific job description. How can they do that? Because SDWT members take direction from the work to be done, not from job descriptions or supervision. They can figure out what to do themselves. It is like being a member of a family. When adults become parents, no one gives them a "mother job description" or a "father job description." They figure it out as they go. And they are more or less effective, of course, depending on their skills and their situations. Similarly, team member roles take on enhanced clarity not from job descriptions but from ongoing training and information if the role and organization structures are properly designed. For other ideas on helping team members change, see Table 22.1.

Table 22.1. Helping Team Members Change

Clarity	Felt need	Support	Self-awareness
Demystify the role by visiting with other organizations.	Present a vivid organization "Case-for-Change," which outlines current business realities.	Allay job security fears with work guarantees for good business performance.	Model behaviors such as recognizing and admitting mistakes.
Empower people to take on special project responsibilities, which are exemplary of the new role.	Provide one-on-one coaching to focus a personal need to change.	Provide reinforcement through performance discussions, policies, practices, and pay systems.	Foster an environment that encourages honesty and self-disclosure.
Create opportunities to highlight good examples of the new role within the organization.	Through visits, speakers, conferences, or training, credibly demonstrate the personal benefits of the change.	Provide training and tools to support newly required expectations.	Add peer input to performance appraisal, promotion, and recognition processes.

Felt Need

The second facet of effective role change has been well documented. Dalton's review of the personal change literature led him to conclude that change occurs only when individuals feel a *personal need* to make the change.[3] This is often overlooked when these SDWT transformation efforts begin. In a number of organizations where I have worked, for example, well intended leaders have assumed that organizational sanction alone would compel role changes across the ranks of employees. On many occasions when this strategy has been used, however, I have observed people respond with "talk" changes but with little real "walk" changes. "This too will pass," they say, noting the common program-of-the-month focus in their organizations. They can often get by with imitating the form without the substance of the change. This is, of course, unhealthy for both the individual and the organization.

People Will Not Change Until They Feel They Need to Change

Until individuals are personally convinced that *they* need to change, they *will not* change. Thus creating what Dalton called "felt need," is an essential part of the transformation process. For some people this is accomplished simply by being exposed to a change champion in the organization who has developed and articulated a compeling vision for the future. Ron, a management team leader, had this kind of influence on some of the members of his team in a division of a high tech company on the West Coast. When he became convinced that SDWTs were essential to the operation of his division, he began to share that conviction with his management team. These discussions became eloquent dissertations on the necessity of creating partnerships throughout the organization, which Ron delivered with the quiet intensity of a thoughtful human rights advocate. "His passion for people involvement is like a virus," said one staff member, "it is hard to be around him for very long without catching it."

Present a "Case for Change"

Other leaders create the environment in which individuals can feel this need by presenting a compelling case for organization change, a vivid description, often tied to the history of the organization, which illustrates the necessity of transforming the people in the group and includes the implications of not changing. Fred Hanson, then vice president of the Portables group at Tektronix, created a felt need by addressing the division soon after he had arrived at Tektronix from Hewlett Packard. He showed them a Gary Larson cartoon, which had a group of dinosaurs standing in an auditorium. They are listening to a stegosaurus speaking to them from behind a podium. The caption reads, "The picture looks pretty bleak gentlemen. The world's climates are changing, the mammals are taking over, and we all have a brain about the size of a walnut." Hanson went on to explain that everyone, including himself as the senior stegosaurus, was going to have to change to meet the emerging realities of the businesses. He presented data about the new Japanese competition and Tek's subsequent substantial revenue loss. Armed with the information from this "Case for Change," people became convinced that a change was a business necessity, not just a style preference of the new leader.

In yet another example of a case for change, the senior management team at the Monsanto Pensacola plant created a series of short dramatic videos that emphasized the risks associated with not changing the organization. The first tape graphically demonstrated the negative aspects of not changing. (We will lose to increasing competition and become extinct.) It then was followed up with a tape one year later illustrating specific examples of where the plant had successfully changed. Plant management describes the videos as a sort of one-two punch that first got peoples' attention and then gave them confidence in their own ability to make the change.

Support

The third facet of successful role change is organization support. Without it the change will likely come undone over time. Change is like a rubberband. Through training, meetings, and even personal coaching sessions, team members are often motivated enough to stretch to the different role, like one end of an extended rubberband stretches to a different position when pulled. When the tension is released, however, the rubberband springs back to the original position. Similarly the team members spring back to the well-known and comfortable role of the past when the organization does not sustain the pull for the change.

Make Employment Assurances

To sustain this change, people need help. This help comes in a variety of forms of support. The immediate support requested is usually organizational reassurance that they will not be put out on the street as a result of transferring many of their skills and responsibilities to other employees. This applies as much to teams of middle level managers as it does to teams of workers. We are all concerned with these basic security issues. Team members cannot be expected to put forth the effort to change when they fear that their reward for this effort will be elimination. Nor will they change for make-work positions of diminished responsibility and status. Organizations who are incapable of offering these assurances should avoid SDWT transitions.

Pay and Other Reinforcements Need to Be in Sync with SDWTs

Team members also need other kinds of formal organizational support. Unless reinforcement systems like performance appraisals, promotions, compensation, and other rewards support the emerging role, we send a confusing message about our expectations to the team members in the organization. In one company the effort stalled when people perceived the performance appraisal system as being inconsistent with the emerging SDWT direction. Though the SDWT required flexibility, and cross-training, and information meetings, the employees were measured exclusively on individual productivity. The system discouraged teamwork and punished people for "nonproductive" time like meetings, which could not be billed back to a customer. Until appropriate changes were made to eliminate this double message, people obviously felt a lack of credible organizational support for the SDWT effort.

Organization Structures Need to Be Aligned with SDWTs

A perhaps even more important form of support is also required during these transitions. Dalton (1970), for example, found that new or modified social relationships were required to sustain personal change over time. Although a number of these transformations have been made with the same intact work groups and their manager, there is a higher probability of success when the role changes accompany organizational changes that modify the makeup and charter of a team.

In one change effort in Tektronix, for example, the role change was supported through a production realignment in the organization, which required managers to shift from their assigned work groups to completely different teams. Though initially confusing, this personnel rotation created an opportunity for team leaders to work out a role change "contract" with a new team that was not encumbered with the habits and work history they had created together over time. In another example, a Digital facility staged the implementation process by moving team leaders to the next section of the organization to be transformed. These operations team leaders would overlap with the existing supervisors to learn the organization, allowing the existing supervisors to manage the business while the team leaders focused on managing the transition issues. After some period of time, the old supervisor group would turn over the work teams to the new team leaders, and the old supervisors would be transferred en masse to the next organization where they would become the new operations team leaders.

While these examples of social change are rather dramatic examples of musical chairs, less significant structural support may be equally helpful. New technologies, new products, or new business programs may provide sufficient change in the organization to refocus the social system to be consistent with emerging role changes.

Financial Reports, Training, and Other Tools Need to Be Consistent

Still another form of organization support is essential to the effective transition of the team member's role. This support is resources and tools. To encourage people to act and think differently without providing them some means to accomplish the change is futile. They need tools and training to work in a way that is consistent with the values of high involvement. A number of people, for example, have found that the financial tools used in traditional organizations are no longer useful for the SDWT. Teams need data that is pertinent to their area of influence and formatted in a way that is readily understandable. Much of the existing financial tooling is geared to report information up and out of the organization, and it is of little use to teams trying to manage quality, cost, and schedule. Even when it is available, it is so abstruse that it is unhelpful. Other resources are needed as well. Tools and resources, for example, for gathering, communicating, and coordinating general information.

Self-Awareness

The final facet of successful role change is self-awareness. Team members who are aware of how they affect others are more likely to be effective than those who do not seek this feedback. This is especially true of team members who have responsibilities for some type of team leadership (at some point in time that includes everybody on the team). The fact of the matter is that most of us think we are probably a little better than we really are. We judge ourselves on our intentions, while others judge us on our behaviors. Team members who think that they are acting appropriately may be surprised when they find that their peers perceive them differently. How do they get this information? Ask for it.

Peer Feedback

One of the most effective ways to help someone complete the role change is to show them how they are perceived by others whom they care about. This is the reason that peer pressure can be such an effective motivator in SDWTs. This can be done through a variety of means such as peer appraisals, but it requires extreme sensitivity and skill to do it properly. Many people, unaccustomed to giving and receiving feedback, can be harmed by ineffective processes.

I have worked with numerous members of teams who have believed that they were fulfilling their responsibilities when their peers thought they were not pulling their share of load. Some team members are seen as lazy when they intend to be helpful, or uncooperative when they want to be honest. Devil's advocates, for example, who honestly believe they are representing the true views of their teammates when they raise issues or concerns on task forces or committees, are sometimes seen as working their own individual agendas that are contrary to the emerging group consensus on the particular issue. Blinded by their own good intentions, team members may have clarity about their new role, and so they have a felt need to make the transition to it. They may also have the organization support to successfully change from a traditional job holder, but they may still be unable to do it if they are not self-aware and responsive to how they are perceived. It doesn't do any good to think you are changing when those you work with feel as though you are not.

Summary

Clarity, felt need, support, and self-awareness are required for a successful role change. Although some of the resistance to change manifested by team members early in the process of the transition arises simply from the normal tendency to dislike disruptions to established life patterns, most of it can be reduced by working through the suggestions listed in this chapter.

In the next chapter we deal with the primary resistance and the most critical barrier to this transition to SDWTs: supervisors at all levels who don't want to change.

Endnotes

1. Christopher Meek, Warner Woodworth, W. Gibb Dyer, Jr., *Managing by the Numbers: Absentee Owners and the Decline of American Industry* (Reading, Mass.: Addison-Wesley, 1988), p. 283.

2. This model and the team member descriptions are used with the permission of BFR, Inc. Copyright © 1989 BFR, Inc. All rights reserved.

3. Gene Dalton, "Influence and Organization Change," in Dalton, Lawrence, and Greiner (eds.), *Organizational Change and Development*, Gene Dalton, Paul Lawrence, and Larry Greiner (Homewood, Ill.: Richard D. Irwin, Inc. and The Dorsey Press, 1970).

23

Helping Supervisors Change to Team Leaders

When I started this business of teams, I was anxious to get it done and get back to my real job. Then I realized that, hey, this is my real job.[1]

RALPH STAYER,
CEO of Johnsonville Foods

A number of concerned team members and team leaders alike express skepticism about whether supervisors can change into team leaders. Says John Homan, a previous plant manager of one of the A. E. Staley SDWT plants: "One of the questions I have asked myself is, can all supervisors be successful in the "new" systems, even with extensive training? My assessment right now is no. I have seen too many examples of people who would not or could not change."[2] Pat D'Angelo, the vice president of the Bakery, Confectionery and Tobacco Workers International agrees. He says that some of the Nabisco supervisors just flat didn't make it. "We had a lot of problems with supervisors," he said. "They either straightened up or they looked for other jobs."[3] Some supervisors in this situation can be moved to less "damaging" positions where they don't manage others. These supervisors can be gainfully employed in technical projects or in other individual contributor roles. But that is neither appropriate nor practical for most cases.

We have already talked at length about why this is such a difficult transition for supervisors at all levels to make. But in this chapter I would like to suggest some more specific ways to help people change from supervisors to team leaders. While it is true that not all supervisors will necessarily choose to change, the experience of many companies is that they certainly can change if they are given the opportunity. Some, in fact, require only organizational sanction to do what they have already been practicing for years. What does it take to help the others?

In a Work in America national policy study, Jerome Rosow and Robert Zager make a number of suggestions for helping supervisors change to team leaders.[4] These include:

1. To redefine the supervisor's job.

2. Reorient and retrain them for the new role.

3. Give them employment security.

4. Provide them some relief from pressures that might compel them to fall back on the comfortable practices of the past.

I would like to elaborate on these suggestions by discussing the change model introduced in the last chapter.

Change Model Affects Team Leaders

All facets of the change model—clarity, felt need, support and self-awareness—are just as important for the supervisor role change as they are for the team member role change. What started out in one company looking like a successful team leader transition, for example, later backfired when only some of the facets were sustained over time. A midlevel manager, who had previously been nicknamed "Little Hitler" by the workers, was motivated by very frank feedback from his management team leader to change his role from sheep herding to shepherding. People were amazed at the transformation. Although he made remarkable changes during the first two years after the feedback, when his boss was replaced by someone who was not a champion of these concepts, the organizational support decreased, and he felt little need to continue with the difficult role. He consequently slipped back to old familiar ways even though he clearly understood the team leader role and was very aware of how others perceived him. He didn't care.

Clarity

Where does clarity, the first facet of the model, come from? It comes from first redefining and then from communicating the new role. In one P&G plant undergoing a transition from a traditional system to SDWTs, supervisors were sent to a three-day session where they role-played some open-ended cases as team leaders and learned about the underpinning philosophy of empowerment. The role plays were critiqued by a supportive panel of peers who gave supervisors individual feedback about how they perceived their behavior. Following this education session, they then visited different SDWT plants where they interviewed team leaders and team members to determine for themselves how team leaders behaved. This demystified the role and allowed them to meet face to face with successful people who shared many of their concerns and objectives. By spending time with these people, supervisors saw how the roles were played out in another organization, and they could ask about the process of personal transition in a forum that was less threatening than their own organization.

Involve Supervisors in Defining Team Leader Role

To the extent that supervisors participate in the development of the specifics of the team leader role, they feel not only increasing clarity about it, but also ownership of it, as in the Kodak example. In the Kansas City division of Allied Signal, for another example, a representative supervisors network has been established to clarify the role in that organization. As more of the organizations are moved to work teams, the supervisors use this network as a forum to understand what specific kinds of responsibilities they will pick up over time. Middle managers and general management also use the network meetings as an opportunity to empower those who become team leaders to assume business projects that were previously reserved for more senior managers. These kinds of activities help managers and supervisors understand more specifically what this transition will mean within the fabric of their own organizational culture.

At the American Cyanamid plant in Niagara Falls, Canada, three supervisors were driven off the original design committees by stinging criticism from their peers. Recognizing that something was terribly wrong, culture team leaders invited supervisors to nominate representatives for a new task force commissioned specifically to look at the traditional supervisory job and redesign it. After a slow start, the process worked. They became fully engaged in the change process. What started out to be a process that disenfranchised supervisors ended up being driven by them. If supervisors are not dealt with properly, they can undermine the entire transformation process.

Not Involving Supervisors Creates a Self-Fulfilling Prophecy

This brings us to another related point. Sometimes supervisors are excluded from the SDWT design and implementation process because teams, unions, or executives fear that they will resist the change. When companies assume that supervisors won't support these changes and they exclude them, however, the supervisors become even more resistant because they are not included. It becomes a self-fulfilling prophecy. A better strategy is to include supervisors early.

Supervisors Need to See How Team Leaders Act

These types of clarifying activities are essential to understanding this emerging role. But they are not enough by themselves. Supervisors need to see examples of team leaders in action to fully comprehend this role. Remember the 13 Room experience at Kodak. Perhaps most important to the process of creating role clarity is the presence of viable role models. Models not for others to imitate, but models that clarify and illustrate the visible and invisible elements of effective team leadership.

In the early stages of the transition, tours to other facilities are a common and effective way to expose managers and supervisors to examples of such leaders. Ultimately, however, the organization needs to have its own role models. "The do as I say, not as I do," method of managing people does not work here. As one successful team leader in a high commitment plant in Weyerhaeuser put it, "We are this way because our plant manager is this way." Managers at Corning echo the sentiment: "We follow his [the plant manager's] feet, not his mouth," a group of them told me about the good example of a management team leader who walked his talk. Conversely, another transformation effort in 1987 just could not get off the ground. I was in the cafeteria one day having lunch with one of the second level managers and I asked him why the effort was going so sluggishly. He put it succinctly, "We won't change until [the general management team] does. The reason we manage like this is because this is the way we are managed." For other change ideas, for each of the four facets of the model see Table 23.1.

Table 23.1. Helping Supervisors Change to Team Leaders

Clarity	Felt need	Support	Self-awareness
Set up a task team of managers to design the responsibilities included in the new role.	Have supervisors work closely with senior mentors who are champions of change.	Allay job security fears with work guarantees for good business performance.	Model behaviors such as recognizing and admitting mistakes.
Establish forums for supervisory role discussions and debates.	Provide one-on-one coaching to focus a personal need to change.	Provide reinforcement through performance discussions, policies, practices, and pay systems.	Create mechanisms for supervisors to solicit feedback from others.
Demystify the role by visiting with other organizations.	Ask questions which allow supervisors to confront their own values and assumptions about other people.	Create mechanisms for peer support like brown bag lunch sessions for supervisors.	Add team member and "peer" input to performance appraisal, promotion, and recognition processes.
Create opportunities to highlight good examples of the new role within the organization.	Use survey and interview data to share perceptions of management style and method.	Provide training and tools to support newly required expectations of leaders.	Create opportunities for senior managers to make their own role change progress (warts and all) visible.

Felt Need

The second facet of the model is felt need. One vice president at Procter and Gamble created a felt need with a thought-provoking letter he sent to several plants in the manufacturing company. The letter stated that the technician work systems had simply outperformed the more traditionally managed operations over the last 15 years. By suggesting that these organizations would replace the traditionally managed ones within the next five years and by requesting retrofit transition plans for traditional plants, he created a felt need in a number of supervisors to transition themselves and their organizations to SDWTs.

For other supervisors, general attempts to create a felt need is not enough. They need specific personal coaching to help them feel a need to change to the new role. One-on-one discussions with people they respect—a boss, a peer, or a friend—can help supervisors create a need for personal change and help them prepare an appropriate transition.[5]

I have been told of skilled managers who have had real heart-to-heart discussions with supervisors that focused, for example, on basic assumptions. "Tell me the truth," they might say. "Do you really think that your subordinates' ideas are as good as yours?" Or, "Why did you say this morning that the team *works for you*? What did you mean by that?" Or, "Why do you often say 'I did this' instead of 'We did this'?" confronting gut-level values is a delicate but useful exercise for developing a felt need to change. Some people use survey data to create an opening for these discussions.

Different Supervisors Require Different Approaches

How to work with these supervisors to create felt need differs according to their situations. Bill Belgard and Janice Klein have developed a useful management typology for understanding how to deal with different supervisors who are changing to team leaders.[6] They posit that there are five types of changing supervisors: trailblazers, pilots, intellectuals, late bloomers, and traditionalists. This deserves more discussion.

Trailblazers, Pilots, and Intellectuals

Trailblazers embrace the concept and have probably been doing it all along. They don't need a lot of help, just a little permission. *Pilots* are the supervisors who know how to get somewhere but they need to know where to go. They are cautious at first, but will be won over without a lot of effort other than the normal vision sharing and role clarification activities. *Intellectuals*, however, believe they support the concept and they say the right things. But they don't walk the talk. They need strong conversations with their own team leaders or consultants to provide a felt need to do anything different. Their mentors can show them the discrepancies in their behavior and language. "You say this, but do something else," might be the words used with intellectuals.

Late Bloomers and Traditionalists

Late bloomers resist for some time and then change. They require a lot of patience. Often their change comes only after they personally are convinced over a long period of time that there is a better way. Lots of felt need discussions are required here, but eventually they pay off. Late bloomers in fact sometimes turn into the strongest supporters later on, much as exsmokers become more supportive of nonsmoking policies than people who have never smoked. *Traditionalists*, however, won't be won over. They feel the SDWT concept is fundamentally flawed. For traditionalists, discussions to create felt need are not helpful. It is better to find them another job.

Support

The third facet of team leader role change is support. One important type of support is job reassurance. Companies won't get far with the supervisory role changes if they allow the perception that SDWTs put supervisors at any level out on the street. Other supports are needed as well. After team leaders are educated about the new role and the need to change to it, they need to be supported by their bosses and reinforced by all the policies, procedures, and processes of the organization.

Get Rewards and Recognition Systems in Sync with the New Role

In one unionized plant, several supervisors thought the transition to participative management would be a short-lived fad. When the next rare promotions from first to second level management occurred, however, both people promoted were individuals who had a strong reputation and demonstrated ability as SDWT managers. Though a few of the managers still expressed skepticism about the longevity of the change, most of them acknowledged that demonstrated proficiency as a team leader would be rewarded and supported. Appropriate SDWT leader behaviors should be clearly identified and rewarded if they are to continue.

Supervisors need formal organizational support. Unless reinforcement systems like performance appraisals, promotions, compensation, and other rewards support the emerging role, we send a confusing message about our expectations to the supervisors in the organization. At least one expert's research clearly demonstrates that, when support systems do not change, supervisors do not change to team leaders.[7] In the organization just mentioned, supervisors were told about the changing expectations for their role sometime earlier. Only a few weeks after that some coincidental promotions were announced, which included two supervisors who had the reputation for being very strong technically, but who exhibited Theory X assumptions and values. Although the promotions were deserved and, in all fairness, had been in the works for a number of months prior to the work with the other supervisors, the juxtaposition of the promotion and the initial discussions with the supervisors was unfortunate and confusing. It wasn't until several months later that the situation was rectified by the new SDWT consistent promotions.

As a contrasting example, in a number of the P&G facilities undergoing transformation, all team leaders are measured by what is called the "what counts" factors. These factors are performance requirements that are consistent with the expected practices of a high involvement manager. In Lima, part of my raise was determined by the same people who helped to hire me: the team. This process allowed an institutionalized opportunity for team feedback to the team leader and helped to keep the reward system in sync with the requirements of the work system. A similar idea was recommended by an engineer I interviewed at Intel. Suggesting that numerous problems would be resolved by changing the performance review process typically used in the United States, he said, "Everyone should be reviewed by the customer(s) they support. Managers should get them from the team, and my team should get them from manufacturing. That would help everybody here to remember whom we work for."

Peer Networks Provide a Different Kind of Support

Peer networks are another kind of support that are very useful to their team leader transition. In one Tektronix organization, for example, a group of managers decided to meet once a week for lunch. They called themselves "AA," for Autocrats Anonymous, and used this lunch time to review challenges and share ideas with supportive colleagues. During times of transition, peer networks give people fresh ideas, renewed energy, and support. They come to realize that they are not in this thing alone.

Use Delegation Schedules to Provide Transition Help

Another important support for transitioning team leaders is some sort of change structure that helps the supervisor track transition milestones. In General Electric's jet engine turbine-blade plant in Bromont, Canada, for example, team leaders agree on a schedule of delegation. This schedule has proven to be a very effective aid to transition. The traditional supervisory responsibilities were listed with a date for when each appropriate responsibility was to be assumed by the team. This provided a much needed organization for the transition and helped team leaders put together training plans for the team to prepare them to assume the new responsibilities. This same idea can be used to then identify the new tasks and projects to be assumed by team leaders after the delegation. This will give them something to look forward to and plan for as they develop their teams to assume many of their former responsibilities.

Self-Awareness

The final facet of the role change diamond is self-awareness. As you might suspect, this is not resident in every changing supervisor. It is least common in senior managers who have been protected from personal constructive criticism for years. But it is a weakness that can occur at every level of supervision. Too many supervisors evaluate their own progress by their good intentions rather than by how they are perceived by team members and others (see Fig. 23.1).

This facet of the change diamond is more critical than it may appear at first blush. I have worked with numerous supervisors (from lead technicians to vice presidents) who really believed they were effective team leaders even though others did not share that opinion. SDWT progress was halted until they could recognize and react to others' perceptions. They walked around "naked," as it were, until they began to hear and believe the cries from the bystanders, "The emperor has no clothes!" Self-aware team leaders know that, even if the perceptions of others are incorrect, that those perceptions drive their behaviors. Thus, the only practical reality is perception. If team members as a whole think you are a traditional manager, you are a traditional manager.

This realization is rare. In a survey completed in preparation for a Supervisory Congress for all of the managers in Esso Resources, for example, were two interesting questions. One was, "Are you a participative manager?" and another was "Is your boss a participative manager?" Ironically, only about 30 percent of the people in management were perceived to be participative by their subordinates although about 70 percent of those same managers wrote that they considered themselves to be participative. Supervisors, like everyone else, are not always self-aware.

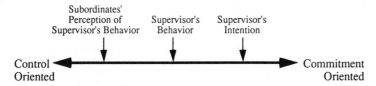

Figure 23.1. The gap between intended and perceived behaviors.

Effective leaders know the truth about how they are perceived and they are not defensive about it. They elicit feedback and take action on it. They also admit mistakes. We saw these behaviors when we visited with Ralph Olney at Kodak, as discussed in earlier chapters. Organizations need to create environments in which it is okay for managers to say they are wrong. In some operations that is career suicide. This must change. Until supervisors are rewarded for candidly admitting their own frailties, an environment of trust and self-awareness is unlikely.

Self-Aware Team Leaders Admit Mistakes Openly

We normally expect our leadership to act consistently with well publicized elements of their values and vision. But when they act contrary to them and then acknowledge and modify their behavior accordingly, it leaves a lasting impression about the depth of their conviction. After all, even the most well intended supervisor will sometimes fall off the wagon. Those who openly confess and rectify actions that are perceived as incongruent with the stated vision are often actually seen as more authentic and committed to their vision than those who cover up or ignore these unintentional inconsistencies.

People in one of the divisions at Tektronix, for example, frequently refer to what is now known as "the coffee incident." In this situation, Joe Burger, a management team leader who professed to support significant employee involvement decreed (seemingly arbitrarily) that there would be no more food of any kind allowed at workstations. Some of the employees in the organization were outraged that he had created this policy without first discussing it with them. After they confronted him he acknowledged his error and rectified it. He publicly told this story about himself multiple times, and his team often used the example to demonstrate that he was truly committed to increasing involvement.

Summary

The role change model applies to team leaders as well as to team members. They need role clarity, felt need, support, and self-awareness to change successfully from supervisors to team leaders. The way we work with transitioning supervisors is different depending on whether they are trailblazers, pilots, intellectuals, late bloomers, or traditionalists. But we must work with them even if we are skeptical about their ability to change. A number of things are important to do to aid transitioning leaders. These include training programs, modeling, and visits to other sites to clarify the new role. Data and coaching discussions can create a felt need to change roles. Job reassurances let people know that while their responsibilities will change, they won't be laid off because of SDWTs. Delegation schedules help to organize the transition. Consistent reward and recognition systems send the message that this is the way we intend to manage. Peer networks provide emotional support. And mentors provide examples and a safe environment for self-awareness. Supervisors, of course will be much more supportive of roles they help to define than those they are given by assignment. Early involvement of the supervisors in the implementation process is a key to generating their support of SDWTs. Without their involvement, supervisory resistance become a self-fulfilling prophecy.

Can supervisors change successfully into team leaders? The answer is yes. And organizations have a moral obligation to assist in the transition process even if some supervisors choose eventually not to change. Even though I have never seen this transition process proceed without some supervisory casualties (mostly by self-selection), it is incumbent on team leaders to assist other team leaders in the process of their personal role change. Why? Because they are valuable resources. The stakes are high here. Simply put, if supervisors don't change to team leaders, you can't have successful self-directed work teams.

In the next chapter we will review a particularly difficult issue relative to team leader transitions. What do you do if your boss is the one having problems changing from a supervisor to a team leader?

Endnotes

1. Brian Dumaine, "Who Needs a Boss?" *Fortune* (May 7, 1990), p. 60. © 1990 The Time Inc. Magazine Company. All rights reserved. Used by permission.

2. John Homan, personal correspondence. Italics added.

3. Pat D'Angelo, *Ecology of Work*, presentation about Nabisco change efforts, June 1991.

4. "New Roles for Managers, Part 1: Employee Involvement and the Supervisor's Job," a Work in America Institute National Policy Study, 1989. Directed by Jerome M. Rosow and Robert Zager. Case studies edited by Jill Casner-Lotto.

5. Gene Dalton, "Influence and Organization Change," in Dalton, Lawrence, and Greiner (eds.), *Organizational Change and Development* (Homewood, Ill.: Richard D. Irwin, Inc. and The Dorsey Press, 1970).

6. Janice Klein and Bill Belgard, "Helping Supervisors to Change: The Missing Link," an unpublished discussion paper commissioned for *New Roles for Manager: The Manager as Trainer Coach and Leader* issued by the Work in America Institute, June 1989.

7. Dr. Pam Posey's ongoing research at the University of Vermont confirms that performance appraisals and other management reward systems must support the new requirements for team leaders if these behaviors are to continue over time.

24

Managing Upwards

When You Don't Have the Support of Senior Management

We're creating a hierarchy of ideas. You say,
"This is the right thing to do here," not
"We're going to do this because I'm boss."[1]

RAYMOND GILMARTIN,
CEO of Becton Dickinson

Nancy is a management team leader in a large financial services company. Before she came to this company, she worked with a corporation that had used SDWTs successfully for several years. Although she is firmly committed to the SDWT concept, she doubts that someone at her level in the corporation can make any significant dent in the autocratic culture of this place.

Walt is an operations team leader of a SDWT in an auto parts plant. When the new plant manager tours the area, she listens to the accomplishments of the customer service team. Although she expresses admiration about the improvements in quality, cost, and speed, she confides in Walt that the team seems a little too independent for her liking.

Can people like Nancy and Walt make a significant difference? There is an old joke about the difference between involvement and commitment. It says that while a chicken is *involved* in producing breakfast, a pig is *committed.* While it is always easy to be involved as a team leader, managers and supervisors are often less enthusiastic about being strongly committed to SDWTs when senior management aren't the champions of the concept. Most will opt for the path of the chicken—especially when the perceived outcome of that commitment is career suicide.

Orderly Top-Down Change Is More Fiction Than Fact

The fact of the matter is, however, that the idealistic notion that championship of the SDWT work culture starts at the top of the corporation and then cascades orderly through the organization is much more fiction than fact. With the notable exceptions of senior leaders like Stayer at Johnsonville Foods, Culkin at Boston Whaler, and Semler at Semco S/A who launched full-scale transformation efforts from the executive suite, virtually every organization that has implemented SDWTs has done so because of early efforts from the management level of team leaders or from middle management staff.

SDWTs Start with Champions in the Middle of the Operation

The work at Procter and Gamble, for example, which started in the late 1960s didn't occur because senior management wanted to change the corporation. It started because plant managers and corporate internal consultants sought ways to reduce labor problems and to improve work flows and processes in the new plants. Union officials and middle level staff members were key promoters of the SDWT concept in Corning before organization-wide efforts were sponsored from the office of CEO Jamie Houghton. Single facilities in General Foods and Digital Equipment Corporation used SDWTs primarily because facility managers like Lyman Ketchum of General Foods; and Bruce Dillingham of DEC wanted to see it happen. The same stories have been repeated at General Electric, Cummins Engine, and elsewhere.

Generally speaking there does need to be sponsorship of the idea at the culture team leader level for the particular unit to be changed. This is usually, however, the plant manager or regional manager level of general management, not the vice president or other senior levels. While it is true that the idea for this alternative management technology must eventually take root at a high enough level of formal authority, where culture changing action can take place, the SDWT seeds are often planted even lower in the organization by people with limited hierarchical power.

Change Influencers vs. Change Drivers

A number of people play a significant role in the evolution of organizations who do not have the formal authority to personally drive a transformation of this magnitude. These individuals focus their energy on influencing rather than on sponsoring the management change. As change influencers, they can affect the change process from almost any level of the organization regardless of their personal authority base. Their techniques do not work in every situation but they have proven effective in influencing upwards in the organization. Once the SDWT concept is fully supported in the organization, even working with specific bosses in the organization who are displaying autocratic or marshmallow behaviors becomes possible.

Naturally the "buck stops" with the person in power. It would be unrealistic to suggest that that change influencers can impact change efforts if those at the top of the organization refuse to accept their ideas. It is equally unrealistic, though, to suggest that top level managers will never listen to or act upon the ideas brought to them by middle and lower level management. Unfortunately, it is often the perception of those in the middle that "their hands are tied"—that what they have to say cannot make a difference. This is simply not true.

How Do Change Influencers Act?

The manner in which the change influencer operates is difficult to characterize. To a casual outside observer it would appear that he or she initiates a series of loosely coupled activities that have little strategic or systematic orientation. Specific actions here might include conversations in the parking lot or local coffee shop, informal networking, making presentations, phone calls, lobbying, and occasional blank stares.

Although by all outward appearances change influencers may seem to be operating in a state of chaos, randomly thrashing about as they attempt to get their ideas heard, there is a method to their madness. They focus their time and energy on three activities:

1. They create a vision of the future state.
2. They take advantage of every opportunity to discuss their vision.
3. They tenaciously support processes that facilitate vision implementation while they discourage processes that inhibit it.

It boils down to three things: vision, opportunity, and tenacity.

Vision, Opportunity, and Tenacity

Let's walk through how Nancy might influence change at her corporation. Once the change influencer is clear in her own mind about what self-directed work teams are and why they are needed in the organization, she then takes advantage of opportunities to make her case heard. Some of these opportunities to discuss the vision are planned, such as meetings in which she can influence the agenda; others are unplanned, in which cases she can "leverage serendipity," such as running into a key executive in the parking lot.

If she is prepared and sufficiently skilled, she will be able to take advantage of both kinds of opportunities. If you follow influential team leaders around, for example, you will find precious little time spent in the activities that the leaders often use to describe their responsibilities, such as planning or formal training. Most of their time, as shown studies by Kotter[2] and others, is spent taking advantage of chance occurrences to further their goals. Change influencers carrying around an agenda in their head, as it were, which includes a list of the people they need to talk to, ideas on how to approach them in the conversation, and their vision of a better future for the business. These unplanned opportunities are what makes the influencing process look so imprecise. The precision and rationale for the seemingly unrelated activities are integrated by the internal work agenda of the change influencer. While the process is certainly not linear or systematic, it is highly rational.

The final cluster of activities relates to simple tenacity. The vision communication process is fraught with frustration, resistance, and passive neglect because the change influencer does not have enough personal authority to make SDWTs happen on her own. But change influencers stick with it until critical mass is created, and then they apply their creative tenacity fully to the implementation process. The path is described by most as frustrating and boring at the same time, but in the end, a clear, well crafted vision with compeling business advantages often wins over skeptics.

Change Influencers Are Politically Astute

A note of caution is that change influences must temper their persistence with politics. By behaving with tenacity, change influencers display their commitment to the vision they are advocating. But change influencers are politically astute and they are sensitive about the appropriate behaviors for this process in their organizations. They recognize that, if they alienate the change drivers with the way they present the vision (pounding the tables, demanding credit for the change, blaming people for doing things the way they do them now, etc.), they will strangle the initiative they are so passionate about implementing. They tend to operate with a kind of calculated audacity. When obstacles appear they search for new paths. They seem to intuitively recognize that the path to cultural transformation is crooked and unpredictable. They adapt, change directions, and explore new alternatives with ease.

Case Study

Let's review how change influencers act in a case study. The organization is a medium sized high tech company located in the West, where managers and staff members with limited hierarchical power were able to influence the creation of SDWTs in significant parts of the corporation through vision, opportunity, and tenacity.

Change influencers realized early on that they would need to get the support of change drivers who had legitimate authority and could authorize the significant support system changes required for the effective implementation of SDWTs. Although the process of influencing the drivers was much more enigmatic and disorganized than it will appear in this account, the activities did fall into the three activity clusters.

Vision

For the vision activity cluster, the change influencers first had to clearly articulate a compelling business driven vision of an attractive future. They began by getting together in a network meeting open to anyone interested in the SDWT idea. The meetings soon filled with managers and staff members who had the interest in and the experience, with the concept, but who had insufficient organizational clout to create the change on their own. As a collective, though, the group had access to several change drivers. The network served as a forum for coalescing the shared experience of the body into a collective vision, which was captured in a visioning tool with behavioral statements along a continuum of employee involvement from low involvement to SDWTs. The tool identified key SDWT characteristics and provided a vehicle for discussion of the concept that allowed the change drivers to participate in the creation and ownership of the emerging vision of greatness for several divisions of the corporation.

Opportunity

Once the vision was emerging the change influencers looked for opportunities to make the vision salient. The "People Involvement Network" meetings continued to provide a forum for discussion of the SDWT concepts and applications. A workshop was developed to share the emerging vision with people across the organization and change drivers participated in the beginning and closing of the workshop. Change influencers also invited a consultant to make a presentation to the senior managers, and the presentation excited and focused the change drivers. In an unplanned leveraging of serendipity, the senior operations officer of the company introduced a four-pronged program to improve the company, and it included "People Involvement" as one of the four key initiatives. Change influencers lobbied heavily to be the ones to define the emerging initiative and in so doing, created an instant champion of the executive.

Tenacity

Even though the SDWT ideas began to take root in various parts of the organization, tenacity was required to institutionalize the fragile transformation. From time to time midlevel management made presentations to keep senior management up to speed, to ask them to set certain examples, or to break down certain barriers to effective implementation. Reward systems, performance appraisals, and job descriptions were refocused, and each required a Herculean effort juxtaposed over the already vigorous demands of the workplace. As results started improving, the transition became easier.

The SDWTs never permeated the entire company. At the time of this writing there are still no corporations of that size with self-direction across an entire operation. But what started out as the dream of a handful of midlevel change influencers became the preferred way of managing in major portions of the operation. Among other things the SDWTs were credited with saving one of the divisions that had been incapable of competing. This division became the most profitable in the company, and hundreds of jobs were saved.

What If the New Boss Is Unsupportive of SDWTs?

While this case is helpful to the team leader who is trying to get SDWTs moving in the operation for the first time, what do you do if the teams are already established but your boss isn't a supporter? What could somebody like Walt, the customer service team leader, do if his new culture team leader is unsupportive of self-direction?

This is not a hypothetical question. In P&G, new plant and brand managers have been transferred into SDWT facilities for more than two decades. Team members and team leaders alike have experienced some trauma over these transitions, because the new transferees are often "high potential" managers with track records as aggressive traditional supervisors. But in the vast majority of these cases, the new team leaders would leave the facilities as SDWT supporters even though they may have been skeptics when they arrived. What changed?

Being Results Oriented vs. Control Oriented

What usually changes is that team leaders personally experience results that are unobtainable in the traditional paradigm of management. The experience convinces them over time. They are smart and practical people. But this is still a difficult personal change process for most. As mentioned in an earlier chapter, while current wisdom suggests that most traditional supervisors are just too "results oriented" to mess around with this touchy-feely SDWT stuff, the truth is that most traditionalists are not results oriented enough. They value control more than results. When the senior team leaders come to understand that their own personal desire to control things gets in the way of better results, they have a choice to make. Results or control? A lot of them choose results. How can change influencers aid this process?

Typically, team leaders who are effective at managing upwards display a few common characteristics. They:

1. Take risks.
2. Keep leaders informed.
3. Create heroes.

Each of these things deserves some elaboration.

Dare Greatly

Traditional organizations have usually created supervisors who are risk averse. In operations dominated by hierarchical decision making and problem solving, supervisors are weary of doing anything that potentially tarnishes their relationship with superiors. Thus they conform. They don't challenge superiors and they pretty much espouse the party line. That is the safe approach. Effective change influencers, however, take personal career risks. They dare greatly. Although they are sensitive to the political realities of their situation, they are more apt to gently confront their superior's doubts about SDWTs. Walt is unlikely to influence his new manager if he doesn't do this. Why should she change her opinion about SDWTs if she has no reason?

Walt, for example, might say to the new culture team leader:

> Maria, if you are anything like I was when we first changed over to these SDWTs, you are thinking that this place is pretty weird. But these teams really seem to work. Why don't you come over to one of the customer service team meetings next week sometime and we'll give you a presentation on what we are doing. I would like you to meet the team. I think you'll be impressed.

Change influencers don't normally use a in-your-face highly argumentative approach to convince executives that SDWTs are the way to go. Nor do they spend time getting permission from senior officers to continue empowerment. But instead they get on with the business of using SDWTs to accomplish extraordinary results. They use the Nike philosophy of management and "just do it." They demonstrate the effectiveness of the nontraditional management paradigm. They get results. And they don't back away from the SDWT way of doing things as an automatic reaction to the new leader's hesitations. Is it risky? Yes. But it has been done successfully in companies like P&G, Apple Computers, and DEC for years.

Working with Resistance from the Senior Levels

More difficult, of course, is the situation in which new leaders have been in the operation for a while, and you find that they are intellectuals, late bloomers, or traditionalists. Exposure and experience alone don't seem to be changing their feelings about SDWTs. How do you address this situation? Sometimes, of course there isn't much you can do. If the person is a full-blown traditionalist, it is better to wait for the next new manager. But I have seen this situation dealt with very effectively where the senior manager was an intellectual or a late bloomer.

Commit to the Success of the Leader

One of my colleagues, for example, is very skilled at doing this. He normally opens up the conversion by asking something like, "Pierre, what is it that you want that you don't already have?" When Pierre says he wants this improvement or that improvement, my colleague commits to help him get it through the SDWTs. I have seen him do this both as a team leader and as an external consultant with equal effectiveness. He also tells him that he wants to do everything possible to ensure the success of the operation, including giving Pierre feedback about what the others in the operation need from him to accomplish the improvements. This is where "daring greatly" comes in. "Pierre," he says, "I know that a lot of general managers never get feedback about how they are perceived by subordinates. I would like to have a deal with you that I will give you that information straight. Are you interested?"

Make the Deal to Share Feedback

If he takes the deal, you have an agreement to share personal observations and feedback from the teams with him. This kind of feedback can be very motivating to the senior manager if it is delivered skillfully. It can help him change. If he doesn't take the deal, however, the relationship with him may be very awkward and uncomfortable from this point on. That's the risk. Some interesting psychology is at work here that you may be interested in. The phenomenon, called *cognitive dissonance*, works something like this. If Pierre takes the deal he will think, "I am a smart guy. I just agreed to let this team leader give me feedback. So this team leader must also be a smart guy. I am going to listen to him." Taking the risk may actually raise your credibility with the more senior manager.

No Surprises

The second thing team leaders do to manage upwards is share information. One of the important unwritten rules of management is, "Never surprise your boss." Effective change influencers are particularly sensitive about this. They are very good at keeping change champions informed about the accomplishments and decisions of the teams. Whenever possible they create firsthand interaction with the senior team leaders and the team members themselves. Something about this personal experience is much more powerful than the secondhand information that is typical in traditional operations (memos, staff meeting reports, etc.). One of the reasons P&G plant managers were usually won over to the SDWT concepts was that they regularly toured each team area to hear presentations about team accomplishments. These tours occurred at least once a month, often with a visiting dignitary from corporate headquarters. Nothing can replace the impact of hearing something with your own ears.

Keeping the boss informed of team decisions is especially important. In traditional operations senior managers always know the decisions because they always make them. But in an SDWT operation, where decisions are being made continuously at all levels of the operation, it is easy for managers to feel as though they are out of the loop. For a traditional manager this is the worst possible place to be. It makes them want to institutionalize controls that give them better visibility of things. To address this issue, many operations use a site-wide operations meeting every day. This meeting is a collection of representatives from each work area who normally are appointed by their peers to represent them in the meeting. The job is rotated regularly (about every six months) to give everyone a chance who wants to to serve in this capacity. While the primary purpose of the meeting is to coordinate issues affecting multiple teams, an ancillary benefit is that it allows managers real-time access to the changing issues and problems of the workplace. This creates a higher degree of comfort and allows the manager to release controls.

Make Heroes

Finally, the third thing change influencers are very good at is making their bosses heroes when things go right. They realize that credit for team accomplishments is shared by everyone who helps (including the team leaders). I saw a Weyerhaeuser pulp mill team recently, for example, talk to another group of team leaders about how important their mill manager has been in the changeover to SDWT. They extolled his virtues fairly extensively. Even though he wasn't there at the time I know that this message got back to him. And I suspect that this positive reinforcement makes him feel good about his role in the mill.

Other change influencers have obtained major speaking engagements at conferences or universities for their senior managers to talk about what the teams have done. Others set up benchmarking and customer visits to their site and enlist the managers in appropriate hosting and presentation roles. Others find ways to have the managers interviewed for the corporate or community press as appropriate. While care should be taken not to transfer the credit for the work accomplishments back to the managers and away from the teams (that is the same old traditional stuff again), appropriate exposure gives the managers positive reinforcement for being a team leader instead of a supervisor. It does another thing as well. The more a senior manager tells other people about how great the teams are, the more she tends to believe it. It is that cognitive dissonance idea in action again.

Summary

Orderly top-down transitions from traditional workplaces to SDWTs are extremely rare. These transitions usually are the result of a middle-up effort, in which management level team leaders or staff members plant SDWT seeds for some time prior to the official champion coming on board. Since these people have no formal authority to make SDWTs happen, however, they are change influencers rather than change drivers. They influence change drivers like the culture team leader of a plant or store (some moderately autonomous site) to champion the changes. Their efforts seem to fall into three activity clusters. Change influencers work on creating a vision for a better future, they create planned and unplanned opportunities to communicate their vision to the change drivers, and they display the tenacity to stick with it until their objectives are achieved.

Once the change is underway, however, it is especially difficult when your own team leader is unsupportive of self-direction. In some cases, the only solution is to wait until someone else comes along. But in other circumstances, daring greatly, keeping the leader informed, and creating heroes can influence significant change up in the organization.

Endnotes

1. Brian Dumaine, "The Bureaucracy Busters," *Fortune* (June 17, 1991), p. 30. © 1991 by The Time Inc. Magazine Company. All rights reserved. Used by permission.

2. John Kotter, "What Effective General Managers Really Do," *Harvard Business Review*, 60 (6), 1982, 156–167.

PART 7

Team Leader Evaluation Tools

25

The Team Leader Litmus Test

Do I Fit as a Team Leader?

Instructions

Choose the selection that best describes your own thoughts or behaviors on the following:

1. The primary role of the supervisor is to:
   - ☐ a. Get the work of the organization done through other people.
   - ☐ b. Meet agreed on goals and objectives.
   - ☐ c. Satisfy customers.
   - ☐ d. Make employees' work life more enjoyable.

2. How would the employees you manage describe the primary role you played over the last two work weeks?
   - ☐ a. Making employees work life more enjoyable
   - ☐ b. Satisfying customers
   - ☐ c. Getting the work done through other people
   - ☐ d. Working to accomplish goals and objectives

3. You have four phone calls, which come in simultaneously. One can be taken while the others must remain on hold. Whose call do you take:
   - ☐ a. The president of your corporation
   - ☐ b. An irate customer
   - ☐ c. An employee you have been counseling
   - ☐ d. A city council member

4. You find out that someone in the organization two levels below you has requested a meeting with you to discuss a problem in the organization. Do you:
   - ☐ a. Recommend that they first resolve the issue with their own manager?
   - ☐ b. Refer the request to the human resources people?
   - ☐ c. Try to find the employee and talk to him or her?

5. The primary responsibilities of management are to:
   - ☐ a. Develop, inspire, coach, teach.
   - ☐ b. Plan, organize, direct, control.
   - ☐ c. Motivate, regulate, discipline, reward.
   - ☐ d. Solve problems, make decisions, go to meetings.

6. How would the employees you manage describe the way you used your time over the last two work weeks?
   - ☐ a. Planning, organizing, directing, controling.
   - ☐ b. Motivating, regulating, disciplining, rewarding.
   - ☐ c. Developing, inspiring, coaching, teaching.
   - ☐ d. Solving problems, making decisions, going to meetings.

7. Your boss comes into your area to tell you that you should stop working on a project that you and your group are very excited about. You disagree with the reasons. Do you:
   - ☐ a. Tell members of the group that you are being pressured to shut down the project and you can't do anything about it.
   - ☐ b. Confront your boss and disagree?
   - ☐ c. Bring your boss into the group to discuss his/her concerns?
   - ☐ d. Quietly shut down the project as requested?

8. A member of the group you manage has a promising improvement idea. Do you:
   - ☐ a. Suggest they write a memo?
   - ☐ b. Put it on an agenda for discussion with the rest of the group?
   - ☐ c. Talk to them and then present the idea personally to senior management?
   - ☐ d. Help them develop the idea and a justification for it more fully?

9. Your group complains that a corporate policy is inhibiting their ability to get their work done. Do you:
   - ☐ a. Ignore the policy and do what you feel is best for the group?
   - ☐ b. Do the work the best you can within a broad interpretation of the policy?
   - ☐ c. Work to change the policy?
   - ☐ d. Ensure compliance to the policy?

10. You are at a social gathering when the name of someone who reports to you comes up. Which of the following would you be most likely to say?
    - ☐ a.   He/she works for me.
    - ☐ b.   We work together.
    - ☐ c.   He/she is in my organization.
    - ☐ d.   I don't really know them very well.

11. When someone in the company asks you to describe your organization, how do you do it?
    - ☐ a.   Talk about how your customers use your products or services.
    - ☐ b.   Explain the tasks your group performs on a daily basis.
    - ☐ c.   Draw a organization chart.
    - ☐ d.   Describe your equipment/technology or work process.

12. Rank the following in order of importance to you from 1 (high) to 5 (low):
    - ☐ a.   Promotions (career growth and increased responsibilities)
    - ☐ b.   Meaningful work (doing the kind of work you find interesting and important)
    - ☐ c.   Accomplishment (making worthwhile things happen)
    - ☐ d.   Being liked (having the people you work with like you)
    - ☐ e.   Status (being more important than other people)

13. Which of the following best describes the way you usually think about subordinates when they have performance problems?
    - ☐ a.   If I don't stay on them all the time they screw up.
    - ☐ b.   They are well intended but they are not very capable.
    - ☐ c.   They are lazy and need to be motivated.
    - ☐ d.   They need better information, training, and tools.
    - ☐ e.   They are devious and need to be controled.

14. When a group of people are having difficulty coming to a decision at work, do you usually:
    - ☐ a.   Come to their rescue and make the decision for them?
    - ☐ b.   Express your opinion but avoid taking over?
    - ☐ c.   Observe and wait until it resolves itself?
    - ☐ d.   Help them come to a decision?

15. Which of the following best describes the way you are most comfortable working with your group?
    - ☐ a.   Staying out of the day-to-day operations until there are problems.
    - ☐ b.   Having all important decisions and information go through you.
    - ☐ c.   Allowing the group to do whatever they feel is best.
    - ☐ d.   Providing resources and support to the group.

16. What would the people who report to you say is the way you are most comfortable working with them?
    - [ ] a. Providing resources and support to the group.
    - [ ] b. Having all important decisions and information go through you.
    - [ ] c. Staying out of the day-to-day operations until there are problems.
    - [ ] d. Allowing the group do whatever they feel is best.

To what extent do you agree with the following statements? (Circle a number 1–5.)

	Strongly disagree	Disagree	Neutral	Agree	Strongly agree
17. People want to do a good job.	1	2	3	4	5
18. Mistakes are caused by bad processes or information, not by employee errors.	1	2	3	4	5
19. I would rather satisfy the customer than satisfy my boss.	1	2	3	4	5
20. People can be trusted to do their best.	1	2	3	4	5
21. Managers need to be teachers, not directors.	1	2	3	4	5
22. I know what people think about my management style and skills.	1	2	3	4	5
23. I know when I am getting in the way.	1	2	3	4	5
24. Business results are more important to me than the status that comes with being the boss.	1	2	3	4	5
25. I like to see team members perform my responsibilities.	1	2	3	4	5
26. I get a real kick out of watching people grow and develop.	1	2	3	4	5
27. A primary job of management is to share information.	1	2	3	4	5

Scoring

Add your selections:

1. a. 1 Point
   b. 2 Points
   c. 3 Points
   d. 0 Points
2. a. 0 Points
   b. 3 Points
   c. 1 Point
   d. 2 Points
3. a. 1 Point
   b. 3 Points
   c. 1 Point
   d. 2 Points
4. a. 2 Points
   b. 0 Points
   c. 3 Points
5. a. 3 Points
   b. 1 Point
   c. 0 Points
   d. 2 Points
6. a. 1 Point
   b. 0 Points
   c. 2 Points
   d. 3 Points
7. a. 0 Points
   b. 2 Points
   c. 3 Points
   d. 1 Point
8. a. 0 Points
   b. 2 Points
   c. 1 Point
   d. 3 Points
9. a. 1 Point
   b. 2 Points
   c. 3 Points
   d. 0 Points

10. a. 1 Point
    b. 3 Points
    c. 2 Points
    d. 0 Points
11. a. 3 Points
    b. 1 Point
    c. 0 Points
    d. 2 Points
12. 3 Points for b, c, d, a, c, or
    c, b, d, a, e (high to low)
    2 Points for b, c, a, d, e, or
    c, b, a, d, e (high to low)
    1 Point for b, d, c, a, e,
    c, d, b, a, e, b, c, d, e, a, or
    c, b, d, e, a (high to low)
    0 Points for others
13. a. 0 Points
    b. 1 Point
    c. 0 Points
    d. 3 Points
    e. 0 Points
14. a. 1 Point
    b. 2 Points
    c. 1 Point
    d. 3 Points
15. a. 2 Points
    b. 0 Points
    c. 1 Point
    d. 3 Points
16. a. 3 Points
    b. 0 Points
    c. 2 Points
    d. 1 Point
17—27. Add the circled numbers

Scoring Interpretation

90-103   Good fit
80-89   Minor change required
70-79   Major change required
60-69   Poor fit
0-59   Consider opening a bait and tackle shop in the Alaska Wilderness.

26
Assessing Team Leader Effectiveness Sampler

Instructions

Think back over the last six months and determine how frequently you demonstrated the behaviors described in each statement. Place a check the last six months and determine how frequently you demonstrated the behaviors described in each statement. Place a check mark in the appropriate circle for each statement.

To what extent is this an accurate description of you as a team leader? (Check one box for each statement.)

	Never 1	Almost never 2	Frequently 3	Almost always 4	Always 5
Living Example					
1. Provides a personal example of the way people should act in a team setting.	☐	☐	☐	☐	☐
2. Manages by principles and information, not by asking people to conform to unnecessary rules and regulations.	☐	☐	☐	☐	☐

	Never 1	Almost never 2	Frequently 3	Almost always 4	Always 5
3. Clearly states the limits (boundary conditions) within which the team can make decisions.	☐	☐	☐	☐	☐

Coach

4. Makes sure the team has the training needed to work effectively.	☐	☐	☐	☐	☐
5. Deals with poor performance appropriately.	☐	☐	☐	☐	☐
6. Develops the team so that they can manage the day-to-day operation without him/her.	☐	☐	☐	☐	☐

Business Analyzer

7. Discusses specific data about product/service performance with the team on a daily basis.	☐	☐	☐	☐	☐
8. Helps the team decide how to be responsive to marketplace information.	☐	☐	☐	☐	☐
9. Is a resource for helping the team redesign the workplace to make it more competitive.	☐	☐	☐	☐	☐

Barrier Buster

10. Works actively to remove unnecessary policies, procedures, or work practices that hinder team performance.	☐	☐	☐	☐	☐
11. Helps the team understand the difference between real and perceived barriers.	☐	☐	☐	☐	☐

	Never 1	Almost never 2	Frequently 3	Almost always 4	Always 5
12. Recognizes when he/she is a barrier to the team and takes necessary improvement actions.	☐	☐	☐	☐	☐
	☐	☐	☐	☐	☐

Facilitator

	Never 1	Almost never 2	Frequently 3	Almost always 4	Always 5
13. Makes people feel empowered.	☐	☐	☐	☐	☐
14. Works to procure necessary tools and equipment for the team.	☐	☐	☐	☐	☐
15. Helps the team solve problems.	☐	☐	☐	☐	☐

Customer Advocate

	Never 1	Almost never 2	Frequently 3	Almost always 4	Always 5
16. Acts like serving the customer is the most important priority.	☐	☐	☐	☐	☐
17. Regularly initiates face-to-face meetings between the team and customers.	☐	☐	☐	☐	☐
18. Emphasizes quality of product/service over quantity of output.	☐	☐	☐	☐	☐

Leader

	Never 1	Almost never 2	Frequently 3	Almost always 4	Always 5
19. Is obsessed with a clear, future-oriented vision for the team.	☐	☐	☐	☐	☐
20. Creates commitment and energy in the team.	☐	☐	☐	☐	☐
21. Helps people do things that may have seemed impossible.	☐	☐	☐	☐	☐

Assessment Interpretation

The most effective team leaders tend to have all responses in the 4 or 5 range as perceived by the self-directed work team members reporting to them.

27
The Team Leader
Survival Guide

Self-directed work teams cannot be implemented successfully as another management or corporate program. This is a fundamental culture change and not just an organization structure. Operations that treat it as such are doomed to fail.

Things to Remember

SDWTs are inevitable. We need to learn how to make them work. This means that supervisors and managers at every level of the organization need to change their roles. (Chapters 1, 3)

All else being equal, SDWTs outperform their traditional counterparts. SDWTs are a response to a need for faster, more flexible, and more committed operations. The fact that most people like them better is a nice by-product, but it is not the reason businesses are using them. Bureaucracy and hierarchy don't work well in today's competitive world. (Chapters 1–4)

SDWTs apply all over the organization, not just to workers. Management teams should also be self-directed. (Chapter 1)

SDWTs are a journey, not a destination. They are not a thing to do; they are a way to do things. Team leaders that forget this have serious (sometimes terminal) problems. Don't get caught up in a means/end inversion. Don't measure things like training time and numbers of teams; measure the true business results like quality, cost, and speed to determine the effectiveness of the teams. Don't focus on individual teams to the detriment of the whole organization either. These are common but avoidable mistakes. (Chapter 2)

SDWTs take their direction from the work to be done and not from the supervisor. A better name for them would be work-centered teams. (Chapter 2)

SDWTs need management even though their name doesn't sound like they do. But they need a different kind of management. They need team leaders, not supervisors. They don't need planning, organizing, directing, and controling. They do that themselves. They also don't need bosses, directors, or police. They do that themselves. They do need trainers, coaches, and leaders. (Chapter 5)

The role of team leader is a different way of thinking. It is a shift from thinking that the role of the leader is to control (the control paradigm) to thinking that the role of the leader is to elicit commitment (the commitment paradigm). The inability to make this shift is probably the single greatest reason for individual team leader failure. (Chapter 9)

Certain values and assumptions can inhibit a persons ability to be a successful team leader. Assuming that people are lazy, or that their ideas are not as good as yours, for example, limits your ability to manage a SDWT. (Chapter 9)

Supervisors work in *the system, team leaders work* on *the system.* Team leaders are boundary managers with responsibilities for managing the impact of the business environment on the team. This includes many nontraditional responsibilities like market analysis, technology forecasting, and working community and government issues of importance. (Chapter 13)

Formal performance appraisals are a lousy coaching tool. Give ongoing feedback during the game. (Chapter 14)

The team leader role changes with the maturity level of the team. As team maturity expands, team responsibilities increase. (Chapters 17–19)

Role changes require clarity of the new role, a personal need to change, organizational support, and self-awareness. Keep this in mind when working with either team members or other team leaders. (Chapters 22, 23)

Managing up requires influencing skills like vision, taking opportunities, and being tenacious. Try to leverage serendipity to meet your objectives. (Chapter 24)

Things to Do

Give team members authority, resources, information, and accountability. Empowerment requires all four of these things. Anything less is a sham. (Chapter 2)

Make job assurances and avoid the wingwalker problem of telling people what not to do. The transition to SDWTs is tough on team members and team leaders alike. But it is most difficult on supervision. Some don't make it. Organizations need to help reduce the anxiety. (Chapter 5)

Involve team leaders in designing their own jobs. (Chapters 6, 7)

Develop the capability of team members. Remember that blaming shuts down learning and development. (Chapter 7)

Focus on purpose, not problems. Help the team focus on accomplishing their purpose, not just on problem solving activities. If a team becomes bogged down in blaming or becomes depressed, it is often due to being overly focused on problems. (Chapter 7)

Manage by vision and values. This includes the ability to manage joint visioning processes, which align groups towards common goals. (Chapters 10, 13)

Act more like a shepherd than a sheep herder. Team leaders lead by example, not by driving the flock in front of them. Shepherds develop shepherds not passive sheep. (Chapter 12)

Use substitutes for hierarchy. Team leaders don't rely on the power of position to get things done. They use information, education and other substitutes. They create an infrastructure that substitutes for hierarchy. (Chapter 13)

Develop competencies in leadership, setting an example, coaching, business analysis, barrier busting, facilitating, and customer advocacy. (Chapters 13–15)

Manage by principle, not by policy. This is a way to provide autonomy without bureaucratic restrictions. (Chapter 14)

Ask questions to develop team members. Don't just give answers. Socratic coaching helps you teach without lecturing. People remember it better if they have to work it through themselves. (Chapter 14)

Walk the talk. People don't care what you say. They care what you do. (Chapter 14)

Keep the team riveted on meeting external customer needs. Too much focus on internal customers, or too much emphasis on the day-to-day operational issues, makes team members spend too much energy on low value-adding activity. (Chapter 15)

Plan for a lot of training time. Teams typically need from 15 to 20 percent of their time for ongoing training in business, technical, and interpersonal skills. Only a portion of this is classroom training. Most of it is used for meetings, cross-training, and real-time problem solving activities. This training must be reinforced in the workplace to be useful. (Chapter 15)

Actively eliminate restrictive policies and procedures. If you aren't changing some big things, you won't get big improvement. (Chapter 15)

Institutionalize effective information gathering and information communicating processes. Without facts and data, SDWTs are dead in the water. Good decision making and problem solving requires good information. People also need regular forums to discuss the information. (Chapter 15)

Don't be a marshmallow manager. Team leaders share accountability with the teams but they do not abdicate their responsibility. They are still responsible for good results. (Chapter 16)

Set boundary conditions. This allows autonomy while providing needed clarity and direction. (Chapter 16)

Summary

Remember, "If you think you are already there you haven't started. But if you think you have a long way to go, you are already on the way." (This is a quote from a team leader who understands this messy and uncomfortable change process.)

Index

About the Author

Kimball Fisher (Portland, Oregon) is a leading authority on
managing self-directed work teams and is cofounder of
Belgard•Fisher•Raynor, Inc., a high-performance
work-system training and consulting company that has
trained more than 20,000 managers. His clients include
Apple, Corning, Monsanto, Shell, Rockwell, and many other
major corporations. He has published in prestigious journals
and collections, including *Organizational Dynamics* and
Human Resources Management, and has spoken at
numerous business and university conferences, including
those hosted by The University of Pittsburgh, Brigham
Young University, The Association of Quality and
Participation, and Texas Instruments.